HANDSTANDS IN THE DARK

JANEY GODLEY

EBURY
PRESS

1

This edition published in 2021 by Ebury Press,
an imprint of Ebury Publishing
First published by Ebury Press in 2005

20 Vauxhall Bridge Road
London SW1V 2SA

Ebury Press is part of the Penguin Random House group of companies
whose addresses can be found at global.penguinrandomhouse.com

Penguin
Random House
UK

www.penguin.co.uk

A CIP catalogue record for this book is available from the British Library

ISBN 9781529106862

Printed and bound in Great Britain by Clays Ltd, Elcograf S.p.A.

The authorised representative in the EEA is Penguin Random House Ireland,
Morrison Chambers, 32 Nassau Street, Dublin D02 YH68.

Penguin Random House is committed to a sustainable future
for our business, our readers and our planet. This book is
made from Forest Stewardship Council® certified paper.

MIX
Paper from
responsible sources
FSC® C018179

Introduction

When I started writing *Handstands in the Dark* back in 2004, I was a middle-aged, jobbing comedian, doing a show at the Edinburgh fringe and living in hotels on the road as I gigged on the club circuit. Think of those tired-looking women who danced on stage behind the big star in a faded satin leotard, women who could keep up but never quite got the spotlight themselves ... that was me, a comedy hoofer.

I was plodding along until one day a man called John saw my comedy show, which was about me, a woman who could laugh about her child abuse and got caught with guns in her father-in-law's house. John told a publishing house that this woman's story was fascinating. I couldn't even get a comedy reviewer in the door back then but, after that, I got a book deal.

I was absolutely thrilled to be writing a book, without actually knowing what that really entailed. I had never written for anyone but me. I'm a girl from the wrong side of everything, with no education. Nor was I in possession of a literary agent or anything like that (why would I need one?). But this girl had been asked to write her life story, so you can imagine how excited I was. We had one desktop computer in the house and an old wheezy laptop that I took on tour with me. So, most of the writing was done late at night, when everyone else was asleep.

Sometimes I was overwhelmed and wondered anyone would want to hear about a wee girl from Glasgow who was good at football and negotiating her way through a mire of paedophiles, misogynists and women who sported black eyes as badges. I had been told repeatedly by many of the men in my life – the men in this book – that I was 'nothing but a barmaid', so my self-esteem needed some heavy shoring. And then there was my family. How would they feel about me exposing the rawness, fears and deepest emotional aspects of my background? How would my husband's family feel? Probably nothing, I suspected, as most of them would car boot their own granny for ten pence pieces, but still … what would everyone think of me?

I needn't have worried. My family were supportive, and I can still see the tears of pride in my daddy's eyes as he held my hardback copy in his hands for the first time, before he died. He would often introduce me as 'my daughter, the author'. My husband and daughter have never read the book and never will. They told me they don't have to, and I agreed. They are very proud of me, I might add.

The book was often described as a 'misery memoir', and we frequently joked in my family about 'my sad book'. On reflection, though, it was a happy book.

In fact, actually there is fuck all that is sad about my life, as you'll learn when you read this book. Yes, I was sexually abused and my mum was murdered - but I also had the best dog in the world, had a funny childhood in many ways, and gave birth to a fierce female who became a comedian and broadcaster herself. The women in my family are warriors – we aren't beaten by life.

I ran a bar in Glasgow's East End during the heroin years, but I never touched drugs. I never drank, never smoked and basically had the mild morals of a home counties housewife wrapped up in the package of a sweary, funny working class girl who grabbed every chance she got.

I didn't want my book to be a testimony to sadness or bravery. I wanted it to be a story about a girl who was very optimistic and grew up viewing the world as something to be taken on, not beaten down by.

I think misery safari books, especially the way they have been framed in that 'Dickensian' style, or like made to look like *Angela's Ashes*, those books with poor barefoot children on the cover, is changing. People can relay their lived experience in a way that allows the reader to see both the light and dark, and see a way out of their own situation. I saw a way out, and I took it. I'm really proud of this book.

Things have changed since I wrote *Handstands in the Dark*. Time has moved on. The #metoo movement happened, and women aren't afraid to tell their stories. Now, women are shouting louder and going onstage talking about abuse. And so many famous men have been exposed as abusers: the narrative has changed since this book was originally published.

I realised that, in this new moment, I was no longer the freaky woman who made people uncomfortable by laughing about her paedophile, like I was back in 2002. I think this is a great thing. Collective voices calling for change can make a stronger society, which can hold a mirror up to prejudiced views. That's what good comedy, and good writing, does too.

I still get people who want to tell me I was wrong; I shouldn't have told everyone about the abuse, the poverty and my family's failings, and it's been impressed upon me by some people that these things are best left unsaid. But I'm just not that kind of woman. Trust me – I'm banned from the USA for telling Donald Trump what I think of him. I've made standing up to bastards a hobby – and a full-time job.

I am 15 years older than the Janey who wrote this book and so much has happened to me. So many people still ask what happened after the book ended. Well, I am still a comic and actor and a broadcaster. I got to fulfil many of my dreams. Not the ones including George Clooney, of course – but I have travelled the world doing stand-up, and have been able to write plays and act. I am very lucky. I will always be grateful for the chance to tell my story, to let people know that the wee scruffy girl with untameable curly hair and a good dog would be heard. I hope you find it uplifting.

Janey Godley
www.janeygodley.com
@janeygodley

1
The world upside-down

Faraway, I could hear my Mammy's voice, singing.

My palms were sore from small hard biscuit crumbs on our kitchen floor digging into the skin, but my legs still leaned against the wall. I liked doing handstands. I loved the world upside-down. It made me dizzy but I liked that feeling. The ceiling was marked with grease and smoke stains. The washing hanging from the ceiling pulley looked like ghosts were wearing the clothes. Woolly hand-knitted jumpers stood straight up with their arms outstretched, but they had no hands or heads. Maybe my secrets and sore bits would disappear if I were to stay like this. My big sister Ann pinched me on the knee:

'Janey turn the right way up, eh?'

'Not yet.'

Sometimes I would only talk upside-down. Sometimes I would talk in a code only I knew. Sometimes out in the street I would kneel down and scoop water from puddles with my hands coz I was thirsty but too scared to go home and face what was there.

* * *

My first memory is being about four or five years old and standing inside our small first-floor flat in the East End of Glasgow laughing. I was the only one laughing. Everyone around me was crying. Our first dog was being taken away to be killed by the vet. I was laughing with happiness because I had an ice cream. No one ever bothered to ask why I laughed at strange times. I had two elder brothers, Mij and Vid, and one elder sister, Ann. I was the youngest, so I was allowed to be daft. When I was about seven years old, I laughed when I realised the words *real fun* are an anagram of *funeral*.

The six of us lived in a small two-bedroom flat at the corner of Kenmore Street on the middle level of a three-storey, grey-stone building in the heart of an industrial area called Shettleston, whose only claim to fame was that it was the least healthy place to live in the whole of Scotland – an average man's life expectancy was ten years less if he was born and remained in Shettleston. The area was a mixture of big brown tenements and grey stone buildings, all mostly engrained with a layer of black soot at that time, the 1960s.

My mother Annie Currie was a world-famous actress, singer and dancer in Hollywood movies – but only in her fantasies. She would sometimes clear back the furniture in our cramped wee flat so she could sing and dance and be Judy Garland for at least one afternoon.

Or, on rainy Sunday afternoons in front of her favourite movie on our old black and white television set, she would stop being my Mammy who collected fag coupons and black eyes and become Ginger Rogers, the dancing sweetheart of the movies.

My father Jim Currie was a hard-working man. In 1960s Glasgow, if you had no money, your options were either a job in the steel works or in one of the big shipyards on the River Clyde. My Dad's family had had high hopes for his future because he had been educated past the age of fifteen – very unusual – and he had later paid to go to night school. He did well, got himself a job in the local steel foundry and, because of his extra education, worked not in the big forge itself but in the laboratories. As far as his family were concerned, though, his downfall was meeting my Mammy, getting her pregnant then marrying her in haste. His family disliked my Mammy's lies, her fantasy world and her inability to keep house. My Dad's family were hard-working, clean people who looked after their kids. My Mammy's family wasn't.

In our home there was a constant damp, dirty smell which rose from the grubby, swirly yellow lino on our floors. Like everywhere at that time, we had one coal fire in the living room with a back boiler in the kitchen. Our two unheated bedrooms were freezing cold in the Scottish autumns, winters and springs. The small, square living room had a large, framed print of a flock of pink flamingos hanging always lopsided on the flowery wallpaper over our open coal fire and I used to wonder where exotic birds like that really lived.

My sister Ann, my brothers Mij (my father's name Jim spelt backwards) and Vid (short for David) and I had almost constant infestations of fleas and head lice. I would sit quietly sometimes and catch the fleas as they leapt off my legs, then throw them onto the open fire and listen for the sound of their bodies cracking in the heat. Mammy would laugh when I did this; Dad would look away.

My parents were almost complete opposites. Dad was a well-read man who enjoyed politics and debating the current issues of the day with anyone, including us children.

'This is the Prime Minister,' he'd tell us. 'And this is the shite he's doing with this country,' and we'd all get bored because we were only children. When he debated politics with some of his friends, I would interrupt with lots of questions because I didn't know some of the long words they used.

'What was that word, Dad? What does *Conservative* mean?'

'It means they're bastards,' he explained to me when I was four.

'That's no' what it means, Dad! What does it mean?'

'It's a government,' he explained, 'that believes in giving money to rich people. They don't help the working classes. The other people are called the Labour Party. But they're all bastards too. Naebody will look after you, Janey. Naebody.'

It was quite tense with him in the flat sometimes, because he did have a bit of a temper. He was a hard-working man and he would come back in the evening, tired, to four lively kids and lots of financial worries. Television was still a luxury at that time but we always had a black and white TV because my Dad could repair old sets.

'Right! The News is on!' he would shout. 'Everybody shut up! I wanna to watch the News on TV!'

He hated the News being interrupted. My Mammy was a lot easier-going and she was always whispering to us:

'Wheesht! Watch yer Da. Don't say that to yer Da…'

She told us we had to keep all sorts of secrets from our Dad.

'Don't tell him they found nits in yer heed at school … Don't tell him ye got sent hame from school coz yer shoes had burst.'

I asked her once why we all had to keep so many secrets.

'Shut up, Janey,' was her answer.

She involved us kids in her double life. We became frightened that, if we gave away one of Mammy's secrets, our Dad would take it out on her. I never saw her being beaten, but I remember once she had a black eye and Dad was holding her in his arms, saying:

'I'm really sorry, Annie. I'm really sorry.'

She was a slim woman with dark brown hair, piercing brown eyes, smooth sallow skin, an ability to laugh at any situation and she was completely irresponsible. She fascinated me because all her little movements were so quick, running around looking after four kids and a husband. I used to watch her and think she was like a colourful, swirling spinning top. As her youngest child, I spent hours with her after the others had gone to school and it was good to get her alone, sitting still, and just stare at her. I used to gaze at her as she sat quietly brushing her dark hair by the bedroom window, chain-smoking cigarettes – she smoked about 50 a day – watching the world pass her by.

I loved those times we would sit together at that window and watch the late summer sun set over the skyline of Glasgow: those two giant gas tanks to the left of the five tall cellblock ends and distinctive chimney pots of Barlinnie High Security Prison and all the prefabs and grey, roughcast, two-storey council houses of the High Carntyne. My Mammy would stand all her cigarette butts on end in a circle like Stonehenge and I would look at her face and wonder what she was thinking about and why everything had to be so complicated and often I would make her tell me stories of her own childhood. She had a great memory and could entertain me for hours with tales of her happy times as a teenager during the Second World War. Somehow I could never imagine my slim, funny, harassed Glasgow Mammy ever being a teenager. She told me she had been a fantastic sportswoman, a swimmer and a hockey champion.

Her main local haunt now was the pawnshop. This service was vital in any inner city community of the time; it was a form of credit and the only way locals who owned nothing really valuable could get cash. I used to go with her and loved the smell of varnish and the shiny, waxed, old-fashioned look of the three or four wooden booths which were built so your neighbours couldn't see you pawning your family's possessions. My Mammy would lift me up to sit on the oak-wood counter and the wee Jewish pawnbro-ker behind the half-bars on the window would always be wearing a clean black suit, smart white shirt and dark tie and he would always crack the same joke:

'So you want to know how much money I will pay for Janey, eh?'

Every Monday, my Mammy would hand over a box tied with string, saying it contained 'my husband's best leather shoes'. The wee pawnbroker knew the routine and would hand over to her a £1 note. Every Friday, when my Dad got his wages, she would pay the money back to the pawnbroker and take the box home. He never found out the box actually contained a small brick wrapped with paper.

My Mammy loved my Dad and, to my mind, kept him going with her funny ways. He was a gifted artist and encouraged me to paint and draw. He would sit and draw cartoons of us children and we would scream at him when he sketched us sitting on a toilet pan; he loved to wind us up by drawing us in silly clothes or strange situations. But, like many Scotsmen of his generation, he had a problem. Alcohol. Almost everyone in his family had a drink prob-lem. When I was growing up it seemed most people I knew had an alcoholic in their family. At weekends, the local pubs were bursting at the seams with heavy drinkers.

Our local pub The Waverley was at the bottom of Kenmore Street with a steep uphill climb back to our building, something difficult and precarious for a jiggy-legged drunk to manage. On Friday and Saturday nights, all the kids in our street would hang out of their upstairs windows to watch their staggering, swaying dads and/or mums meandering home. The dim white streetlights would mark out the course of this strange ritual race and we used to make pretend-bets on whose dad or mum could make it up the slope without falling down once or holding on to one of the lamp-posts. I was proud of my Dad coz most times he would succeed in one big long drunken stumbling run. It was only rarely that his legs buckled and he fell down. Normally he would reach our corner building safely and we would hear him singing one of his favourite Frank Sinatra songs – usually 'My Way' – as his feet thumped up the stone steps to the building's outside door then *boom-boom-boom* up the echoing concrete steps of the stairwell inside to reach our first-floor flat. Sometimes he would stagger in still wobbling about and – missing all his usual targets: dog, budgie and kids – collapse onto the only thing I truly loved – the television set. I would watch in horror as it fell with a thud onto the floor then blinked to blackness and I was absolutely terrified it might explode. I had visions of it blowing up like I'd seen on TV in some cartoon – like an atom bomb going off.

Dad would spend all of the next day with a big box of television valves and a soldering iron weakly smiling his apologies to me as I helped him repair the big brown box. I loved the smell of the solder and the burning flex and the valves looked like big science-fiction bombs wrapped in

7

tissue. I was fascinated that electricity could go into the set along thin wires and make a picture of the real world. My insistent questions about television tubes and electricity must have driven him mad – not a very good thing for a man who was usually nursing a raging hangover.

The Waverley pub where he spent so much time intrigued me. On Fridays and Saturdays, I used to peep in and breathe the warm, beer-smelly cigarette-smoky glow. I had no interest in alcohol or cigarettes; I just wanted to be in there and figure out why adults were so obsessed with the place. My eyes would scan the long thin room and see all my friends' dads standing around in their best suits, spending their hard-earned cash on long boozing sessions. The biggest dare we local kids had was to run into the Waverley bar through one door and skip out the other end without getting caught; but I was always too scared to do this in case Dad got hold of me. Whenever he even caught me standing at the door, I would get such a blast of his anger that his disappointment in me worried my soul. But I knew he would never hit me. I was his favourite. I could do most things and get away with it by making him laugh. When he was not drunk he was a really good Dad and he did love my Mammy; I would often catch them in the kitchen kissing and hugging each other and I would run over.

'Let go of her, Dad! Tell me it's only me you love!'

My Mammy had had a difficult life. When she was a teenager her own mammy had died, leaving her to bring up a wee brother aged six and a sister aged eight because her father, my Granda Davy Percy, was a useless bastard. Another sister, only slightly younger than she was, did not want any of the responsibility and left to work in England. So my Mammy became, in effect, a mother to her own family, then became pregnant by my father when she was

19 and by the time I was born – her fourth child – she was 26 and must have been emotionally frayed. She would talk to me with real fondness about her own mother who had died so young but, when I listened to these rose-tinted tales of her childhood, I just felt she had had a better deal than we were getting now. The way she told it, she had lived in a beautiful Sally of Sunshine Street land. The way she told it, her mammy was a clean woman, a good woman who made great dumplings and held glamorous dances for soldiers during the Second World War. It was as if her mammy had been a rock who held the family together by sheer personal strength. I dreamed in my childish imagination that my dead grandmother would come back and take me to her lovely clean home and hold *my* family together.

My Mammy told me wistful tales of how she used to swim in the clear blue Firth of Clyde off Saltcoats, a seaside town just down the coast from Largs in Ayrshire, and how she once saved a man's life.

'A prisoner escaped from jail and fell into the sea off Saltcoats and I rescued him,' she told me.

Sometimes, after telling me these tales of her sunny childhood and the clear blue Scottish seas, she would lean over our dirty window-sill, stick her head out of our grey stone flat and chat to the neighbours downstairs.

Directly beneath us lived Mr Woods, a deaf mute who owned a moped. He made loud noises when he tried to communicate: 'Bpheergh!' he would go, as if you had just stood on a dog's back leg. 'Pheerch! Bweett!' He never actually said words, just whooping noises and yelping sounds. Many of the local kids were scared of him but I was not because, by listening carefully to him and watching his hands, I learned to understand what he was trying to say. After a few years, I taught myself sign language so I could

9

run errands for him, the incentive being that he always gave me a decent tip – threepence or sixpence. Sometimes he would even give me a short trip on his pale blue moped and I loved it. Zooming around the local streets on his buzzing bike was great fun for a wee kid who had never been in a car.

My best pal Rachel lived upstairs with her gran and uncle, her home an exact replica of ours except it was very clean, smelled lovely and they had a dark red carpet and a telephone. She had a loving, caring family who enjoyed being with her and her uncle would often take both of us out to nearby Tollcross Park or to a museum. The trip I remember most was the day he took us to the People's Palace right by the River Clyde, a big red building with sweeping staircases and giant columns – it was like going into a fairytale castle.

As well as Rachel upstairs, at the bottom of our street I also vaguely knew a very pretty girl called Sandra who was wee, blonde and all the adults said she had cute dimples. She was a Catholic and normally my Mammy used to warn me: 'Don't play with Fenians!' I wasn't allowed to play with the boys who lived across the street because they were Catholics. But my Mammy got on well with Sandra's mammy so we were allowed to talk. Sandra had lots of brothers and some sisters and they all looked exactly the same: they all had blond hair and intense, staring blue eyes like the alien children in the movie *Children of the Damned*. She used to play with a little blond boy called Barra and his six blond brothers, who were also Catholics.

There were lots of children in the neighbourhood and soon we had a new dog too. It was at some drunken friend's party that my Dad first saw a wee black German Alsatian which was being neglected by his owner. He felt sorry for the poor wee puppy, so picked it up and brought it home. The dog had smooth black and brown fur and big brown eyes with white dots above each eyebrow. Unfortunately, because he had been abused, he was a biting, vicious, angry dog and aggressive to everyone except me. My mother took to telling him: 'Don't play with Fenian dogs!' We called him Major and he became my eternal hero, my pal and, sometimes, my protector because I had a secret that I couldn't tell anyone else. I could only tell my dog friend, because Major would listen and not tell any human being the damning truth about me.

I don't really know when it started but I do know I feared my Mammy's brother from when I was very small. He lived minutes away, one block from our house. His name was David Percy, named after his father, my Granda Davy Percy. Everyone commented on how good my Uncle David was with children and especially with me. At family parties, he would sing *Baby face! You got the cutest little baby face!* And he would call me Sweet Pea:

'Sweet Pea, go an' get me a glass for ma beer ... Sweet Pea, c'mon here an' jump up on ma knee ...'

He was around twelve years older than me and would wait for my Mammy and my Dad to go out, then take me into my bedroom. I kept my head down but I knew the drill. He sat me on the bed and I can still smell the cigarette smoke on his hands as he stroked my face. The long, brown-stained fingers would slowly pull up my skirt. My legs would go stiff. I tried my hardest to will them never to open again, never to spread my knees apart for him, but I did what he told me.

'Lie down, Sweet Pea.'

My body goes like a plank of wood. He leans over me and starts to open his trousers. I turn my head to the wall.

11

I can hear the zip go down. He lifts the hem of my skirt and puts it right up to my chest. His smelly fingers hook inside the top of my knickers and he pulls them down. He digs those fingers inside me as his other big hand grabs my small hand and puts it inside his open flies. He rasps words through his smoky breath. I know how to rub him up and down. He has shown me. I keep my face away from him and stare at the wall. My sister Ann has stuck a picture of TV's David Cassidy and The Partridge Family on the wall. I focus on the Partridge mother's face, smiling and gentle, her arms around her family. I shut my brain down and pretend I am in Disneyland, that perfect place I have seen on TV with the big magic castle. When thinking of Disneyland does not distance me enough from the pain between my legs, I rub him harder and link letters to numbers in my head … a = 1 and b = 2 and c = 3 … I like codes and can think in numbers.

'You like it when I touch ye?' His fingernails scratch bits of my inner flesh I had not known were there.

'495,' I tell him quietly.

'Whit?' He looks confused. 'Just keep rubbing it hard!'

I know he will never get the code.

2

The girl who came to school

I loved learning and was eager to get to school. At home, Dad had always played competitive number and spelling games and anagrams with the family and had made no concession for the fact I was the youngest. He was always banging on about how education was important. So my first teacher Miss Cubie was amazed that, at the age of five, I could read and write long words from the school's word boxes like

ENTHUSIASM

Some children are scared of big words but, at home, I was used to making words out of other words for anagrams, so I knew how to break words down in my head:

EN – THU – SI – ASM

As soon as I met any new teacher, I made an anagram of her name. I thought of Miss Cubie as Miss Bue-ic. Janice Malone was my pal and I made her surname into 'a lemon'. Miss Cubie let me go round my class with the chalk board on which I had written ENTHUSIASM and she even took me into an older classroom.

'Look at this wee girl,' she said. 'She's only in the First Class but she can write a big word like this.'

I loved the attention and I remember other teachers saying 'Wow!' and I thought *Fantastic! Get me more of that attention!*

I loved everything about school from Day One. It had an order and structure which contrasted with the chaos of my life at home. At school, you had a lunchtime when you actually got fed a proper lunch rather than just an Oxo cube. Before teatime I would sometimes go to Shettleston Public Library and look at the big books with maps of the world and imagine where I could go when I was older. The library smelled of polished oak and had a silent stillness – there were no dogs barking, no children with squinty-eyes fighting and screaming in the stairwell, no adults shouting at each other and you could sit and read books in complete silence.

At school, I also found my gift was storytelling – I was the funny girl, the one who always managed to tell a story to deflect the pain I felt inside. I wanted to be the wee girl with the bright bows in her hair wearing clean socks and pants, but I wasn't. There *were* kids in my class who did not live in poverty. They had lovely clean homes with a garden. They had mums and dads who smelled nice and did not shout. Sometimes I would walk up roads where my school-friends lived and see clean teddy bears sitting on clean window-sills; I used to imagine what it would be like to live in those houses, with clean sheets on my clean bed and lots of tasty food which I could eat off clean plates. I didn't want to live in a smelly house with an uncle who did things to me.

Sometimes one of my friends would invite me to her home and I would see the look on her mother's face when she met her little girl's best friend. The mother would smile yet flinch at this skinny, scruffy waif who was introduced to her, but I always won these mothers over by smiling happily and talking about school and homework and everything they wanted to hear. This also avoided any probing questions about my family. In reality, these people were just ordinary, hard-working Glasgow folk but, in my mind, they were very, very lucky, special people. I was more comfortable going round to little, blonde Sandra's house which had that familiar, sweet, sickly smell of beds wet with children's piss. I didn't like girls' dolls. I destroyed them quite a lot when they seemed to be too clean and pretty; I felt they needed to be dirtied. I broke dolls' arms and legs and drew on their faces. I preferred playing football.

I was a plucky child and one that – to the outside world – seemed to survive most situations but, in the middle of the freezing winter of 1966, I stripped down to my vest and underpants and stood beneath a gushing chilly gutter flood to enjoy a 'wee shower'. Within hours I had collapsed on the living-room floor with a raging fever and became delirious. That week, I almost died of pneumonia and my Mammy had to be sedated as I drifted in and out of consciousness. They told her I was very close indeed to death but, slowly, I managed to pull through. Prior to that illness, I had had frequent urinary infections and kidney problems and, in light of the pneumonia and the bruises which they found on my body, I had more doctors' attention from then on. I was only five years old. My GP suggested prescribing the drug Valium.

'She has behavioural problems,' he told my parents.

It was around this time that I got the nickname 'Shakey Cakey' coz I trembled so much but no one ever thought to ask *why* such a small child would shake so much. I also had a tendency to harm myself. But no one ever thought to ask me *why*. After the illness, I just continued with my life as usual and getting back to my beloved school was very important to me although, by now, I seemed to annoy many of the teachers just by my very presence. They would ask me haughtily:

'Does *no one* in your family own a hairbrush?'

'Do you not own a *single* clean dress?'

I annoyed them even more because, although I was right-handed, I had taken to using my left hand for writing. Several teachers tried to stop me continuing this strange ritual, but I could never truthfully explain to them why I did it: I hated the fact that my Uncle made me touch him with my right hand. In art class – my favourite – I started drawing pictures with my left hand while trying to paint them in, at the same time, using my right hand.

'Stop using both your hands!' the teacher would tell me and hit me on the back of my knuckles with a ruler. 'Just use your right hand!'

I felt I needed to get everything done quickly. I used to paint at home and would not do anything else until I had completed the whole painting. At school, my teacher would say: 'The lesson is over. You can come back next week to finish the painting,' but I would scream and scream until I was allowed to finish it there and then.

Eventually, I decided to tell my Mammy about what my Uncle was doing. I stood in our small, dirty kitchen with my eyes focused totally on the wallpaper with its pictures of onions and carrots. I felt dirty and bad as I explained to Mammy that my Uncle was 'tickling' me in a place I did not like. I can still see her watching me with eyes I had never seen before. This was the woman who had carried me inside herself for almost nine months, the woman who had held me as I was vomiting the week before with a stomach ache. My Mammy stood still, put both her hands firmly on my shoulders and looked me directly in my eyes as she hissed:

'If you ever tell this to your Dad, he will kill my brother and then he will go to jail *and you will have no daddy*! Is *that* what you want, Janey? Are you sure you know what you are saying? Don't you *ever* talk to me like that again!'

I stood completely still and held my breath.

The emotions I had been feeling before I told her were totally re-confirmed. It was entirely my fault – just mine – and that's the way it would always be. I knew then that I had to live with the shame and shoulder the blame: a big responsibility for a child who could only draw well, play football and run fast but never fast enough.

I had already begun to cut myself and pull chunks out of my hair. At first I would just scratch my arm with a piece of broken glass then, after doing that for a while, I would sometimes gouge a little deeper. My Mammy and Dad told me off when they found big scratches on my arms and tufts of hair under my bed; but I would always have some excuse to cover the truth.

Soon, my Uncle David Percy took the abuse further by penetrating me. I was being raped regularly. There are no words or sentences or paragraphs which can describe the pain and feeling of suffocation. I would lie there stiff as a board and clench both my fists. I would push my finger-nails into the palms of my hands, hear the blood rushing through my ears and feel my heart pounding with fear. His hands always smelled of tobacco smoke and, with his rough fingers, he would rapidly pull off my panties. I would turn my face to the side and focus on the multi-coloured swirly wallpaper. As he pushed himself into my body I would imagine I was melting into that patterned wall. The pain would become intense but the worst feeling was the suffocation as he lay completely on top of me, sometimes covering my face. I had started to try to look him in the eyes, as I knew he hated this, but sometimes he would put a pillow on my face as he raped me. I can clearly remember contemplating suicide at this age. I was six. I decided the best way to do it was to throw myself on the main road and get hit by a car.

* * *

I had short brown curly hair and everyone confused me with a boy. I did not want to be a girl. Girls had something men liked so men touched them there. I did not want to be a girl. I denied any of my gender traits for fear it would attract more abusers. I didn't care what happened to me. I would be the one who would climb onto fast-moving lorries that left my street every day from the local creamery and trundled down the main road with me hanging on precariously. I would climb the creamery wall to find a metal bar or girder to tie a rope for a swing and leap down off a high wall. Nothing scared me except being with my Uncle. I was always nervous, constantly shaking, biting my nails, forever clinging to my Mammy, trying hard to follow her wherever she went. But, when I was among other kids, I was fearless.

One hot summer day – so hot the black tarmac on the road was actually starting to melt – we were playing rounders. I stood with a baseball bat in my hand ready to whack the ball. Out of the corner of my eye I suddenly spotted a wee black mongrel dog that belonged to our neighbour Mr McGregor racing through the kids. I knew this dog was a tad loony. It was usually kept on a leash. But today it dodged and weaved through all the kids until it stopped stock-still and faced me. It snarled and barked and snarled, then took one giant leap forward and bit into my hands as I held the bat. I thought *It's got rabies!* coz I had recently seen a rabid dog on TV. It was all blood and pain and saliva and bubbles and teeth and I dropped the bat and started screaming in terror as the blood pumped furiously out of my right hand which the dog was still biting into. The pain from his pointed teeth digging into the back and palm of my hand was unbelievable. I picked up the bat in my left hand and battered the dog on the head to force it to release its grip. The other kids were all shouting out:

'Mr Currie! Mr Currie!'

My Dad was on a night-shift that day, so he was lying in his bed with the window open because it was so hot and he heard and recognised my screams amid all the other kids who were shouting. He ran barefoot down the hot sticky-tar street, swept me up and carried me running back to our house as Mr McGregor arrived and leashed the dog. My Dad ran down to the Waverley pub where my Mammy's younger brother was drinking and Uncle James took me to hospital in his lorry to have the wounds all over my hand stitched. I still have the scars.

I was heartbroken when I heard the wee dog had had to be destroyed by the vet, but my Dad had caused such a scene with poor Mr McGregor who had been tending his garden when the dog ran out into the street. Mr McGregor apologised profusely but Dad was ready to kill the dog himself. It all seemed a bit strange and unexpected to me because our dog Major – always hungry and angry – had bitten at least four people in Kenmore Street and nothing had been done about it. I never wanted that wee black mongrel to be killed on my account and I felt guilty every time I saw old McGregor in the street after that. *I was responsible for getting his wee pet killed.* But the good thing was that he was so embarrassed he let me help him in his beautiful, well-tended garden and even allowed me to play in his back court – something that was normally sacrilege, as he hated kids in his back court.

Each of the blockhouses in the street had a back court-yard area. During the summer months, all the mothers would come round the back courts puffing on their ciga-rettes and the kids would put on a show for them, using washing lines draped with sheets as stage curtains. I could not really sing so I would impersonate some of the local women, dressing up in my Mammy's clothes and talking like a wee Glasgow housewife, a floral headscarf tied tight with a big bow under my chin and a big brown handbag with one strap swinging on my arm. I would sing drunken songs and swagger about knocking kids over as I shouted out husbands' names. I remembered all the recent titbits of gossip and would blurt them all out and my Mammy would gasp and hold her face in shame. But I loved to shock. I could tell my words had hit home when some of the women burst into fits of laughter and others just silently smiled. My performances would infuriate the mothers whom I chose to ape, but would get claps of delight from the mothers I had left out of my comedy sketches. I loved those days of complete innocence, playing outside in the streets or working at school, especially when I could draw or paint.

At that time, the *Sunday Post* newspaper ran a weekly competition: every week, a child would have a drawing published and their school would be awarded an ency-clopaedia. My new teacher Miss Miller had encouraged me to draw a picture of the dark winter mornings in which Scottish children had to walk to school – some kids had recently been knocked down by cars in the gloom. I drew a good picture with my right hand and Miss Miller was so pleased she sent it off to the *Sunday Post*. It won the competition and our headmaster invited me into his office. I was so excited at the prospect of bringing something good to the school and, when I was led into the headmaster's office by slightly built Miss Miller with her round-rimmed glasses, I was deeply impressed. The room was very imposing; very official-looking and the walls were covered in big bookshelves. The headmaster Mr Maitland stood by his desk and welcomed me in. He looked down at me with an air of grave authority and explained that the prize encyclopaedia was to be presented to the school at a special end-of-term ceremony but, as I did not have a proper uniform, the head boy would present the prize to the school instead of me.

I stood and looked down, ashamed at my dress, humiliated, yet I felt no real disappointment: I was used to that feeling of worthlessness. Miss Miller tried to protest, but was quickly put down. She took me out of the office trying to mask her anger, but I could tell she was annoyed. She bent down, held me close and told me:

'Forget about the school, Janey. One day, you will be on stage and everyone will see you and clap.'

I felt better as Miss Miller walked me all the way back to class holding my hand tightly, like she was willing me to stay afloat in this shit world she was forced to have a part in. At the special end-of-term ceremony, I watched our shiny, well-dressed head boy in his smart blazer hand over my prize to a smiling headmaster as the school cheered on. I did not feel too bad after the event. I already had no self-esteem. *Why should they let a girl like me be up there?* I sometimes imagined other people could see the bad girl inside me. Those were the words that my Uncle spat out as he raped me.

'You're a *bad* girl! You're a *bad* girl!'

I knew I was the girl who came to school with sperm on her jumper.

I walked out of the school hall that day with my hand-made Christmas calendar in my hand, all glitter and cotton wool. I felt something sad inside me but was not quite sure what it was. Christmas passed and I told no one at home about the prize-giving. I felt it was not really worth discussing. I knew it would upset my Mammy if I told her. She and my Dad were the reason I was so shabbily dressed; I did not want them to feel this strange, cold sadness I had inside of me.

* * *

My main ambition at the time was to own a bike on which I could ride outside and away from home. This was impossible with the family budget, but I was very determined and I did manage to gather together various bits and pieces of old bicycles and assemble them into a new bike; it must have been the weirdest-looking one in the city, all sizes of wheels and frame cobbled together. I cycled everywhere on my 'new' bike with Major, an apparently mad snarling dog, running, barking behind me. We travelled through the many green parks in Glasgow and along all the busiest main roads. I had no sense of left or right and would often ride on the wrong side of the road. I would pedal for hours and hours, wishing that I could cycle right out of the city and see the rest of the world with my own eyes and not just in books or on television. Sometimes I would cycle so far I would get lost and have to find my way home by following buses I knew went to Shettleston. I never asked anyone for help because I didn't risk talking to strangers and, by this time, Major would be so tired, hungry and thirsty he would have bitten anyone who came close. So I would find and follow a 61 or 62 bus and arrive home late and hungry. My bike gave me freedom, but it also brought me heartache.

Pretty little blonde Sandra at the end of our street had particularly nasty *Children of the Damned* brothers. One of them used to punch me whenever he saw me and let the tyres down on my bike. I was scared when I met him because he kept doing it and kept doing it and kept doing it. He was younger than me, but he was bigger and a mindless bully.

'He keeps letting doon the tyres of ma bike,' I told my Dad, 'and I have tae keep pumpin' them up again coz he bullies me.'

'Well,' my Dad advised me calmly, 'just fucking pick something up and hit him with it the next time he's bent doon at yer tyres.'

And that's exactly what I did. The next time he bent down to deflate my bike's tyres, I hit him on the side of the head with a half brick. *Crack!* He started screaming, holding his head, his face and hands covered in blood – his blond hair matted with it. He fell down and lay on the pavement screaming in agony and I just ran away terrified and screaming because I thought I'd killed him. Later, his mammy brought him to our door. She'd cleaned him up a bit but there was still brown, dried blood on his face and in his hair and my Mammy yelled at me:

'Whit the *fuck* did ye *dae* to him?'

'He kept letting ma tyres doon,' I explained, knowing it now sounded a really limp excuse.

* * *

By this time, my Uncle David Percy had started to use perverted games. He would declare a game of hide and seek. I would have to go hide somewhere and he would search for me in our flat of only two bedrooms, a kitchen, living room, bathroom and hallway. The game always ended with me being molested or raped. When my Uncle told me he wanted to play games, I would panic. On one occasion, I thought if I made myself small enough he could never find me. So I decided to hide in my bedroom's old-fashioned clothes closet. Major followed me, so I had to squeeze him in too. I folded up my skinny legs on the ledge inside the closet and bent down my head and pulled in this big, grumpy, unbendable, slavering dog. We both sat there and breathed each other's air. I stared into his eyes in the near-total darkness and wished I too were a dog, one who could run free across the grass in nearby Tollcross Park. Major's body was uncomfortably contorted but he never moved, never whined and sat sharing my anger at the big people who made our lives hard. We both knew my Uncle was coming. We both heard his annoying child-like voice taunting me.

'Ja-ney …Where are ye, Ja-ney? … C'mon, Sweet Pea … C'mon oot … Ja-ney … Ja-ney …'

He is outside the closet now, his footsteps have stopped and he is bearing down on us. Major's ears have pricked up, his brown dog eyes flick at me; I notice at this moment how long his eyelashes are. The door is wrenched open. I sit motionless and keep my eyes fixed on Major. My Uncle puts in his hand to pull me out. Major unfolds his gracious limbs, leaps, snarls and bites all at the same time. His teeth make contact with flesh, he gurgles that dog noise that makes him remember he is an animal and not just a pet. We both jump from the wooden ledge and leave my Uncle screaming and bleeding behind us. Feet running on lino … dog nails skidding on floors … I make it to the door … pull the handle ... we run down the concrete stairs screaming, barking, two fugitives, one noise! The last stairs are in front of us; we can hear him cursing, shouting and running behind us. We dive, jump out and land on the sunburnt grass, laughing and gasping. We have escaped for at least one more day.

3
Everybody dies

We occasionally went on holiday in the summer months when Dad got time off work. Then too, I was safe from my Uncle. One year, we all went to St Andrews on the Fife coast – the home of golf. It had one of the most beautiful graveyards in Scotland and I had a real fascination for graveyards – I felt very calm and safe in them. The graves in St Andrews were really, really old and the bereaved wrote on the stones with such passion in old-fashioned writing that I couldn't quite understand and gave great details that weren't necessary like *Here lies a dentist*, which isn't really important when someone's dead. I would spend hours slowly walking round reading all the ancient stones. I found one that told about the death of a nurse. I was appalled. Until then, I thought nurses did not die because they knew about medicine. I spent hours afterwards asking my parents about death.

'Does *everybody* die, Dad?'

'Everybody dies, Janey,' my Dad told me. 'We're all born to die. Everybody.'

'When am I going to die, Dad?'

'We're all going to die sometime, Janey.'

I looked at my Mammy.

'Everybody dies,' she told me. 'All of us.'

* * *

At home I was always surrounded by alcohol. In our street, there were a few shebeens – drinking dens – someone's apartment where all the local alcoholics and hard drinkers would congregate to get truly drunk when the pubs were closed. The door to a shebeen was never closed, so we kids would troop in and wander among the seated, standing, stumbling and sometimes unconscious drinkers, trying to collect empty bottles to take back to the shops. In those days you got money or sweets for returning the bottles. Once, my pals and I went into a shebeen next to my home, stepped over all the drunken people lying on the floor and peeped under a bed looking for bottles but, instead, we saw about five tiny dead kittens being eaten by the cat and dog of the house. It was like a jigsaw of dismembered, half-chewed paws, limbs and body parts which you couldn't match. Wee black and white kittens' heads with glassy, staring eyes and bloodied necks rolled about as the cat and dog ate their bodies. I ran screaming out of the building.

Later that same day, a man was murdered in that same room on that same bed. A drunken argument broke out, a man was accused of hurting a woman in the house and someone killed him with an axe which we children found when we were digging around on wasteground at the back. Later, we stood outside the house as the police – always called 'the Polis' in Glasgow – questioned local kids. At first, I thought we were in trouble for not helping the kittens. I was traumatised over the poor dead cats. The drunk's death just washed over me and the rest of the kids. We never told the Polis about the axe. Drunkenness and its consequences were just accepted as normal.

I hated alcohol and blamed it for most of my problems. I hated to see my Dad drunk; he lost all control and all common sense. My Mammy had never been a drinker but now she had a nervous breakdown and became addicted to the Valium prescribed by our GP. It was the 1960s and, when women felt depressed, they brought in Mother's Little Helper to help carry the burden. Everyone's mammy in my neighbourhood seemed to be on Valium. Mine became a dull, anxious woman on it. I would come home from school and find her slumped on the floor, completely unconscious. Her stress levels must have been enormous. Each day was a new challenge on the debt trail. On bad days, when she had really bad financial problems, she would go round to various members of her family begging for cash, always hiding it from my Dad who never really knew the full extent of her problems and was left happy in the knowledge that she took care of money matters. The Valium was my Mammy's only true friend and she always took too many tablets to get herself out of the depression. She couldn't just take one tablet; she had to be 'oot o' it' – completely unconscious. She became addicted. She used to take me up to other people's homes where she knew they got prescriptions too and beg tablets off them. She got the doctor to prescribe Valium for me so she could get more tablets for herself. Maybe she had more demons to grapple with than I knew about. Dad was always shouting at her and got so angry with her doctor he eventually went to the surgery to confront the man who kept his wife doped up.

'Women need these tablets,' the doctor told him.

'She is *unconscious*!' my Dad yelled. 'Fallin' doon all aboot the place. She cannae cook. Unconscious. She's *fucked*!'

So my Dad beat up the doctor in his surgery. The police were not called; violence was commonplace.

* * *

Sometimes Dad *would* discover some of Mammy's debt problems – like her forged signature on the insurance books or her wad of pawn tickets or the fact we had a sheriff's officer coming round to evict us that very day. Mammy's cash problems just seemed to escalate. One Christmas, she told us to open all our Christmas toys very carefully so as not to rip the boxes – they had to be pawned that week.

'Dad is never to know,' she told us.

Over the next few months, I was anxious in case Dad asked to play a board game with me, because I knew it would not be out of the pawn shop until mid-June. I had no idea what Mammy did with the cash. But the Valium addiction clearly wasn't helping. She knew this and tried to come off the pills cold turkey, which was a mistake. One night, she and I were alone in front of our big roaring coal fire and I was standing looking through an album of tea cards someone had given me. They told bizarre *Believe It Or Not* stories of people and events from around the world. One of the cards was about a flea circus in America and I was engrossed. *All those hundreds of fleas I have had on my body and in my hair and I killed them all!* The picture showed tiny fleas riding in tiny chariots. *I could have had my own flea circus*, I thought. *And people would have paid me to come and see it – Janey Barnum's Flying Circus. I could have made money!*

Suddenly, my Mammy screamed. I turned and saw her throw her head back. I stood rooted to the spot and watched in the detached way I did when I was being abused. She was having an epileptic fit. She fell down and thrashed about. I seemed to cut all my senses off. It was as if it was not really happening. She was wearing really cheap black plastic shiny knee-length boots and, in the throes of the fit, one of her feet went into the open coal fire.

Her screams were deafening but I remained stock-still and watched her burn and thrash about. Her foot stayed in the flames, the plastic by now morphing into a grotesque shape around her charred flesh. I started gasping for breath as the whole scene played out before me, as if I was watching it on television. Eventually I ran and left her – with her foot still burning in the fire – to get my big sister Ann who was downstairs in a friend's flat. My sister was 13 years old at the time; I was nine. She ran back in with me and pulled my Mammy's burning leg from the coals and ripped off the boot, taking some skin and flesh with it. The smell of burning plastic and meat was overwhelming. My sister looked so in control but inside she was panicking too. My Mammy was taken to hospital, having suffered terrible burns to her ankle and foot. When she came home, she had to endure weeks of bandage changes and terrible burn treatments. Then she was taken to a mental hospital for a 'rest'.

I felt awful guilt. I felt I should have helped her. I felt a complete failure as a daughter and as a person.

* * *

The asylum was in the north of Glasgow. Whenever I visited her, I found she was making tea or chatting to some other woman who sat in a complete daze. I was terrified that Mammy would end up like those other women in there. During one of my visits, in the corner of her ward sat a poor wee woman with a glazed look in her eye who held a book in her hand and she was trying in vain to flick over a page. Time after time she lifted the paper up but let it drop without turning it over. This drove me to distraction and eventually I got up and flicked it over for her. The woman looked at me in amazement, then screamed into my face. She went ballistic and threw a big hysterical tantrum.

I sat there, a small child, scared and guilty that I had hurt someone yet again. The nurses came over and told me:

'Just stay back. Don't help her. Stay close to your mother.'

The images still haunt my nightmares.

I can't remember when the nightmares started, but they are with me today as an adult and they started when I was a small child. Sometimes I am very small, looking up at people with big feet stamping on me; big cats dragging me in their teeth as I try so hard to shout out and be heard; and I die in my dreams. I see my funeral; I lie in a coffin and will my body to get up out of the box but my stiff limbs are frozen in rigor mortis; I hear the dark demons whispering in my ears, but the box is closed and no one can hear me.

* * *

By the time Mammy was in the mental asylum, my Uncle David Percy had decided on a new game. He would hold me down and choke me until I passed out and I would regain consciousness while he was raping me. Today, in my nightmares, I can still see his face as he strangles me into unconsciousness.

* * *

While my Mammy stayed on in the asylum for an unknown length of time, I was carted off to live with an aunt of my Dad's in Uddingston on the outskirts of Glasgow, a big open wooded area totally different to Shettleston. There were lots of houses which all had front *and* back doors *and* upstairs sections. I had never lived in a home where the family ate so much and bathed twice a week. My aunt and her husband were very kind to me and made me feel very welcome. They had a son – my cousin –

around the same age as me. Their house was very clean and they even had a rabbit and a strawberry patch in the garden. I was mesmerised by the total difference of lifestyle. Within days, I had eaten all the strawberries and accidentally killed the rabbit. It was not really my fault; I picked it up to stroke it and the animal got a fright. When it struggled I dropped it. And then I picked it up and accidentally strangled it by holding it too tight round the neck. It was very old. I can still remember the total shame I felt when I saw my cousin cry. I thought *Only I can make everyone hate me within a couple of days.*

My aunt did her very best to fit me into their lifestyle but she was disgusted by the fact I was lice-ridden and very mouthy and I soon discovered she had a secret. Alcohol. What I found weird was that she was a *secret* drinker – before this, nobody in my direct family had ever been ashamed of their booze problem. After I discovered my aunt's secret drinking, I grew to like my cousin – we had at least that one thing in common – and, during that summer, we would go out to the nearby woods with his pals, but I found he was not very confrontational and could not fight for himself. One day, a big friend of his walked us into a dark, densely wooded area and grabbed at me.

'We don't think you are a girl!' he snarled. 'You have short hair and you always wear trousers and you play football! Show us your fanny or we will call you a boy!'

The big boy pushed me and told my cousin to hold me down while they had a look at my fanny. I was way too fast for them and was annoyed my cousin did not defend me. I grabbed a large stone, leapt at the big boy and whacked him on the side of the head. He squealed like a little girl and I just kept hitting him around the head – *crack! crack! crack!* – cracking the stone down on his skull; *he had tried to look at my fanny!* My cousin had to pull me off him. The big boy bled so badly that I had to wrap my T-shirt around his bloodied head and we had to take him home. His mother was furious and, despite my protestations of self-defence, I was not believed. She marched down the street, confronted my aunt at her front door and, within hours, I was back in Shettleston with my Dad.

In the meantime, my Mammy was benefitting from her stay at the mental asylum. She resisted any real therapy and ended up helping the nurses organise the in-patients' routine. Helping other people helped her. She would chat to everyone in her usual familiar way, pretending to herself that she was not really 'one of them' – only a helper temporarily staying in a mental ward who happened to have some burns on her legs and a bit of a stress problem. She got to know all the nurses by their first names, something that wasn't common in those days. They genuinely liked her and had great laughs with her. She came out with a whole catalogue of funny stories about all the poor women she'd met and how they were all totally mental.

I was overjoyed to have her back home. I loved to hang around with her and go shopping every Saturday. I liked the local Asian corner shop in Darleith Street, the next road to Kenmore Street, which was owned by a wee Indian man called Aslim – Mammy took to calling him 'Asylum' and he politely corrected her for at least the next eight years. But I hated the local butcher's shop round the corner from Darleith Street. It had beautiful hand-painted ceramic tiles on the walls depicting cows and bulls grazing happily in a field and standing beneath lush trees with blue skies in the background. I would look at these stunning animals in the picture and then at the big scabby dead and bloody carcasses hanging on hooks in the shop. I hated the dead animals touching my face, which they sometimes did. The butcher's shop smelled of blood and had dirty sawdust on the floor. One day, when it took forever to get served and I got really bored, I took a look up inside one big cow carcass. I actually stuck my head in the animal's hollow flank and slowly climbed up into its ribcage until I was completely inside the dead beast. When I was completely encased, I boomed out in a low, deep voice:

'This is the cow talking! You must all stop eating me or I will haunt you! MOOOO!'

There were gasps of horror from all the women in the queue.

My Mammy was embarrassed and angry. All the women shouted at me as she pulled me out of the cow. I was all greasy and bloodied. The butcher came and slapped me round the head, at which point my hungry dog Major, who was waiting outside for his weekly scraps, ran in snarling and took a bite at the butcher but missed. He then realised the cow was a better target – and tastier – bit into the carcass and hung onto its sides as everyone tried to remove both mad dog and child from the shop. The butcher yelled at my Mammy:

'You're barred, Annie! Get out! Don't come back!'

This was a big blow to her – in those days women some-times cherished a good butcher more than their partners. Good sausages were to be revered and good men were rare.

When we were clear of the shop, I thought Mammy would be absolutely livid, laden down with various bags of food, saddled with a dishevelled child and a barking dog, barred from her butcher's. I thought she would slap me round the head. But, instead, she laughed all the way home. In all the fracas, the butcher had forgotten to charge her, so she knew he would let her back into the shop because she owed him money.

On another cold, wet, windy day, she huddled me under her coat and pulled me into a particularly dirty shop. There were voices all around and, in the dark of my Mammy's coat, I could hear men shout and swear, while the sound of a TV or radio blared in the background. The commentary was being done by a very fast-talking man; I couldn't make out the words. The room smelled of smoke and wet coats. I looked down and saw piles of cigarette butts on the floor. My sandal shuffled them into neat little piles until all the strewn fags made perfect little squares. Suddenly my Mammy spat out: 'Fuck it! Fucking shitty horse! Shoot the bastard!' as she spun me round, took me out from under her coat, pulled me by my arm and swore all the way up the road. I wanted to hate horses too, just like my Mammy. 'Fucking horses!' I whispered under my breath into the driving rain.

* * *

My Mammy's sister Rita was totally different. She came home from the Isle of Man aged about 30 to stay with her dad, my Granda Davy Percy – the father of Uncle David Percy, her brother and my abuser. Rita was very thin and always coughing, but she was good to all of us. My Dad was very fond of her and built her a radiogram – a long box, which housed a radio and a record player. On the inside lid of the radiogram, Rita pasted pictures of current pop stars: the Beatles, the Rolling Stones, Gerry and the Pacemakers and lots more I didn't recognise.

Rita got married when I was around ten years old. Robert was his name and the only defining thing I can recall that made him different from us was that he was a

Catholic. He lived with his dad and mentally handicapped brother just one street away and we kids treated their house like a big extension to ours; wherever Rita went we followed. After she married, Rita became a bit more like my Mammy – she had cash problems and was always living on her nerves. I loved to be with her when it was just the two of us, but I never felt that she was ever really happy. There were always problems for her to deal with: she had to look after Robert's mentally handicapped brother and her own ageing father – my Granda Davy Percy – whom I used to like going to see coz he was full of stories about the Second World War which fascinated me at the time. He did seem a wee bit creepy, though.

All this to-ing and fro-ing between homes was commonplace. My extended family always seemed to be coming and going through our house. Whenever he ran out of money – which was often – my Mammy's younger brother Uncle James stayed in our home – he was the one who'd taken me to hospital after Mr McGregor's dog had attacked me. Uncle James regularly came to stay in our two-bedroomed flat which already housed my Mammy and Dad, me, my sister Ann, my brothers Vid and Mij and Major the dog. It was a crowded home. Uncle James would arrive with his wife 'Crazy Katie Wallace' and their two kids Sammy and Jackie, who were virtually brought up alongside us. Our crowded home became an even noisier one filled with the sounds of raised human voices and Major's distinctive bark: he always barked quickly in short, two-bark bursts – *Woof-woof … bark-bark … woof-woof … woof-woof* – like it was in a code. Major and I were best friends in a big throng of people.

* * *

One rainy day, I scratched my name into the wall of the landing outside our flat's front door. I carved:

JANEY CURRIE – 1970

'Janey, fucking stop it, ye wee bastard!'

Mammy had just climbed the stairs and was dripping wet holding two plastic bags full of cans and butcher meat.

'Ye cannae write yer name in the wall!' she shouted.

I wanted to be myself, yet I wanted to 'belong'. I joined the Brownies, who used to hold their meetings in an old church in Shettleston, because I enjoyed all their reassuring rituals and games and I loved the code flags. My Mammy could not afford to buy me a uniform but I made do with a second-hand shirt and skirt. I would pore over my Brownie Rule Book and would vow to try hard to be a 'good girl'. I studied hard for all my badges and one night, in the dark cold December of 1970, I was preparing for my Road Safety Badge. Such was my concentration reading the booklet and trying to remember all the rules for Road Safety that, as I crossed the road, I walked in front of a car. I can still feel the impact of the vehicle. It felt as if something sharp had just cut off my right leg and had crushed my thigh. I was unconscious for a couple of seconds, then sat at the side of the road staring down at my mangled leg. I was in total shock but could not feel any pain. I couldn't understand why people around me kept telling me to lie back down.

'I have to cross the road,' I told them. 'I don't want to be late for the Brownies.'

Fortunately for me, the speeding drunk who smashed his car into me was a doctor but, unfortunately for him, soon afterwards my Dad walked past going to his late shift.

He spotted me lying on the pavement and asked the crowd calmly:

'Who knocked down the wee girl?'

'That man over there,' he was told.

My Dad beat the doctor up so badly at the scene of the accident that the police – the Polis – sent the drunken and battered man off to hospital in the same ambulance as me. I sat in my second-hand Brownie uniform and shouted at him for the whole journey to the casualty department:

'Ye fucking bastard! You hit me with your car! Ye fucking bastard!'

At the hospital, a nurse washed my legs and feet saying disdainfully: 'Look at the *dirt* that came off you!' as if it was my fault I came from a dirty home. It upset me. Worse still, the Brownies wouldn't let me back into their club as I had to wear a big plaster cast on my leg for months because the hospital had not set my leg properly. The Brownies said I was a liability and there were insurance problems with me having a plaster cast on their premises; I had to attend Hospital Out-patients for a year – it took that long for me to learn to walk properly again, not helped by my frequent handstands.

'Watch this!' I'd tell my friends in the stone stairwell of our block. 'I can go all the way upside-down with my plaster on!'

'Yeeesaaah!' they'd all yell.

It felt great doing handstands. The plaster counter-balanced my body's weight when I was upside-down, but coming down tended to crack the cast, so I would put water on it to soften the plaster and hide the crack. Eventually, after a year, I was back playing football and running around but, even then, the Brownies would not let me rejoin them.

* * *

When my Uncle was not sexually molesting and raping me, he kept himself busy by joining in and wanting to 'belong' just like me. He became a member of the local Orange Order, a very influential Protestant organisation; there were around 30 Orange lodges in Glasgow's East End. Religion divided and defined communities in the city. Catholics supported Celtic Football Club – which flew the Irish Republic's tri-colour flag over its stadium on Saturdays – and Protestants supported Rangers Football Club – which flew the Union flag of the United Kingdom. I knew a young boy who was stabbed to death just for wearing a Celtic scarf and walking along our street. He was 18 years old, studying History at university and his mammy had bought him the scarf for his birthday. He died with 15 stab wounds underneath a parked car. The young guy who murdered him demanded he be put in a prison which held Protestant UDA terrorists because he claimed the killing was part of a political struggle against the Pope, the IRA and all Catholics.

As a child, as far as I knew, Catholics went to chapel and were at least taught about their religion but most Protestant adults did not attend church. We kids all went to Sunday School groups, sometimes in the local church, sometimes in the local Shiloh Hall or Tabernacle Hall. It was somewhere to go in those days before computer games, videos, DVDs or even high street amusement arcades arrived. There were not many community activities for kids, so most of us piled into a Sunday School, collecting our penny candy on the way in and on the way out. But I did not really take to religion. The preacher – he wore no religious dog collar, just ordinary clothes – would stick figures depicting Bible characters onto a big red fuzzy felt board at the front of the hall and talk about the Lord's divine love. Every week, I used to listen to a sermon about opening my heart and letting Jesus in and, every week, I prayed for Him to stop my Uncle raping me. But it never stopped. I thought Jesus did not like me or maybe I was not important enough to be saved.

My Uncle David Percy played flute for the local Orange Lodge; he also taught Orange children the flute. I hoped he never hurt any other child there. But I knew he *had* abused at least one other child. I had found this out three years before when, one night, my big sister Ann sat with me in the toilet at home in Kenmore Street and I had started to cry. Ann sat me on her knee to comfort me while I stared at the swirly orange and red linoleum pattern on the floor.

'Why are you crying, Janey?' Ann asked. 'Are ye sore?'

I crouched on her knee with both my hands jammed between my legs.

'Aye, I'm sore,' I told her. For the last two years I had had a burning pain whenever I peed. The swirly orange and red pattern on the floor blurred out of focus as tears magnified the colours.

'Where are ye sore?' she whispered to me.

I pointed to my lower abdomen, then pulled up my skirt and pointed at my knickers: 'My pee pee hurts all the time and Uncle David Percy tickles me there an' I hate it!' I sat still, scared to breathe. I could feel Ann's arms tighten around my waist as she balanced on the toilet pan.

'Oh Janey! No, no, no! I thought if I let him touch *me* he widnae touch *you*!' She pulled me round and hugged me; my legs went round her waist and she sobbed into my neck. 'If we never let him get us on wur own he willnae do it again, so let's just stick together when he is here, eh?' She hugged me tighter.

But that had been three years before; the abuse had continued, had turned into regular rape and Jesus had not stopped it.

4
The gangs, the Gadgies and a gun

I used to read newspapers in the toilet because it was one of the few places in our crowded flat where you could get peace and quiet. By reading the papers, I knew Glasgow in the 1960s was a crime-ridden city. It was notorious for its razor gangs – they used open, cut-throat razors as weapons. I read that the ageing pop singer Frankie Vaughan had gone to the rough Easterhouse area and tried to get the gangs to give up their weapons but failed; I read about Jimmy Boyle being put in prison for killing people and my Mammy had told me she had gone to the Barrowland Ballroom and must have danced with 'Bible John', a red-haired serial killer who attacked women who were having their periods and who quoted from the Bible before strangling them and kicking their faces in.

There was a gang in Shettleston called The Tigers and my brother Mij would tell me tales of how they would go into nearby Tollcross Park at night and fight with machetes, but Mij tended to exaggerate, so I was never sure how true these stories were.

Glasgow also had 'Gadgies' – travellers but not actual gypsies – who lived near Shettleston so, every summer and sometimes at Christmas, their fair would come up to us.

The Gadgies were hard-working folk who made their living from carousel and big wheel rides and penny stalls; they sold hamburgers and candyfloss and ran dodgems and they captivated me. They lived in caravans and long trailers and wore beautiful, brightly coloured clothes; they were very well dressed, well spoken and well educated and they had crazy dogs – anyone who could keep a mad dog was OK with me. But when I went to a Gadgie fair once as a wee girl of about four or five, there had been a clown holding balloons with his big painted clown face going *hahahahaha* and it had terrified me. So, even when I grew older, I was a child who was frightened of clowns.

In the summer, the Gadgies would offer us children threepence or sixpence to beat the bushes beside a pungent, dirty off-shoot burn of the River Clyde that ran through our local council housing scheme – scared rats would run out and the Gadgies would shoot them for fun. I loved watching the big Gadgie men using Diana rifles to shoot tiny silver steel shuttlecock-shaped pellets into the frightened, running rats. You didn't see any blood: the rats just fell over as the pellets went into them. I swam regularly in the burn and there must have been so many diseases floating there among the dead rats and rusty broken prams that it was amazing I didn't catch something fatal.

Local adults had different entertainments. Every July, almost the whole of our adult community would converge on the streets, drunk, as they marched with the Orange Walk, the big annual Protestant parade where Orangemen would sing about someone called 'King Billy'. My Uncle David Percy banged on about the perceived wrongdoings of the Catholics for many a night. In reality, he was a layabout who raped children and drank too much, something his King Billy might not have approved of. He used to try to make me sing Protestant songs, but my hatred of him instead made me learn Irish Catholic rebel songs from my pal's dad and I would sing them really loud into his face.

My defiance simply provoked him to be even more brutal when he played his 'games' and I started being very badly bruised by his punches as well as the rapes themselves. He had no conscience about hurting me and cleverly kept most of the bruising to my lower abdomen or legs, where it was hidden under my clothing or would seem natural because I was a rough tomboy and often covered in bruises from football and my own escapades. I did show all the signs of abuse by scratching and cutting my skin and by my hair-pulling habit, but that was overlooked very easily – my family continued to assume I was just a nervous child. At school, my teacher Miss Miller would sometimes take me aside and ask about the bald patches on my head but I would always tell her it was just me getting into fights and nothing to worry about. I did not like the other teachers who saw the cuts and bruises and bald patches and turned their eyes away. I wanted someone to notice the pain I was suffering. I craved the chance to speak out, even if I then hid the truth. I did not want my Dad to go to jail for killing my Uncle. And he *would* have killed him. My Dad never did like Uncle David Percy: as far as Dad was concerned, he was a lazy, workshy layabout.

I loved my Dad: he was the big father figure that we were supposed to be scared of but I never was – he was a pussycat to me. My Mammy used him as a threat to keep us kids in line, but he never carried out the punishments she promised he would give us.

Then, one day, my Dad told me he and I were going to play a game of hide and seek. I ran into the bathroom and locked the door tight. Dad called through the door:

'Janey! Open the door – it's your Dad! Unlock the door and let me in!'

I just sat there, frozen in fear, saying: 'No, no. No!'

No amount of reassurance could get me to open the door. I sat there, crying, terrified. I sat tight.

'What is it you're afraid of, Janey?' he asked. He was getting angry because he couldn't understand why I would be scared of him. His voice was starting to have an edge: 'Janey! It's me – yer Dad! Open the door!'

He eventually had to borrow a ladder, come up the side of the house and climb in through the bathroom window. I sat staring at the floor as he tried patiently to coax me out of my terror. I was relieved when he just sat on the floor and held me for what seemed like hours. I was clinging to him like a life raft. Somewhere inside of me he felt my fear but could not rationalise it. I sat thinking: *I should have known my Dad would never hurt me.*

He only frightened me slightly when he was drunk, not because he was violent but because I was convinced he would fall over, bang his head on something sharp and die. In some of my nightmares, he fell and cracked his head open. In others, I was chased down dark streets by demons, I screamed as I ran with dead legs dragging me through invisible toffee that slowed me down; I would stop struggling, turn round, face the demons and shout: 'I know this is a dream! I can wake up!'

Then one dark demon's mouth would stop snarling and smile. The jaws would open and, slowly, it would taunt me: 'Wake up, then!'

The conscious part of my brain struggles to awaken:

'Please, please wake up, please wake up, please wake up!'

But nothing happens

I turn and face the dark demon.

It sniggers, reaches over and grabs me by the throat.

I can hardly breathe.

I can feel my life drain out of me.

Blood pulses behind my eyes.

I scream so loudly.

Eventually my own screams wake me up.

In my childhood, my nightmares never woke my parents. My sister Ann would waken, but not my parents. Major was my protector. Whenever Uncle David Percy came into our home, Major would attack him, snarling and biting, and get beaten for his aggression towards a close family member. He would be kicked under the kitchen table and I would crawl under with him, rubbing his kicked ribs and whispering, 'Thanks, Major,' into his black pointy Alsatian ears. He would look at me, blink and lick my face, then bury his head into my armpit and stay there for a while until his sore bits mended. For all the kickings he got, he never once gave up attacking David Percy. I would often sit with Major in my bedroom at home and plan a way to kill my Uncle but, of course, I knew it would not happen. Each time he demanded I obey him, I would comply in terror like a silent lamb to the slaughter. He would tell me I was a 'bad girl' and said I liked the things he did to me.

'Say you like it.'

I would be forced to put my head down and tell him to 'do it' because I 'liked it'. When I was being physically held down or punched or raped or suffering extreme pain inside my body I would try to shut off my mind or focus on a ripped piece of wallpaper or, in my mind's eye, still try to believe I was standing in Disneyland watching all the colours of the bright parade and those flying Dumbo elephants I had seen on television.

* * *

47

My brother Vid knew nothing about the abuse, but, one day, he tried to sell me to a wee man with a lame leg who was caretaker of the local Catholic chapel and who told Vid that he would pay him £1 if he brought him girls. To my brother, a pound was a fortune. Vid had never shown much interest in me – I was too young and silly to be in his gang – but, later that same day, he started brushing my hair and wiping my face because, obviously, he did not want to deliver shabby goods on his first day of trading. My eagle-eyed Mammy spotted Vid in mid-brush and asked him why he was getting me all dressed up. He, in all innocence, told her:

'The wee limpy man at St Barnabas told me he would give me a pound for a girl.'

This time, my Mammy saved me. Maybe she hated the thought of a Catholic touching me. Vid was promptly taken off to the local Police Office to tell them the tale of the paedophile who worked at the chapel. My brother sat in stony silence, frightened of the police but admitting nothing. They became more and more agitated at the whole sorry tale and eyed my Mammy as if she were lying. Annie, the queen of improvisation, grabbed the wire of the Anglepoise lamp, wrapped it around Vid's wrist and told him:

'This is a lie detector: every time you tell a lie you will get electrocuted!'

Vid took a deep breath and did not stop talking, his face ashen with fear. The wee limpy man was questioned but let go with only a warning.

Three weeks later, my Dad was standing in a queue at a bus stop, huddled against the driving snow, waiting to go to work, when someone with a walking stick shuffled by him. As he passed, my Dad recognised the caretaker and immediately bolted after him and punched and kicked him all over the street. The folk at the bus stop were horrified and tried to pull my Dad off him:

'He's a cripple! ... What the fuck are you doing? ... Get off him!'

Dad did not even bother to explain; he was too busy kicking and kicking and kicking the old man in the head and body. The police were called and Dad was charged, taken to court and fined. No one ever spoke about it again but, for years afterwards, every time my Dad saw the crippled caretaker he would beat him up. There were never witnesses; he was never charged again; and the chapel paedophile eventually left the area.

* * *

By the time I left primary school aged eleven and started secondary school, my Dad was no longer spending much time with us. My brother Vid was almost leaving secondary school and my sister Ann was working while my eldest brother Mij was 19 and getting into all sorts of bother. We all still lived at home, but it was at this point I felt the most alone. My sister and brothers were growing up very quickly and developing their own lives away from me; and my Uncle was still raping me regularly. For me, puberty had still not happened. I had no breasts; I still looked like a boy. I was also the smallest girl at my new school, Eastbank Academy. Other kids would stop and look at me then ask:

'What age are ye? Ye're awfie wee!'

All the pals I had were exceptionally tall for their age which only made me look even smaller. I tried hard to fit in, but it was difficult looking as I did – dressed like a burst jumble sale on skinny legs. The local second-hand shops were where my clothes came from – and some clothes were hand-me-downs from Mammy's pals' kids, which became most embarrassing when my own pals pointed out I was wearing their old jumpers.

* * *

My Uncle David Percy did not attack me weekly, nor were there specific patterns. At times it was frequent; at times I almost believed it had stopped altogether. He did not molest me every time he came to my home, only when the circumstances suited his needs. He liked to scare me and would sometimes threaten to kill my Dad or my sister Ann. To reinforce his threats, he once brought into my bedroom a black handgun with a brown wooden handle. He was holding me in a corner of the room; I was being subjected to his usual form of playtime and feeling desperate and I had a horrible terror in the pit of my stomach. *A gun means death.* The only time I had seen a gun was on television: if someone fired a gun, the other person was dead. *He's going to kill me!* My Uncle had left it lying on the bed while he molested me and, when he got up to pull on his trousers, I grabbed the gun and held it with both hands like I'd seen in the police series *The Sweeney* on TV. I held it up high, pointing it at his face and stood up, gripping the trigger with my right index finger. His face went ashen and his breath started to quicken. I guessed he must be figuring out if the gun would fire, just as I was. I held it steady and he kept eye contact with me:

'It has no bullets in it,' he whispered. 'But I can go get them and come back.'

I dropped my hand with the heavy metal in it, held out the gun to him and replied:

'One day I will get you.'

It was the first time he actually had to acknowledge that I hated him.

I turned and walked out of the room. I felt for at least one second on that one day I had scared him. It was a small victory but I had not won the war.

5
The family

By the age of twelve, I planned never to get married. I was going to go live in Australia and learn how to talk to Skippy the Bush Kangaroo so that I, too, could be the friend of TV's talking marsupial. I was going to fly round the country in a hot-air balloon looking for other talking animals. I was going to hunt evil child-beating clowns (I knew they did exist) and burn them while the talking kangaroo shouted *Burn, you evil clown!*

It was also when I was aged twelve that, one Friday night, my Dad disappeared. For a week, my Mammy phoned hospitals, the police and the steel factory, desperate to find him. After that week, he simply reappeared but never told her or us where he had been. It was clear, though, that he had finally given up the long struggle to keep his marriage together; he could not understand how he worked hard all week and we still could not afford to pay the electricity or rent. Other people seemed to manage, but not us. His salary would sometimes be 'Wages Arrested' (confiscated) by the sheriff's officers and often we would be threatened with eviction. Dad moved out of our home. Maybe he just hung on until I was old enough; maybe he just could not cope with the cash problems; maybe he should have stayed and been a bigger man and sorted it all out. I don't really know the reasons. But he went. He left but dutifully kept in touch every week. He came back and gave Mammy weekly cash to help out but, of course, it never really did help her. Nothing did.

She took the separation terribly; she saw the collapse of their marriage as a huge personal failure. But her fear of being without my Dad soon turned into anger. She would rant and rave to us about his shortcomings and then spend the rest of the night crying because she had been abandoned. She would turn on all of us at the slightest excuse. Some weeknights, when Mammy was either short of cash or – even worse – had run out of cigarettes, she would shout and bawl at us and run through the flat and slam doors and scream:

'You're all bastards!'

I would suffer badly if I had been to see Dad and did not return with cash. I was torn and confused and hated the whole situation. I wished everything could go back to the way it had been.

Mammy did have the good sense to go to Social Services and register as a lone parent which, in theory, worked out more financially viable as she was no longer responsible for the rent and upkeep of the family. She got State Support, but it did not amount to much and we did not notice any difference at all.

The strangest part was that, when it came to Saturday nights and Dad got drunk as normal, his homing instinct would often lead him staggering back to our flat. Mammy would put him on our old battered sofa and wait for him to pass out from the alcohol, then would gingerly go through his pockets and empty each one in turn. I would stand there rooted with fear in case he woke up and they started fighting. In the morning, when he regained consciousness, he would never refer to her stealing his money and, later on, I realised this was, in part, his way of giving an extra pay-off to Mammy. Neither had other partners that I knew of. To me, it seemed like having a Dad who worked away from home during the week.

Mammy was not good at disciplining the family on her own and the flat soon developed graffiti on the inside. My brother Mij and his friends used knives to carve names like JOE-D and CHAS TINNY on the wooden window frames and used pens to scrawl words on the walls. Mammy never cleaned them off or covered them up. Everything seemed not quite under control and our home began filling up with strangers who would sit with Mammy and take tablets and pills and drinks and would get freaked out of their heads and lie back on the floor and talk bollocks. Mammy had now started drinking alcohol. I hated all her stupid pals coming into our house with their even dafter boyfriends who just hung on because they knew eventually they'd get to fuck women who were full of tablets. None of them were bad people; it was just that we had enough problems of our own to be dealing with. I missed Dad so much it hurt. I felt abandoned. He had not just left her – he had left me. He knew how chaotic it was – that was why he'd left – but he'd left me, at twelve years old, to cope with it.

In Dad's absence, my eldest brother Mij tried to fill his place as the big man of the house, but he was a mixture of spoilt first-born and petulant mummy's boy. He had grown from a sensitive child into an insecure teenager and now, as a young man, he was vastly overweight and had become a big, violent bully. He would argue with Mammy and punch her; she would punch him; she would take her shoe off and hit him; he would chase her and punch her full-force in the head; and the two of them would roll about on the floor hitting each other. I had never seen Dad physically hit Mammy like this. It was terrifying. My other brother Vid and I would try to butt in and stop the violence but nothing on this earth could stop the two of them antagonising each other.

'C'mon, then,' Mammy would spit out at Mij. 'Hit me – go on – hit me!'

'I will!' he'd say. 'If you don't shut up, I'll hit ye!'

'Go fuckin' on – *hit* yer own Mammy! Does everybody *know* ye hit yer *mammy*, ye big fat *bastard*!'

Mij would hit Mammy so hard she would be bruised; she would fight back so fiercely he would be scratched all over his face. My sister Ann would mostly avoid it all but, when Mij got too close, she would lash out at him too; she would fight back as hard as my Mammy and took no prisoners. When the fighting got very violent, my dog Major would join in and one or more of the brawling humans would get bitten. I was never sure if the fighting scared Major or excited him or if he was just hungry. The house was like an asylum; it would never have happened if my Dad had been there but, of course, Dad was told nothing about it because Mammy loved Mij dearly and would always protect him. At times, I wondered if Mammy did it just to get attention. If everything was quiet, she would create a drama. But, if Mij gave her a black eye or a cut arm or a badly bruised leg, she'd say: 'Aye, but he's ma son! I love ma son!' and then she would cry and so would he.

'I'm sorry, Mammy!' Mij would sob to her and they'd hug and be sorry and sad together.

He was truly lovable when he was good, but Mij was insecure and was having problems outside the home too. He was easily led, broke into a shop with some friends and was sent to a local Borstal home with a monkey-puzzle tree outside. Mammy was grief-stricken and visited him weekly for about a year until he came home. The only real effect

Borstal had on him was that, afterwards, he started putting on even more weight.

My other brother Vid, despite having tried to sell me to the paedophile caretaker, was bright at school but not really interested in education. He tried his best to keep the family together and would help by going out and stealing food and money for Mammy if Mij had been particularly nasty to her.

In all this madness, my schoolwork began to suffer. I started missing two or three days a week – sometimes because I had no lunch money or because Mammy asked me to run errands instead of going to school – and eventually my Guidance Teacher, Mr Burgess, started to ask questions about my home life. I sat with him in a bare office containing only a desk and two chairs. He offered me a cigarette, but I told him I didn't smoke and, for the first time in my life, I told someone something about myself.

'There's trouble in the house and I don't think I can cope with it any more,' I told him.

I fell apart and cried.

'You have bruises,' he said gently.

'My brother is hitting my Mammy,' I explained to him, speaking slowly. As I spoke, the frustration started to spill out of me; it was like a wall of grief coming down. I stuttered out about Dad leaving and Mij hitting us all and then, just I was just about to open the floodgates to reveal what my Uncle was doing to me, I took a breath and stopped. I felt this kind, caring man, Mr Burgess, could sort it all out for me, but fear held me back. I had already told my own Mammy years ago and she had been angry with me. Mr Burgess looked at me with the saddest eyes I had ever seen in an adult. He held onto my hands and tried to wipe away my tears at the same time. He told me:

'If someone hits you or attacks you, Janey, go to the police. Don't let anybody hurt you. Always go to the police.'

I sat there knowing this was not an option: Mammy would go mad at me if I 'told' on Mij, but I pretended to accept Mr Burgess's advice. I promised to try and get more schooling in. He promised to keep an eye on me. I begged him not to get social workers involved. By this time, both my brothers had social workers coming to the house. I didn't want to give my Mammy another problem.

* * *

I had no school blazer, but I finally got an anorak and sewed the school badge on the breast of the lurid blue quilted material to make sure Mammy could not pawn it. Even so, it was in the pawnshop four weeks after the summer holidays began – with the badge still on. Mammy must have persuaded the pawnbroker he could sell it to someone else from the same school for some other poor kid.

On one of my twice-a-month visits to my Dad during that winter, he asked me:

'Where's yer coat? It's freezing cold.'

'I don't have a coat, Dad.'

'And why are ye wearing open plastic beach sandals?'

I was 13 and all the other girls were wearing fashionable high platform wedges. He took me into Glasgow city centre and bought me a coat, some new jumpers and shoes. He was puzzled when he saw me immediately scuff the shoes and tear the labels out of the woollens. It soon dawned on him that I was damaging the goods so that they could not be taken back to the store for a cash refund. We kissed goodbye and I hopped on the bus home, blissful in the knowledge that Mammy would shout at me for not getting cash, but that the clothes would stay mine. That weekend, when Dad came round to our home, he must have had a showdown with her, because she went berserk at me when he left:

'Tell yer Daddy *every*thing! Go on! Tell yer Daddy *everything*, will ye? Tell yer fucking wonderful Daddy that cares so much aboot ye! Yer Daddy that fucked off and left you! Yer Daddy that leaves ye here!'

And she slapped me round the head a few times. I was left feeling torn by the whole thing, I was mad at my Dad for leaving me with all this shit; angry at Mammy for not being able to cope.

* * *

One week shortly afterwards, the school organised a sponsored swim in aid of a charity. The kids had to collect sponsorship cash, swim the lengths promised, then hand the cash over to the school. On the day of the swim, a friend and I decided to skip English class and just fool around under the pretence we were going to see the gym teacher – we just hung around the toilets laughing and running about. We thought we had got off scot-free but, later, the headmistress came stropping into my biology class and demanded that the friend and I come outside into the corridor. Once there, the headmistress grabbed me roughly by the neck of my shirt, pulled me up to her face and said:

'You are a thief, Currie. You are nothing but a common thief!'

She marched the other girl and me up to the school office and told us that, when we had skipped English class, another girl's sponsorship money had been stolen.

'You lied about your reasons for leaving class. You did not go to see Miss Stewart in the gym. So I know you are *thieves*!'

I protested my innocence: 'But I wa—'

The headmistress slapped me hard on the right cheek and the pain rang through my head. 'You're a thief!' she screamed right into my face. 'You're nothing but a common thief! That girl collected money for charity and you stole it!'

I turned and ran from the school and belted all the way home. I was in tears when I got there and blurted the whole story out to my Mammy. She looked me straight in the eyes and asked: '*Did* you take the money, Janey?'

'No, Mammy, I never took it.' I felt my own anger rise at the same rate as my Mammy's. She lit a cigarette, grabbed her coat and marched me back to confront the headmistress. *At last my Mammy was my hero! She would save the day!*

All the way along the road to the school, Mammy was puffing on her cigarette, muttering to herself: 'Hit you, did she? ... Fucking hit you, did she?' and then she would mutter: 'I'll fucking show *her* what fucking hitting is.'

Slowly, it dawned on me that my Mammy was walking so fast and her voice was getting so vicious that she was going to lose her temper completely. I stopped her halfway to the school and pleaded: 'Mammy, please don't get too upset. Don't swear. Remember, I have to stay at the school. Just take it easy, Mammy.'

She paused long enough to take one deep drag on her cigarette and to spit out the words: 'No one hits my wee lassie. No one! I mean it! And she won't hit you ever again!'

By now, I was shit-scared of the whole thing and began to wish I had never told her about what had happened. But it was too late. We were already at the door of the school office and she was dragging me in behind her, demanding to speak to the headmistress. Out of the big brown door appeared my dragon headmistress, all long tweed outfit, coiffed blonde hair and polyester white scarf, strutting for a showdown. I stood there as this large woman eyed my wee Mammy. I followed the tweedy woman's eyes down. Mammy had unkempt grey hair pulled to the side, no make-up on her lined face and wore a very shabby pale blue cotton coat, no tights and cheap brown plastic shoes which her toes had partly burst through. I realised at that moment what other people saw when they looked at my Mammy and for one awful second my Mammy saw the look of distaste in the headmistress's eyes as well. I felt sad for my Mammy. One disdainful look from this figure of authority and she almost crumbled. Mammy had been about to launch into her big defence speech, but the tweedy woman's nasty look momentarily floored her.

After that fleeting second passed, though, she pulled herself up to her full height and asked matter-of-factly:

'Why did you hit my daughter?'

'She is a thief.'

Both women then dived into a shouting match, accusations flying from Mammy, the headmistress drowning her out with her side of the story; Mammy eventually cornered the woman into a lame admission:

'Yes, I pushed Janey.'

Mammy took one step back and punched the woman hard in the middle of her face. My elegantly dressed headmistress went flying backwards, hitting and tumbling over a chair to land flat on the floor with her long tweed skirt right up over her chest revealing light brown tights with white knickers underneath. Mammy jumped on her and started delivering more punches into the woman's head with her wee fists. I stood totally gobsmacked. The school office burst into wild activity and, as Mammy was dragged off the headmistress, the woman lay on the floor, gasping, with her hair pulled up and tufts of it on the floor. Mammy looked down at her snarling: 'Charge me! Get the Polis! I hit an adult and you hit a child! You hit my daughter and she has a witness!'

With that, Mammy turned on her heels, grabbed me by the hand and marched out of the school leaving everyone in the office in a state of shock. The police were never called. The girl whose cash had been 'stolen' admitted she spent the money on food because she was hungry and the headmistress told everyone at our school assembly that there had been no theft. I sat smugly as I was vindicated and my Mammy became a legend at Eastbank Academy. The aftermath was that the headmistress and my Mammy had another meeting. My Mammy came out and told me:

'Look, she's accepted that you never stole the money, but you dodged a class and I punched that cow, so you're going to have to take six of the belt.'

I was given six lashes with a leather strap on my right hand and the headmistress looked like a crazed animal when she was hitting me. Even the assistant head, who was present, looked unsettled when he saw her eyes. I stood there, aged 13, thinking *How many other people are going to hit me? What is it about me?*

* * *

After that, my Mammy just kept taking more Valium and lurching from one crisis to another. At least the State made sure the rent was covered and I now became eligible for free school meals. So, in a way, things were a bit easier on the cash front. She made sure we had electricity by getting a pal of hers to break into the central panel for our block and illegally connect us directly – so we never had to pay another bill except on one occasion when an Electricity man spotted the wire. She was prosecuted and ended up in Glasgow Central Court where she turned into Greta Garbo and Rita Hayworth for the day. Watching all those angst-ridden movies on Sunday afternoon TV had paid off. She wrung her hands and cried:

'Ma own mammy left me in ma teens an now I've got ma own weans and I've had a nervous breakdown and I'm havin' the change of life!' She always mentioned her womb when she wanted to make people uncomfortable. 'And here's me,' she wailed, 'and ma man's ran away and left us all and I've got a wee lassie at school!' She held her hand to her forehead and gave them their full money's worth.

I sat in court thinking *Fucking hell, Mammy! Where did you get that voice from?* She did everything short of looking up to the skies to see her sons flying off to die in the Second World War.

She was given a warning and was told never to reconnect her own supply of electricity ever again. All the way back from the court to the bus stop, the two of us laughed.

'What a performance I did there, eh, Janey?' she said with some pride. 'They all had to feel sorry for me when they saw me fallin' apart.'

'Yes, Mammy.'

It was only a few steps later that I realised everything she'd said (apart from the 'change of life') was true. She'd performed the tragic role of someone who was exactly who she was.

After this, Mammy fell into an even deeper depression; she started really going mad with the drugs and accumulated even more 'Valium Pals' around her: other women who were equally doped up all day on tablets. Sometimes I would come home from school and find them all in our dirty living room with the graffiti on the walls, huddled around our wee fire talking gibberish.

'There's a snake sliding up that wall, Janey! Hit the spider off! There's a spider on it … There's spiders! … There's spiders everywhere!!'

I kept to myself more and more, sharing my thoughts only with Major. We would go on long walks as I poured it all out to him; he must have been fed up listening to my shit life. Even dogs have their limits. Some mornings, when Mammy let him out for a while on his own, he would try to follow me to school. This worried me a lot, as he was always hungry and did bite people at random. I often had to chase him back up the street, hoping he could make it home without snarling at someone.

* * *

By this time, I had a sort of boyfriend. He was my Mammy's pal's son and we would hang out together but I avoided the contact side of the relationship as I felt I was not worthy of having affection given to me and I was scared that the sex situation might arise. I really liked and was very physically attracted to some of the boys at my school, but would never have had the nerve to ask them out. I had absolutely no self-confidence. I did not believe I could be worthy of anyone's attention at all.

My sister Ann already had a steady boyfriend and was working as a sewing machinist in a factory; she was 18 and in love. In that one year, she and Jay got engaged, she got pregnant and they got married.

Dad was now living with Aunt Rita and Uncle Robert at Redcar, a small seaside town in North Yorkshire. He came up to Glasgow for Ann's wedding and it was so good to see him, just as it was great to see Ann happy with Jay, but there was a problem. Jay was a Catholic. It was not *such* a big deal, but enough to create some tension in the family: his Catholicism hung in the air like a bad smell. When she gave birth to her son Jay Junior in July that year, I was ecstatic: he was so tiny and beautiful. I loved him on sight and would spend hours just looking at his face.

My Uncle David Percy also got married that year. His wife Margaret was also a pregnant bride. She had a son around the same time as Ann. I liked Margaret: she was really just a teenager like Ann trying to make the best of her life. My Uncle David Percy and Margaret lived next door to his father – my grandfather – Granda Davy Percy. I would visit Margaret when Uncle David was out of the house – this was easy to do as Granda Davy would tell me if his son was at home or not. We both kept up the façade of happy families; he would make a point of being nice to me in front of his wife. When we were accidentally alone for a moment, he would mostly give me a silent, sinister stare; sometimes he would look out the side of his eyes and snigger at me. I never thought once of telling Margaret about the abuse, I just carried on as if it was all in the past and part of a big bad dream.

On one occasion, Margaret asked me to stay the night with her; my Uncle David was away and would not be coming home. She did not like staying there alone so I agreed. They only had one bed in their flat. That night, while I was asleep, my Uncle David Percy did come home; he crept into bed beside his wife and me. I awoke in the early hours of that morning to feel fingers creeping into my knickers. I thought it was his wife; I could not believe it. I sat upright to see my abuser's face staring at me in the early morning light. His wife was asleep beside him. He did not care and carried on trying to pull me towards him. His new baby was in a cot in the same room. I jumped out of the bed and shouted:

'Margaret! Wake up!'

The baby screamed.

My abuser hissed at me to be quiet and looked shit-scared.

'Shut up!' he whispered at me. 'Shush! Shush!'

Margaret sat up in bed and I saw her eyes. She knew. *She knew.*

'Are you all right?' she asked me.

I stood in their cold flat and pulled on my jeans. I had the words of my Guidance Teacher, Mr Burgess, swirling in my head. *Go to the police. Don't let anybody hurt you. Always go to the police.* I told Margaret that I just wanted to go home now; she tried to reason with me to stay as it was about 5.00 a.m. I turned to my Uncle and shouted at him:

'If you ever touch me again, I'll go to the fucking Polis, ye bastard!' I turned to Margaret. 'He was *touching* me,' I said and pointed at him.

Margaret looked at him with cold eyes; I walked out of the flat and ran all the way home. I will never know what he told her but, the next time I saw Margaret, nothing more was said. Nothing more was *ever* said about it. She never asked me why I left that early to run back to my Mammy. It was as if it had never happened.

* * *

In the winter of that same year, I took a really bad attack of the mumps. They went away, but complications followed and I was petrified I was going to be put in hospital; I was scared of nurses touching me and doctors probing my body. I started being sick and sick and sick and lost too much weight and this, together with the after-effects of the infection, left me very weak. I would lie on a pull-down sofabed in the living room watching television; I loved *The Sweeney* because bad people always got caught and I would try to keep myself from vomiting all the way through the show so I could follow the plot. My Mammy was really concerned and I had many visits from our GP who gave me some health drink which I never managed to keep down.

On one particular night, I lay in the darkened living room with the smell of vomit on my bed and all I could see were Major's eyes silently watching me as I tried to make it to the toilet. I could not stand up – it was as if my legs were too thin and shaky to support me – so I crawled on all fours until I made it to the bathroom door. Major slowly walked beside me all the way. I sat at the door and passed out for a moment. When I came round, I was dizzy and scared, but Major sat curled around me on the cold floor. I thought I was going to die. I didn't care if I died or not, but I felt so desperately weak and ill. I made it to the toilet and crawled back to bed, with Major sitting there all night watching me and whimpering as I hung over the bed to vomit into a white plastic bucket. Occasionally, he would put his paw up onto the grubby candlewick bedspread and get me to rub his head as I lay there waiting for the illness to slowly work itself out of my body. I had always loved Major but never before needed him that much. He was there for me. He knew that I was ill and would hardly leave my bedside.

* * *

My brother Mij came to visit my sick-bed with his new, live-in girlfriend Cathy, and my Aunt Rita and Mammy's Valium pals all came along to make comments about how skinny I was, how sickly I looked and what form of cure I should take.

'Castor oil is what you need ...'

'Black treacle will cure you ...'

'You should get some good Irish stew down you ...'

Dad also came to see me, as he was now back living in Glasgow and, during my time ensconced in the living-room pull-down bed, I was privy to most of the adult conversations that took place while they thought I was asleep. That was how I heard that Mij's girlfriend Cathy was pregnant. *Was no one safe from the dreaded teenage mother syndrome?* The pregnancy caused more antagonism between Mammy and Mij. He was determined to make this relationship work, but he did not bank on Cathy being as headstrong and bad-tempered as he was. Their fights were just beginning when I started to come through the illness.

We now had Cathy staying, pregnant and feeling stifled in our dirty, overcrowded flat. There were seven of us living in two bedrooms and a living room. Then along came my Uncle James – Mammy's younger brother – with his wife 'Crazy Katie Wallace' and their two kids Sammy and Jackie – and then we also had my Dad's brother Uncle John on a temporary stay in our flat.

I loved Uncle John – a quiet, funny man with a sparkly character though he had always been a drifter and no one knew much about him. He would look after me and stop Mij from hitting Mammy; I think Mij realised Uncle John was not someone you messed with. He had spent some time in prison when he was younger but, unlike most of the people we knew who had been Inside, he never talked about it at all. He encouraged me to go to school, would listen to all my homework projects and discussed all my written stories. In return, I would steal cigarettes for him from my Mammy. She and Uncle John had a strained relationship. They would circle each other like vicious cats.

Mammy would shout at him and accuse him of eating too much or getting in her way; he would never argue back; she would throw cups at him to get a reaction; he would just smile at her and amble away into his bedroom to read his books. This unnerved my Mammy, because she was used to – and liked – a man who fought back. We all lived alongside each other in a cramped, disjointed, dysfunctional kind of harmony.

Major enjoyed snarling at all the new legs as they came and went through our home; he would sniff round the new baby when Ann visited and she would panic in case he took a bite. But poor Major was getting old – he must have been about twelve years old by now and his limbs were getting stiff. One morning, he went out as usual around 6.00 a.m. but, this time, he returned limping. As the week went on, his hindquarters seemed to be getting more painful so my brother Vid took him to the RSPCA vet. Vid loved Major as much as I did and was distraught when he was told the dog had been bitten by a rat. It seemed Major had been fighting with vermin down at the burn where the Gadgies used to shoot rats. The vet advised that 'The dog should be put to sleep,' but Vid was determined to keep Major alive. Two nights later, I was lying in the living-room bed when Major came in all limpy and sore. I climbed out of the covers and hugged him. He looked at me as I stroked his hot, matted hair. He put his head on my knees and died, right there on my legs.

I screamed at the top of my voice.

Vid came running in and held Major with me. We both kept trying to rub him and make him alive again. We could not believe he was dead. Mammy even shed a tear as we stood round his dead body. I could not be consoled. I had to help Vid lift Major and we both took him to the old burn bridge and buried him in the mud. I spent months after his death looking at the one photo I had of him, missing him so much that it was a physical ache in my chest. He had been my only true pal, my protector, and now he was gone for ever. He haunted my dreams. In sleep, we would run together over the football fields; I would laugh as he pulled his leash from the door handle and swipe it at me. But the nightmares were still there, too. I would dream I was being buried under the floor of a cellar beneath a castle. It was dark and then I would be in a prisoner-of-war tunnel as if I were trying to escape from Colditz and I would get stuck in the tunnel. Always underground. I am trapped underground. I try to escape by going through a door, but the door is too small to get through and the tiny passage is too narrow to get through and I can't escape.

* * *

By now, Mij had returned to his old ways. He would hit his girlfriend Cathy; my Mammy would batter Mij for hitting Cathy; Mij would then batter my Mammy for hitting him; and Cathy would hit Mij for battering my Mammy; so Mij would hit Cathy again; and it became a circus. Mij's wee baby Debbie would sit there looking at everyone hitting everyone else and not even scream. Just look silently. Taking it all in behind her baby eyes.

During the week, Mij worked as a porter at Glasgow Royal Infirmary, so that gave us all some respite from his temper tantrums. He was still a fantasist. He boasted he had performed brain surgery on a patient; the man lived and was cured. And, one night, he brought home some equipment from the surgical wards. One of these items was a very sharp and scary scalpel. Mij wielded it, for fun, as if he were some homicidal heart specialist. A few nights later, in the midst of a heated argument with Mammy in our kitchen, he held the blade right up to her face, almost touching her cheek. I was so terrified he would cut her that I put up my left hand to stop him. He accidentally sliced through my wrist, just missing the artery, but blood spurted onto his face, onto the wall and down onto my Mammy's jumper. As I turned my wrist, some blood spurted upwards and hit clothes hanging from the ceiling pulley. I had to be rushed to the Royal Infirmary with a dirty, very smelly pillowcase wrapped tightly round my wrist, which I'd done myself. Mij was frantic, Mammy was panicking and I just bled. I had to have the slash on my wrist sealed with butterfly straps and I still carry the scar.

I had, by this time, had more than enough of Mij's violence. A few weeks later, I did run up to the Police Office and reported to the desk sergeant that my brother had been hitting me.

'We cannae dae nothing unless ye charge him,' the policeman told me.

'Well, I'll charge him, then,' I replied.

An officer came down to our house to confront Mij and I was beyond caring what reaction this would cause. Mij was sitting on the living-room couch.

'This wee lassie came up to see us because you've been hitting her,' the policeman said.

'Ah well,' Mij replied. 'She was cheeky.'

'*I'm* cheeky,' said the policeman. 'Hit *me*, ye big fucking fat bully. Stop hitting her! If you lift yer hand to her again and she comes tae me, I'm gonna jail ye.'

Mij sat there looking petulant and put down. Afterwards, they all went mental with me.

'Ye fucking grass!' Mij yelled at me.

'Ye fucking brought the Polis here!' Cathy yelled.

'That's all we need,' my Mammy told me. 'Our Mij going to jail. Ye know fine well that he's been in trouble before. You're a fucking dirty bastard. You're a bad, bad lassie, Janey.'

By now, I really didn't care. I felt I had just managed to escape one man who abused me sexually for nine or ten years; I was not about to take on another who abused me physically. That weekend I surpassed myself. My Dad was in Shettleston and I went down to The Waverley and told him, 'That cut on my hand. It was Mij. He held a knife to my Mammy's face. I got in the way.'

He put down his pint, walked up to our house and threatened to beat Mij up if he touched any of us again. As usual, when Dad left, Mammy stuck up for Mij and gave me a real mouthful for having 'grassed' on her favourite abusive son. I tried to understand but couldn't: it was the same way she had reacted when she learned her own brother was a paedophile.

* * *

I was still very small and skinny for my age. I had no shape or breasts nor had I menstruated. My body was still a child's.

'You've got nae tits!' boys would shout at me in the street.

I was glad to look androgynous, as it meant I avoided any real sexual attention. My social life, though, was beginning to pick up. I was slowly starting to gain a little confidence in myself and was making new pals; I went to school discos where we danced to Mudd, Showaddywaddy and the Rubettes. I had always hated the Beatles and the Rolling Stones because my Uncle had often played their music in the background while he abused me. My own taste was now folk music, Yes, Genesis and watching *The Old Grey*

Whistle Test on TV, when I could. I even snogged a few boys because I knew, if you snogged someone, you could become the centre of attention by talking about it later.

Vid's best friend Charlie had now moved in to join Vid, Mij, Cathy, their small baby Debbie, Uncle John, Mammy and me in our already crowded two-bedroom flat with one small living room, one usually broken non-functioning bath, no hot running water and a skanky kitchen. We had to wash in the kitchen sink and heat up hot water in a pot. Vid and Charlie had been friends since they were tots but were total opposites. Charlie was a Catholic and supported Celtic. Vid was a Protestant and supported Rangers. Charlie – aged 17 – was a flash ladies' man who looked after his appearance, bought really expensive clothes, always dressed cool and wore Denim Deodorant for Men; Vid had to rely on his gift of the gab.

A lot of the local kids were starting to sniff glue: getting high by inhaling the fumes of strong solvents. I never understood this and always avoided people who did it, but some of my pals had also started drinking alcohol. I tried this but it wasn't for me either: it made me feel sick and I disliked the feeling of having no control. I also refused to smoke cigarettes because the smell of nicotine on my fingers reminded me of my Uncle David Percy. So my pals would slag me off:

'You've got nae tits, ye don't smoke, ye don't drink, what're ye gonna dae if ye ever *do* grow up?'

My teenage years were relatively simple in comparison to what some other teenagers got up to – I was not moody, not stroppy, had no real interest in make-up or sexually revealing clothes. I had no need to get involved in the usual conflicts between parents and kids that reflect the child's need to appear adult; I was not a virgin. Around me in the streets, the punk era was beginning. I had worn ripped clothes with safety pins in them for years out of necessity, now middle-class kids were paying fortunes to buy them from designer shops. They were paying to look poor. I didn't like punk fashions or music. I loved Supertramp, Steely Dan, Abba, Meatloaf, Kate Bush and many more non-punk singers. Dad bought me a cassette tape recorder so I could sit in my room and tape Radio Luxembourg, which had very bad reception but played fantastic music. The result on my cheap machine was listening to good music interspersed with foreign-language voices breaking in from other European stations.

'Fuck me, it's the Pope!' we'd say. 'Aha! He's gone! We'll dance again!'

The one good thing about having Charlie in our house was that he brought along his Philips stereo record player and I was in awe of his music collection. The Stylistics, Abba, all the best new disco hits and LPs by cutting-edge Glasgow comedian Billy Connolly. *Wow!* I'd think, *He can tell a story that isn't funny but the way he tells it makes it funny!* I would rush back from school before Charlie got home from his work as an apprentice electrician and play the vinyl records on his big rubber-matted turntable through his big loudspeakers. Mammy would shout at me:

'Don't touch that boy's fucking records! It's the only thing he's got, the big stupid Catholic!'

But Charlie was OK about it and, in fact, liked to discuss music with me. Sometimes he would even let me go with him to buy his weekly record at the music shop; I was in heaven and felt I had found my vocation in life: I wanted to be a disc jockey! I would have my own record collection and play at all the best discos in Glasgow! But Mammy told me: 'You'll never make any fucking money playing records.'

So I went to my school's career teacher for advice. This gloomy old man in a tweed jacket which smelled of musty pencil-shavings sat opposite me in a poky, mushroom-coloured office. His worn-out face asked me what I wanted to be. I came up with my favourite dream jobs. He put aside his books, opened up an old red card index box, flicked through to my chosen careers and, with a straight face, replied:

'Disc jockeying, psychic reading and stand-up comedy do not constitute a career in Glasgow, but you can be a secretary or a sewing machinist.'

Rather disappointed, I went back to studying food, nutrition and history. I was doing well at my Standard Grade studies and looking forward to taking my exams, but the start of my January term was a bad time for Mammy. She always had no cash but this time was worse. I had no shoes at all to wear to start school and, on Thursday, 20 January 1977 – the morning of my sixteenth birthday – I went into the school office in my Mammy's plastic sandals and said, 'I'm 16 now. I'm leaving school.'

'You can't,' they said.

'Yes I can,' I told them.

'But you're taking six Standard Grades,' they said and got my art teacher to come and talk to me.

'Janey, don't leave. Stay on and get your art exam, then do your art Highers and go on to art school. You've always wanted to go to art school.'

'No,' I said. 'I need money. I have to leave.'

My maths teacher tried to persuade me, then my food and nutrition teacher – a wonderful woman, Mrs Jackson – begged me, 'Please stay. Everybody else in the class is going to fail these fucking exams. You're the only person who's going to pass this exam. I'm gonna look like a fanny. Stay and at least pass the exams so I don't lose my job.'

'I'm sorry – I'm leaving,' I told her.

'Oh fuck!' she said.

I liked her.

It was a quick, impulsive decision. I regretted it the next day but felt I couldn't go back. I still had no shoes, only my Mammy's plastic sandals. At the end of the week, I got hold of a pair of desert boots and that settled things. You couldn't wear trousers to school – only a skirt – and you couldn't wear desert boots with a skirt.

Nobody in my family had ever stayed on at school and gone to university. So I (and they) figured it couldn't be that important, though my Dad had gone to night school. I had imagined that getting a job would be better and easier than staying at school, but I found it was easier said than done for an unqualified teenager who did not have any idea what form of employment she could – or wanted to – do. I heard about something called 'Community Industry' where kids who came from abusive backgrounds or had learning difficulties got to work in the community. I came into the first category, although the authorities were unaware of this. It was, at heart, a community project for daft people with no hope.

When I went for the interview, I told them: 'My Mammy and Dad have split up and I've got nae education but I want tae help people.'

As I was a good talker, good with people and looked very shabby, I was accepted for the work and got sent to Castlemilk, a sprawling housing scheme on the outskirts of Glasgow. I was one of a group of 15 girls who, each day, were sent with two supervisors to work either in an old folks' home or in a children's nursery. Some of the other 14 girls had been put into children's homes when young, were still in homes, had got pregnant very young, been abandoned by their families and/or had really serious learning difficulties. Two of them had had children by their own fathers. They treated me like an equal and I loved that feeling; nobody looked down on me for not having the right clothes or for wearing unsuitable shoes. I particularly loved working at the old people's home. One old man told me about the days when he used to deliver milk around the cobbled streets of Glasgow with a horse and cart, keeping the milk cold with blocks of ice and with pre-arranged places to water the horse. The most consistent advice they all gave was *Live your life to the full, because you get old really quickly – and always make good friends because sometime later you will need them to look after you when you're old.*

Every morning, I would get up quickly and happily rush out to get the bus to go to work. It was the first time I had had my own money and I made the best I could of dressing myself and helping Mammy out financially. I was finally beginning to feel grown up and making my own cash gave me some independence. Like my Dad before me, I soon decided to go to night school and pay to finish the education I had given up. Twice a week I travelled to Cardonald College on the other end of the bus route from Shettleston to study for my art and English Standard Grades.

At home, only Charlie and I had jobs and the house was even more overcrowded, as Charlie's girlfriend sometimes stayed overnight. Mij had been sacked by the Royal Infirmary and we would spend our evenings listening to tales of his adventurous fantasy life. It was a couple of years after the film *Jaws* had been released and Mij tried to convince us he had once fought off a shark at the beach in Largs, Ayrshire.

'The shark died,' he told us, 'and I buried its body outside the County Bingo Hall at Castlemilk.'

He told us he had also tamed a wild lion from Glasgow Zoo.

'It became my friend and I disguised it as a big dog and kept it on a leash.'

Mammy called him Walter Mitty after the movie character. At one point Mij convinced himself that he was the pop idol Bryan Ferry.

I was also starting to worry about myself as I still had neither breasts nor periods and I knew that I should be developing, but I kept all this to myself as no one in the family ever discussed sex or periods. Mammy and I grew apart a lot that year; she was no longer financially responsible for me and neither was Dad, so some of the pressure was off them now. My way of giving Mammy some help was to keep out of trouble, not cost much and try to be less of a burden all round. I made no big demands, had no big expectations and I was not moody.

My favourite day of 1977 was one morning when Mammy and I got up early and found a cheque in the post from the Welfare. She whispered to me in the kitchen that we'd have a day out. Just us both! I ran to the public phone box and called work to say I was sick, then Mammy and I cashed her cheque and caught an early train.

When we got off at Saltcoats, it was a beautiful, sunny, clear, seaside day that welcomed us. We giggled as we ran like two teenagers down to the shoreline and paddled in the cold grey water of the Firth of Clyde under a hot sun and cloudless blue sky. We ate breakfast in a beachside café then headed for the funfair in the afternoon, playing bingo and eating chips. She then talked me into going on a big wheel for the first time in my life. I was so scared as I soared alone into the sky that I screamed and laughed at the same time, looking down at the now tiny figure of my Mammy as she waved and laughed up at me. When I staggered off the wheel, she held me close, laughing loudly, 'Never be scared of anything, Janey!'

I wanted to believe her and wanted to tell her I thought the abuse was over now. But I couldn't. She held my face close and smiled, telling me it was time to sit on the beach; she bought a can of beer to drink.

'Why d'ye have to drink just now?' I sulked.

She smiled and said nothing.

We both sat in silence as the summer sun soared above us and almost burned us to the bone. We watched the sea lap up to the shoreline as we lay back on our coats thinking about everything. The day had been one big adventure but then it was over and we both knew it was time to catch the train back to the place where we had to be 'us' again. I had savoured the whole day as if I knew I was never again to have that precious time with her.

6

A new boyfriend

Nineteen seventy-seven was the year that changed both our lives. I grew up and my Mammy got a new boyfriend.

His name was Peter Greenshields. I really did not want to meet him. Nor did the rest of the family. She and Dad had been separated for at least four years, although they still got back together most weekends when he arrived back at our home drunk. It was hard for me to imagine that Mammy was sexually active or to cope with the knowledge that she might want a man other than my Dad.

When I met Peter, he was a neatly dressed but slightly creepy man, only about five foot six inches tall, thin and wiry, with thick, dark wavy hair and cold blue eyes. I thought he had a very lined face for a man who was only about 37 – my Mammy was 40. Peter explained to me that he was just out of prison but avoided telling me why and answered with a blank cold look when I probed. There was something sneaky and unsettling about him and I tried hard to be nice to him for Mammy's sake but I disliked him on sight. He used to set a small wire noose outside his back window to trap pigeons and then he cut their throats with a Bowie knife and ate them. Mammy could see no wrong in Peter at all. She and I were walking with him in Tollcross Park one day when he saw a swan swimming on the pond, jumped into the water, grabbed it and strangled it.

'I hate swans,' was all he said by way of explanation. The white bird's fat body lay by the side of the pond, with its long slender neck flopped around like someone had deflated it.

Mammy told me he had lived with some woman who was really bad to him and had taken away his young son when he was in prison; she told me he was a nice wee man who had just fallen on hard times and she really warmed to what I saw as his odd personality. They didn't actually live together – for one thing, there was no space in our house – but, soon after they met, he moved into a ground-floor flat directly across the street from us. His window looked straight up at ours and I felt as if his eyes were on us at all times.

Mammy would walk across Kenmore Street and watch television with him in his flat, which had wooden floorboards immaculately bleached clean. His home was very sparsely furnished. Characterless. A couch. Two chairs. A table. They smoked cigarettes together, but his flat always smelled of carbolic soap and Old Spice under-arm deodorant. I never really liked being there, but Mammy sometimes insisted that I join them for a cup of tea and a Fray Bentos meat pie. Occasionally he would try to make friends with me. On one occasion, because he knew I liked reading, he gave me a dog-eared, second-hand copy of James Herbert's horror novel *The Rats*.

'Thank you,' I said.

Mammy was always very guarded in her conversation about Dad in front of Peter. I wasn't and would eagerly chat about him while Mammy gave me cold stares. Peter would glare at me for talking about Dad and then suggest Mammy went home and take me with her.

She had bruises from the start of the relationship. Peter didn't just hit her. One day, she was acting really scared, pacing up and down, clenching and unclenching her fists, very agitated, finally bursting into tears. I looked down past her, through our first-floor window and saw Peter across the street, standing in his ground- floor flat just glaring up at our window. I looked in my Mammy's eyes and saw her fear. I opened the window and shouted down across the street, 'What's your problem? What the fuck's your problem?'

Peter walked away from his window and my Mammy grabbed me.

'Don't upset him!'

'Why, Mammy? What's he gonna do?'

One night at his flat, in an argument after he shouted at Mammy when he was drunk, I smashed a large china bowl with a floral pattern onto the top of his head. It shattered over his skull and I pulled him down by his neck to the floor. While he remained stunned, Mammy and I scarpered out of his flat and across the dark street to our building. She was hysterical with fear; I explained the whole thing to my brother Vid and to Charlie; they took one look at Mammy's face and tried to reassure her that Peter could not get to her – he had no key to our flat. But she was inconsolable and sat petrified in her bedroom, looking over at his window, a big kitchen knife in her hand, waiting for the madman to arrive. About half an hour later, he did come running to our door, banging on it, shouting:

'Annie! Come oot! I'm no' leavin' – come oot, Annie!'

Charlie and Vid opened the door and chased him down the stairs. Peter was beaten, but only for the moment. The whole charade continued with Mammy feeling alternately sorry or scared and then taking Peter back into her heart. We all grew weary of her acceptance of his behaviour. She would always stick up for him.

'He's no' that bad, Janey. It's me. I make him mental.'

All the time, I thought to myself: *What is wrong with women who think they can 'change' a bad man into something good? I never want to be like that.* All the time, Mammy made excuses. She had ignored her own brother's sexual abuse of me; she had made excuses when her own son Mij beat her – which he still did; and now here she was making excuses for Peter – a man who could only hurt her more and more. I thought: *How low can her self-esteem be?* My nightmares had started to include Peter. He was trying to trap me in a box, trying to suffocate me.

In time, the whole family just grew to accept Peter as part of Mammy's life. I still fantasised that Dad would come home and sort out the whole sorry, shitty mess, but he never did. I tried my best to just keep my head down. I was still working hard during the day and going to college two nights a week to get my qualifications.

* * *

In September that year, I accidentally met a boy called Barra outside the Palaceum Bar in Shettleston. He was a blond guy who had lived in my street ever since I was a small child; he and his six blond Catholic brothers had played with little blonde Sandra and her *Children of the Damned* brothers. Barra's brothers all had odd nicknames like Snider, Bug and Jason and they had a really bad reputation locally. I knew Barra had been in trouble with the police and had been put into a St John's boys' home for shoplifting and house-breaking with his brothers. His two oldest brothers were serving life sentences for armed robbery; another was on the run from the police for armed robbery.

Barra was not really a talker and was, in fact, rather shy. But, after he and I had walked around for a while that first night, with me doing most of the talking, he asked, 'Can I kiss you?'

I was taken aback because I hadn't realised it was a romantic walk. 'Fine,' I told him.

We became a couple. Teenagers in Shettleston could not afford to go on dates: they just walked up and down the streets talking. After work, I would meet him at the bus stop and we would spend the early evening walking around the streets with me doing the talking and hanging around the back of the local creamery with his friends who were always older; then he would spend the rest of his night getting very drunk without me while I hung out with my girl pals in the local Italian café. He looked older than his 15 years and could go into bars and get served. We had absolutely nothing in common: I didn't drink, I didn't smoke and I was relieved to find he never once tried any sexual advances on me. He was actually nothing like his 'hard' reputation although, one night when I was with him, he got into an argument with a local fantasist called 'Puppet' McGill who, like my brother Mij, was convinced he was the pop singer Bryan Ferry. Barra stabbed 'Puppet' in the neck with a knitting needle. I ran away. I never asked why he was carrying a knitting needle. The police were never called; violence was commonplace.

Another night, as normal, Barra went off to drink with his male mates while I went to see my girl pals in the local Italian café and listen to the jukebox. Later, Barra mentioned he had got involved in a fight with an older man and the following Saturday a policeman arrived at my home to question me. He said Barra had beaten someone up badly. He tried to get me to confess to being a witness to the assault. I refused. I had not been there. After that, every time the same policeman saw me in the street, he charged me with loitering or breach of the peace. I was taken to court seven times, found guilty and fined every time except the last.

On that occasion, I had again been charged with loitering. I explained to the magistrate: 'I was standing on the pavement, at traffic lights, waiting for the green man to light up.'

'Are you calling the police liars?'

'Yes, I am. I've never done anything wrong. I don't smoke; I don't drink; I work as a social carer in Castlemilk and I got arrested for waiting to cross the road. If I'd run across the road when the red man was lit, I'd have got done for jaywalking. That Polisman picks on me and he keeps arresting me. If you look, you'll see all the past charges are from him.'

The magistrate looked at the policeman, said, 'I don't understand this,' and dismissed the case.

Barra said he felt awful about it and knew he had caused me grief. When we were together, he was kind and polite and shy. With me, I felt he became the child he never got to be in front of the gang he hung around with. We always talked about my future, never his. He would tell me that I could be a really good artist and encouraged me to keep going to college. He often spoke about how we never had anything in common, but said he would miss me if I left him. He never tried to get me to drink alcohol and would shout down anyone who used peer pressure to wear me down. I did enjoy being with him. One night, as we sat huddled together in a cold hallway and the snow was deep on the ground and sensible folk were heading for home, he held my face, kissed me gently and told me: 'I really, really love you, Janey, and I want us to get engaged.'

I was 16 years old and he was 15. I looked at him in complete horror.

'No,' I told him. 'I don't ever want to be an East End wife sitting in Easterhouse or Shettleston havin' your weans and wondering how I'm going to afford to redecorate the hoose some day.'

He was crushed.

'What's wrong with that?' he asked. 'What's wrong with getting married and havin' weans and staying in Shettleston?'

But all I could see was my sister Ann, pregnant at 18, standing in our hall with her new husband, Jay, then being trapped by a baby. I did not want that – ever. I wanted something more. I wanted to see the world.

Barra and I continued the relationship. I had already met his parents and they were not much different from my own: two people in Glasgow trying to do the best they could. His mammy had actually told me to get rid of Barra as she liked me and did not want me to end up like her, stuck in a violent family always visiting one son or another in prison.

That New Year, after we had been together around four or five months, as we were stepping off a bus, Barra suddenly told me: 'I'm no' goin' oot with ye any mare,' and walked away. I never asked him why he dumped me, but I later found out that he had started seeing another tiny local girl – Lizzy. She and her pal Lauren were OK, but sometimes Lauren would bully me a bit and I was really scared of her. She threatened to beat me up once. It was the beginning of bad blood between us.

* * *

A few months before this, I had met my new best pal Maggie. She came from a big family in Shettleston. Her brother was already my brother Vid's pal. Maggie had been in care for some reason which she never explained but, by the time I met her, she was free and unemployed. We became good pals so it seemed natural that she moved into our already overcrowded home. Mammy, Maggie and I all slept in the same room. Just after splitting with Barra, I had stopped the community work, so we were all claiming Unemployment Benefit and all just about scraping by.

Maggie smoked a lot but never actually said much – I was the opposite – but I loved her strange sense of humour; she was very dry and sarcastic but simultaneously very childlike and, because I was one year older, I always felt very responsible for her. She always looked vulnerable – like a victim – with big brown puppy-dog eyes and perhaps I was trying to mother her. She had been through her own shit in life but strangely neither of us discussed our past problems. She did not know I had been sexually abused, but what she *was* appalled at were our washing facilities and so we both shared regular trips to the local 'Steamie' – an old Victorian washhouse much like a launderette which was housed in Shettleston Public Baths. While our washing was being done in the Steamie, we would buy a ticket to have a hot bath ourselves. It was great just to sink into it and get the smell of the city off your skin, even if it was for just one day.

The next year, I decided to leave Glasgow.

* * *

One sunny May morning, Maggie and I packed the few clothes and belongings we had into one suitcase and headed for Glasgow Central Station. We caught a train to Redcar, the small town on the North Yorkshire coast near Middlesbrough where my brother Mij had lived for a short period, as had Aunt Rita and her husband and even my

Dad. We had hope but no jobs, no accommodation and no cash except what was in our pockets. It terrified me, but not enough to stop me getting on the three different trains which took about six hours to take us to Redcar's old Victorian station. When we emerged, Maggie and I just stood and looked around. Lack of forward planning seemed suddenly to loom large as a major problem for us. The only person I knew in Redcar was a woman I had met with my Mammy five years before.

'Can you remember how to get there?' Maggie asked me.

'Yes.'

So Maggie and I walked through the streets of Redcar and, when we arrived, just stood looking for a few minutes at the rubble. The whole area had been torn down.

We counted the cash in our pockets, walked down to the seafront and approached the first of many guest-houses that lined the promenade. A fat woman with curly blonde hair opened the door and stared at us both suspiciously as I explained that we had left Glasgow and had nowhere to stay.

'I'm 17, she's 16,' I said. 'How much is it?'

We were shown to a small room at the top of the stairs: all brown wallpaper and old Victorian furniture. Maggie and I both sat on our foamy single beds with the sound of howling seagulls almost drowning out our words.

'Where do you think we'll get a job?'

'D'ye think this place'll be all right?'

'D'ye *know* anybody here any more?'

'No.'

We decided to take a look around town before it got too dark. We visited the seafront, the rock shop, the café and the amusement parade then realised we had seen almost everything. Redcar was more run down than I remembered. We strode along the main street, spent the last of our cash on a bag of hot chips, headed for our new home, then talked into the night about how we would try and get some work here. Despite the fear, we both looked forward to the challenge. Eventually, Maggie slept. I lay awake there in the dark feeling absolute fear take over me. I was 17. But I was still a child. I lay awake and thought: *How can we manage tomorrow without any money? How did my Mammy ever sleep in her life when she was faced with all these problems?* I had never before been anywhere without my family. I thought: *What on earth am I doing here?*

* * *

I awoke the next morning, looked round and sat up completely confused as to where I was. I looked across at Maggie and the enormity of the whole situation came crashing down on me. But I took a chance and asked Bessie, the owner of the B&B: 'If we go and register at the Social Security will you let us stay here and give this address to claim benefit from? You'll have regular payments – the Government is a more secure source of income than a job.'

The DHSS gave us £17.50 each a week; the room cost us £15 each a week. That left us with £2.50 each to feed us, launder clothes and live on. Bessie was an overworked nurse in nearby Guisborough, so we offered her our services as B&B chambermaids. Every day we got up, ate all the breakfast, cleaned all the rooms, hoovered all the carpets and washed all the dishes. She paid us each £2.50 a week. It was better than nothing, but we had to buy food every day for our evening meals and this, with other daily expenses, left us really living on the edge of poverty. Bessie's husband Des was a kind, hard-working builder who felt really sorry for us. He knew that, for three days a week, we starved all daytime and evening until breakfast time came round again and we could eat. So, every evening when he came home and before Bessie arrived, he brought us in a huge pot of tea and a plate of biscuits. Maggie and I would wolf them down. I tried to ask Bessie for more wages but she would not bend.

'You do seven days' work for £5 between you each week. Take it or leave it.'

Bessie was a big wobbly-jelly person who had double chins which juddered when she spoke. She was certainly not unkind; she just liked a bargain. She knew we were desperate to stay and exploited that knowledge. At the height of the summer season, she shifted us into a wee caravan in the backyard, but we still had to pay her the full money. Our caravan had no gas and she told us we had to buy our own; she understood our financial set-up and realised there was no way we could buy gas, but still left us in a damp caravan with no light or heating. We were so young, so overwhelmed by our elders and so desperate that we never argued.

We must have made an odd couple: Janey with the chatty mouth and Maggie the silent smoker. She hardly spoke two words to anyone except me and would sometimes only speak to other people through me. Our only belongings were the cassette player Dad had given me and our treasured wee transistor radio. We listened diligently every Sunday afternoon to the chart show on BBC Radio 1 and could not believe how long Olivia Newton-John and John Travolta were at Number One in the charts with 'Summer Nights', the song from the film *Grease*. Every night, we would hang out at the beach or go to the café and play one song – usually ELO – on the tabletop jukeboxes. It was good to feel like a real teenager for a change. Life in Redcar had turned out to be not so bad; I even noticed that the local college ran a free art course in the evening, so I enrolled for that. Maggie – who could not draw to save her life – came along too because she did not want to be left alone. I used her as my model and, when she was forced to take part, I would paint her contribution as well as mine to keep her happy.

I called Mammy a few times at her local pub (we had no phone at home) and she sometimes wrote to me; the rest of the news from Shettleston was passed on to me through the monthly phone call from my sister Ann. I was also given the address of some people from Shettleston who knew us and who now lived in Redcar. Maggie and I went to visit them a few times; they had met all of my family at one time or another; I didn't feel quite so isolated then. But Maggie never received any news from home: no letters, not even a phone call to our guest-house.

I loved the B&B and, despite her shortcomings, I did like Bessie. She even took me with her on a three-day trip to Blackpool; basically, I was there to keep her company. We shared a wee room on the seafront and went shopping together. I only had about £3 to spend, but she kept me fed. I went on a few rides at the Pleasure Beach which I enjoyed, but when I turned a corner and saw a mechanical laughing clown I was terrified and even the fairground game where you throw balls into a clown's mouth frightened me. That night, Bessie took me to a dinner dance at the Winter Gardens and she introduced me to a tall man.

'This is Janey Currie from Glasgow – she works in my guest- house,' she said to the man. 'Janey, this is James Callaghan, the Prime Minister.'

I looked at him and thought *Fuck! So it is! I recognise you off the telly.* I didn't know if he was Labour or Conservative. I shook hands with him and thought he looked clean and shiny though a bit worn out. He said, 'Hello, Janey,' did that smiley thing that politicians do and moved on. Bessie spent the rest of the night dancing; I sat at the side of the dance floor drinking Coca-Cola and thinking *I just met the Prime Minister – how weird is that?*

On the train back to Redcar I decided that Maggie and I could no longer live like this and figured it was time to move out of Bessie's but, when I talked to Maggie about it the next day, we both realised it would be too difficult trying to get a flat when we were on Benefit.

Later, I was out shopping for our dinner in the town centre when I walked past a betting shop and a voice behind me rang out, 'How are you, Sweet Pea?'

I turned and there stood Uncle David Percy, in the doorway of the shop.

'What are you doing here?' I asked him, shocked.

He just looked at me, laughed and asked: 'Where are you staying?'

I mumbled something and ran off back to the guest-house where I gibbered to Maggie: 'You'll never gue- You'll never guess who's here. David Percy's here. My Uncle David. David Percy. I don't like him. I don't like him.'

Maggie could not understand why I was shaking or how seeing my Uncle could be such a problem.

'I hate him,' I told her. 'I don't want to talk about it.'

Maggie, typically, just sat quietly and accepted my answer without further probing.

I was terrified. *Was he after me? Was he expecting me to let him rape me again?* My emotions were everywhere. I felt I had grown up a bit in Redcar and had became more mature, but seeing him really set me back and made me feel like a small child who could not find her own way in the world. I tried hard to pick myself up and kept my focus on trying to get a flat for Maggie and myself. We scoured Redcar and, before long, secured a nice wee room of our own near the chip shop for £6 a week.

Maggie had no real idea who my Uncle was, but she chatted to the Shettleston family we had gone to visit in Redcar and they told her that, yes, he had been to see them and that he was here in Redcar, on his own, looking for work. I knew this was untrue, as he had never really worked in his life. My nightmares became worse and I became more and more paranoid and would wake up in our new flat sticky and sweating, scared to breathe loud in case the terror was there in my bedroom. I decided to go back home to Glasgow. Maggie was upset and made me promise that I would come back to Redcar to see her occasionally; I tried hard to reassure her but felt within myself that, as long as my Uncle was there, I was not going back. We had come to Redcar in March; it was now October.

Leaving Maggie behind was awful because I still felt very responsible for her, but she had grown in confidence, was now making friends of her own and I could not face meeting my Uncle again. I packed my clothes into plastic bags and got on the last train to Glasgow. The city looked like home as I drew into the Central Station. It felt odd coming back, as if I had failed, but I could not wait to get on the bus and find my Mammy and let her know I was home: none of us had phones. Inevitably, she was in the local pub, but she was happy to see me and we both went back to Kenmore Street.

'I've got something bad to tell you,' she said. 'That wee lassie that went oot with Barra – Lizzy – she crossed the road wi' him over to the bus stop one night and she was killed by a hit-and-run driver. That could've been fucking you!'

I did manage to see Barra later that week and he looked awful; he would not talk to me about what had happened and we never really spoke again.

* * *

So much had changed in my family in the eight months I had been away: Debbie, my brother Mij's wee daughter, was getting taller and chattier; my sister Ann was again pregnant; Charlie had moved into his own flat; my brother Vid had left home to work in England; Mammy and Peter were 'keeping company' more often. The house seemed empty and strange – there were only five people living in it – my Mammy, Mij, Cathy, Debbie and me.

Mij had settled down a bit since I had been gone. He had been hanging around the Palaceum – the local bar where I had met Barra. It had been taken over by a new family; it had always been a big bar with a separate function room but now the new owners had converted the function room into a disco.

Wow! I thought. *A disco in Shettleston!*

I was desperate to go!

I had never been in a bar before as I was still only 17 and licensed premises were only for people 18 or over, but all my pals had been and, at weekends, Mij's girlfriend Cathy worked at the Palaceum as a waitress. So, that Friday night, my friends and I all got dressed up and rolled up at the door – a big bunch of 17-year-old girls covered in eye shadow and lip gloss except me. I did not wear make-up because I didn't know how to put it on.

We could hear the disco music booming from inside the club and came face to face with a doorman who looked even younger than me, all dressed up in a suit, his eyes staring short-sightedly at everyone. He passed them all through but took one look at me and mumbled, 'You're too young. Ye cannae come in.'

I was devastated. All my mates went in and left me alone on those cold steps outside the disco. I wasn't confident enough to try and blag my way in, but I vowed to hate that stupid doorman for the rest of my life. I turned and walked away in the dark, sat at home alone – everyone else was out on a Friday night – and played my cassette tape while drinking a Coca-Cola. The end of 1978 was quite a sad time for me. I spent a miserable Christmas with Mammy and Peter. Mammy had no cash and I sat in my bedroom and watched *The Sound of Music* thinking maybe if I ran away to Austria and became a nun my life would all come together.

Uncle David Percy was far away in Redcar. Granda Davy Percy had moved closer to us in Shettleston. Ann's marriage seemed to be going well. Everyone seemed to be moving on with their lives, but I was still being treated as the baby of the family one minute and expected to be a big adult the next.

Dad came over to see me at the New Year; he told me I had to start thinking about getting a steady job. *I was old enough to hold down a job but too young to get into bars!* I was confused and in a rut, but I had a plan in my head. Everything would change on Saturday, 20 January, my eighteenth birthday. Then I would be able to vote, drink and even finally make it as the first female to reach 18 in our family without being pregnant. I would get a job, save the cash, go back to Maggie in Redcar and we could then move on to Scarborough, the next big seaside town down the coast in Yorkshire. I decided I had definitely finished with Glasgow and would move on again after Saturday, 20 January 1979.

7
The big night

The night of Friday, 5 January 1979 was cold, the snow was thick on the ground and the Scottish winter bit into the flesh of my feet. Yet again the shoe problem was with me. My shoes had holes in the toes and the only solution was to pack them with red teddy-bear fur from a teddy that belonged to my niece Debbie. How odd I must have looked with the red fur peeping through my shoes, but at least I was warm. I had a new friend called Marion who was gorgeous and slim and had boobs and was everything I wasn't. She lived with her gran and grandad in a small flat, in the next street. She had boys falling over her and I was so envious of her clothes and style and obvious beauty. We were good mates and, on Friday, 5 January, we got dressed up in cheap shiny tops and jeans, covered our hair in clips and boogied on down to the Palaceum. My nemesis door-man was there on guard, but this time he could not stop me. I had made 18 ... well, two weeks to go, but that was just a technicality *surely*? I kept my head down and shuffled forward; the doorman squinted at me, lifted up my chin and smiled as he mumbled, 'Have a good night.'

Hurrah! *Finally* I had made it into glittery disco heaven! I quickly learned the etiquette of publand: you drank three vodka lemonades and danced energetically to every song that hit the turntables. *I was made to dance!*

It was weird being there among my older brothers and their mates, but I felt I had finally arrived; I belonged here.

Every weekend another mate had a house to herself as her parents left her home alone. We had amazing parties and I was quickly introduced to the adult world of passionate kissing and men. I got to snog at least 15 men in my first three weeks of arrival in the adult pub world. One big problem, though. The kissing thing was fun and a great teenage pastime, but I was scared of sex. Every boy I kissed (and I kissed loads) left me feeling odd and detached. I had still not physically developed, with little to no breasts and definitely no period. I felt totally weird; all my mates were sexually active and gossiping about it. When boys tried to touch me, I would go away to a place in my head. Very soon after starting, I could see no point in kissing. *Maybe I was a lesbian? Is that what happens? If you don't fancy men do you automatically become a lesbian?* These questions whirled inside my head until I was driven to distraction.

But, on the exact day of my eighteenth birthday, finally, after much praying and pondering, my first period arrived. *I was not physically distorted! I had a vagina that worked! I had a womb! I was a woman!* I had worried my Uncle had damaged me internally, but here I was now, a fully grown female adult. I celebrated by quietly but proudly marching into the local chemist to buy sanitary goods, although I found inserting a tampon only halfway and trying to sit down had its drawbacks. *Yaagh!* It seemed I still had much to learn.

* * *

Life at home had not changed much. Mammy would gush, 'Oh, Peter's a great man. See me and Peter? Peter's lovely! Peter makes great soup. I love Peter! He's a great wee man.'

She came home from Peter's one day, her hand wrapped in a white dishcloth with blood seeping through it. She told us she had fallen in the back court but it was the back of her hand that was cut. *Who falls on the back of their hand?* I realised it was a razor or knife slash and she must have put up her hand to protect herself. But the whole incident passed without questions; she had covered up for her brother and for her son; now she was covering up for yet another abusive man. *God help her.* I left her to it. I could do nothing to stop her.

One late night soon afterwards I came home and Mammy wasn't in, so I walked across the road to Peter's to see if she was there. The lights were on in his ground-floor flat, but there was no answer when I knocked and shouted, 'Mammy?' and this annoyed me. I knew they had to be there because they rarely went out. I went round the back of the flat and pulled myself up onto the window and peered through. My Mammy was lying on the floor naked and Peter was holding her down. For a moment, I was horrified that I had just seen them having sex and was about to drop down from the window ledge when Peter raised his right hand and I saw he was holding a short-handled axe and he whacked her on the head with the sharp edge of the blade. The blood went everywhere. I screamed and ran to the door shouting. No one came out.

Mammy had looked terrified, so I stayed quiet in case my shouting made him do it more. I really don't know what happened next. I think I was in shock. I stood in the street and just stared at the house, waiting for her to come out. I don't know how long it was, but the police eventually arrived; maybe someone else in the blockhouse had called them. Mammy came out and there was smoke everywhere. Peter had tried to kill them both by setting fire to the house. She was taken to hospital. He was charged with attacking her and with attempted arson.

After Mammy was let home, she had to keep going back into hospital, but didn't talk to us kids about it and made it clear we should not ask her. She had no burns, recovered well, had a big cut on her arm and axe wounds in the back of her head which were stitched. I never told her, the police or anyone else that I had seen what had happened and, within a week, she and Peter were back in love. She gave evidence for his defence in court – we were never told the verdict, but he was released – and they both spent her Victim's Compensation money together. I thought: *That must be what love does to you.*

Peter made sure Mammy slowly alienated herself from her friends and family: she stopped seeing her Valium Pals and members of her family who lived any distance away. She had had quite a big circle of friends but, as time went on, she just had Peter. Even with us children, she no longer sat and chatted or asked us questions as she used to. She became less and less involved in my life. One night I really laid into her about Peter and his violence. She had come into my room as I was taping Radio Luxembourg. As we started to speak, Kate Bush was singing 'The Man With The Child In His Eyes'. I left the tape running as I told her, 'Mammy, you'll need tae get away from him. You just need tae get away from him. I swear to God, all these cuts and bruises—'

'Och, Janey,' she interrupted, 'he's no' that bad. Peter isnae that bad. C'mon, I mean he's had his problems, we've had wur fights, but I'm as bad as him.'

'You're no',' I told her. 'You're no' as bad as him. He's never had any cuts and bruises. Every time I see you, you've got a bandage or a black eye.'

'No, no, no. You don't like Peter. You've never liked Peter. That's it. You always upset him,' she started shouting at me. 'You upset Peter!'

'You're going to end up fucking deed!' I shouted back at her. 'You're going to end up fucking deed lying in your fucking coffin, because you're going to let him fucking kill ye!'

'Don't swear,' she told me. 'Don't get upset.'

'You're going to end up fucking deed, Mammy—'

'No I won't. Peter's no' a bad man.'

'Ann and I are going to have tae explain to your grandweans that you are deed an' the reason they never got tae see you was because you let a man kill you. That's what I'm going to have tae say in years to come – *I'm sorry you never saw my Mammy, but she let a man kill her!*'

Mammy burst out laughing: 'I cannae imagine you being a mother! … You don't seem like the mothering type tae me. I don't think ye'll be a mother. You're good wi' weans but I cannae imagine it but, don't you worry, I'll be there the day you have a wean.'

So we all carried on with life and waited for the next big disaster to strike. I had no idea how my Dad felt about it all. By this time, he was living down in Bridgeton, at the other end of Glasgow's East End, working in a chemical factory and he worked a lot, so I rarely saw him. He still came back to our house when he got really drunk. Most weekends, I would waken up and see him and Mammy in bed together. I have no idea how Peter took this. As he lived opposite, it was hard to miss my Dad arrive, staggering, loudly singing his drunken megamix medley of Frank Sinatra and Protestant marching songs. Mammy did love Dad being there on Saturday nights because, on the Sunday, she would still dip his pockets for cash, then both of them would get pissed and reminisce as I sat with them and we all imagined we were one big happy family again. On Sunday nights he would go home, leaving Mammy feeling sad and me feeling confused. *Why could she not make him stay?* Adult relationships flummoxed me.

* * *

One weekend in early March 1979, I was passing the Palaceum bar to go for my weekly wash at the swimming baths (our bath no longer worked and we had never had hot water anyway) when I met my nemesis doorman. We got chatting and he offered me a job as a weekend waitress. Mij's girlfriend Cathy already worked there and he said she would show me the ropes. *Brilliant! I had a job!* That first weekend was fun and the cash was good. I found out that the new owner of the Palaceum was a Catholic called George Storrie; he had seven sons, one of whom was also called George, so they were differentiated as Old George and Young George; my nemesis doorman was the sixth son and was called Sean Storrie.

I asked around and local people told me Old George Storrie had been in prison when he was in his late twenties for armed robbery. He had graduated into various other crimes including safe-cracking and jewellery robberies and had lived and worked as a driver and general worker on the Gadgies' travelling fairgrounds for many many years until he became accepted as a Gadgie not by birth but by association. After his marriage, he settled down more and eventually became a troubleshooter for the city breweries. In Glasgow at that time the pubs were hard-drinking, hard-fighting places; Old George was known for his fist fights and for always confronting gang leaders head on.

One famous tale I found was that, when Old George was around 30, he was dragged into the back of a police Black Maria van. Inside were five uniformed policemen with truncheons and wooden sticks. The van was driven to a back street in the south side of Glasgow, where they tried to beat him up. He fought his corner. He knocked two policemen unconscious and beat the other three to the ground. When he got out of the Black Maria, he was blood-ied and badly beaten, but they were in an equally terrible state. Old George had survived and his relationship with the police was established.

In the 1960s, Old George was once in the company of Arthur Thompson when Thompson met with the Kray Twins and some other well-known criminal 'Faces' from London. Arthur Thompson was regularly called Glasgow's 'Godfather of Crime' by the Scottish press and lived in a house called The Ponderosa – named after the family home in the Wild West TV series *Bonanza*. They discussed flood-ing Glasgow with Purple Heart tablets (popular illegal stimulant drugs of the time); George was opposed to the idea and withdrew from the meeting. He hated drugs and drug dealers. He had no criminal gang. He had his seven sons, some of whom worked at the Palaceum. My nemesis doorman Sean Storrie was a real bastard to work for and his nickname was 'Mad Eyes' which was a fair description of the prolonged, angry stare he sometimes gave. But they were also sometimes soft, brown, reassuring eyes. He made me do all the shitty jobs like wipe up vomit and broken glass and any other crap that needed doing. I would tell anyone who listened what an arse he was. He also had the Storrie family habit of mumbling and tended to talk in telegramese so he might say to me:

'Guy bar near payphone, red hair Guinness, called Frank, name on pool board.'

Which meant:

'Go and serve the guy with the red hair, near the phone, a pint of Guinness, then put his name up on the pool list.'

It was infuriating.

He would say, 'Shops. Ye want?' instead of, 'I'm going to the shops. Do you want anything?'

After I had worked at the Palaceum for a week, he asked me out, but I was not really interested – he wasn't my type. He was very very quiet and very moody. He also always sneered at me when I was in with my mates dancing and chatting to young guys. So, out of curiosity, I said *Yes*.

Sean was the sixth of seven brothers – just as my first boyfriend Barra had been; Sean and Barra were both Catholics; I had become Barra's girlfriend outside the Palaceum where Sean now worked; and Sean was even born on exactly the same day of the same year as Barra.

On our first date, I had to wait until he finished his shift at the Palaceum and he got Shuggie, one of his drivers (the Storries had drivers who worked for the family), to sweep us off in a big golden Mercedes. We were chauffeured to Sean's home. He lived at the other end of Tollcross Park in a big house that everyone called Toad Hall and which stood alone on the corner of a main road surrounded by an eight-foot-high brick wall. It had what seemed to me a vast back garden and looked like one of those houses you draw as a child: four big windows and a door, but it was no ordinary door. It was impressive by any standards. A giant wooden door with beautifully ornate carvings of roses on it. We went into the living room and I was amazed that he owned a video player – they were not common at the time.

We watched *In the Heat of the Night*. He never really spoke – like Barra, he was not a great talker and was a year and a half younger than me. I think I talked nervously all the way through the movie. I felt truly out of my depth. This boy lived in a mini-mansion and I lived in a house with graffiti on the inside. Eventually, I decided to stop talking and call it a night. He leaned over before I had a chance to speak again and held my hand then kissed me on the lips. It was weird, coz normally at this point I pretended to be dead. But this was good! I liked him holding me in his arms and he was a really sensitive, lovely kisser. *Wow!* I thought. *So this is what it is meant to feel like?* That night, he walked me back to Shettleston through Tollcross Park and, within weeks, we were truly, madly, deeply in love.

He never pushed me into sex. I told him about the abuse. He listened patiently and never made any judgements. I fully expected him to dump me. *Who wants 'used and damaged' goods?* But, slowly, he made me feel more at ease and my first 'consensual' sexual experience was such an awakening. *I actually liked sex!*

About three weeks after our first date, one night after a late shift, Sean and I sat in the back of his large golden Mercedes, listening to music on the radio and kissing as we were driven by Shuggie for what seemed like hours through a beautiful spring night. Eventually, we arrived at the small town of Blairgowrie, sat by an old wishing well and held hands as we made our wishes. I thought: *This will be the most romantic night of my life!* I was still a wee, curly-headed tomboy, but I was holding hands with this young guy who had a Mercedes and a chauffeur and we were kissing in the moonlight. That was the night we got engaged. Three days later, he gave me a wee solitaire diamond ring round the back of the Palaceum. *Me!* I thought. *I have a diamond!*

My family never really formed much of an opinion of Sean as he was very quiet and never made any effort to impress them; he also disliked my father as he felt Dad had never protected me from Uncle David Percy. I had been very embarrassed taking Sean to my home for the first time, because of the graffiti, the dirty smelly toilet and the general poverty it revealed. But it never bothered Sean and he seemed to accept all the wacky ways of the Curries. His own family was hardly perfect. Early on in our relationship, he told me, 'People will do things, but you've got to ignore them.'

'What do you mean?' I asked, confused.

'My brothers. People will do and say things. Ignore them. In this family, trust naebody.'

Young George in particular would sneer at me. When I persuaded Sean to get the spectacles he'd needed for a while, Young George told him: 'Now you know what she really looks like, you'll fucking want your ring back,' and, in the Palaceum one night, Young George shouted out at me, in front of all his mates:

'Your ma is a daft old cow, your brothers are arseholes an' you are a begging bastard. Everyone in Shettleston has fucked ye!'

'Well,' I shouted back, 'at least I havnae fucked you, coz I'm allergic to pork an' you're a pig's arse and if ye think *my* brothers are cunts ye should see my Sean's brothers – he has *six* daft bastards in *his* family!'

It was a never-ending battle. All of the other six Storrie brothers would make sniping remarks at me. I was either too loud, too mouthy or too giggly. I was not good enough. Sean was too young. I was too poor. Sean had a great future in front of him. I would only hold him back. I would only get pregnant to snare the rich boy. The objections went on and on. In actual fact, the one thing we were very careful about was birth control. I was determined not to get pregnant. Sean felt the same. But his family put so much pressure on us both that, after about six weeks, he left Toad Hall and we both moved in with my maternal grandfather

Granda Davy Percy – the father of my abuser – who was a friendly if slightly strange man. He had talked openly about sex to me when I was younger. When I was around 16, he had told me, 'You should go on the pill and get oot and enjoy yourself.'

What grandfather says that to his granddaughter? When I was younger, he had often sat by the fireplace with the zip of his trousers down and, inside, I could glimpse his floppy old penis as he chatted to me. I used to think he never knew his flies were undone; I just put it down to sloppiness on his part.

This was the house in which Sean and I were going to live. We were desperate to be together and I knew my Uncle David Percy would not come near his father's house when Sean and I were there together. In fact, David Percy had not been heard of in ages. Sean knew of the abuse, so I felt if my Uncle *did* show his face, it would be OK. Sean would protect me. And, for once, things happened as I wanted them to. Uncle David Percy never did once visit my grandfather while we lived with him in Shettleston. And Granda Davy Percy's strangeness did not reoccur.

It was a small flat with Granda sleeping in the living room and Sean and I taking over his bedroom. We created our own wee home within Granda Davy's house. For the first time in my life I owned a fridge and we spent that summer lying in the garden enjoying the sun and making love every spare moment we had. Sean was very shy and, by nature and family upbringing, ever so quiet but my Granda was good company and he could get Sean chatting.

Granda Davy was a Protestant – his son David was still a very active member of the Orange Order – and Sean was Catholic, though not a practising one. They debated religion and politics vigorously and I liked that side to Sean.

I had been brought up in a home where my father always expressed strong political views. But I did feel sorry for Sean at times. He had never really got an education and had a lot of literacy problems – those were the days when dyslexia wasn't recognised – but he was intelligent. I felt he could have done anything he wanted, but he had never even got to choose a job; his father had decided he would work in the Palaceum … and he also had very bad migraine headaches. One night when I went over to see him at Toad Hall, I found Sean lying on his bed alone in the dark.

'It's the headaches,' he told me.

He told me he had tablets for them.

Meanwhile, I carried on working alongside him at the Palaceum. The previous owner had been forced to hand over weekly protection money to a local gang who were friends of my brother Mij. When they tried this on the Storrie family, a 'heavy' came in and said to Old George, 'You gie us 50 quid every week and yer bar will be safe – there'll be nae fights in here.'

Old George calmly walked round from behind the bar, coshed the heavy then battered the fuck out of him. 'I like fights in my bar!' George said as he kicked him. 'I start most of them!' Old George was very well 'connected'; these local boys were small potatoes in comparison. His philosophy of life, which he had inbred in his children was: *If ever anybody fucks you about, face up to them. Never show weakness. If you do, then they will get you.*

The Palaceum was safe under Old George's management, although accidents did happen. A regular called Jonah McKenzie had his left eye knocked out in a freak accident when a heavy glass ashtray – not intended for him – was thrown across the dance floor and struck him on the eyeball.

Not long before I met him, Old George's nephew Harry was taken into police custody for dealing with a trouble-maker at the Palaceum; both Harry and the bloodied hatchet he had used were taken to Tobago Street Police Office. Old George walked into the building and insisted his young nephew was released. They refused. He then walked into the chief investigating detective's office and, after a short discussion, left with both the bloodied hatchet under his coat *and* with his nephew. It was rumoured locally that Old George had been carrying a gun during the discussion. Harry later had to pay a small fine. It was some-times easier even for the police to let Old George do what he needed to do, as he could be extremely vengeful.

He liked to control people. He liked to play his seven sons off against each other. But I rather liked him. Although he was a very hard man, he did not have a cruel mouth; he had a smiley, happy-looking mouth. When he smiled, his mouth made you feel you had to smile as well because it was so infectious. I used to go round to Toad Hall a lot with Sean. One night, Old George was sitting in his dressing gown and I noticed his lower legs were mottled blue and severely bruised.

'What happened?' I asked.

'The fucking Polis,' he told me, rubbing his legs. 'It happened years ago.'

'And they're still sore?'

'Aye.'

The Storries were almost as dysfunctional as my own family. Around the same time that I started going out with Sean, his brother Michael Storrie started going out with a girl called Mags. She was from the north side of Glasgow; I tried hard to make friends but we never hit it off. We had absolutely nothing in common to talk about. I had more in common with Old George's new girlfriend Patsy Paton who was 25, blonde and real fun. Old George was 55 and Patsy was younger than some of his sons – in fact, Patsy's older sister Mary was going out with Old George's son Philip. The older sister went with the son; the younger sister went with the dad. But young Patsy and Old George were a good match. Mouthy, opinionated and very much the dominant female, she was from Bridgeton, near where my Dad was living.

One night, she and I were swapping family stories and trading backgrounds. I explained about my Mammy and Dad being separated and told her, 'Mammy has a boyfriend called Peter, but he beats her up and I fucking hate him.'

'Oh ah fucking hate that too,' she replied. 'My mammy had a man called Peter as well an' he fucking nearly killed her. All us kids got put in foster homes coz o' that wee cunt and he got put in the jail for the beating he gave my ma – he nearly killed her. Thank fuck he's still inside.'

I looked at her and said quietly: 'My Mammy's Peter is not long out of jail.'

Her face froze. 'What's his surname?'

'Greenshields,' I said quietly.

'Fucksake!'

She was inconsolable for about two or three minutes, then told me, 'My mammy was petrified of him and she was a fucking fighting fishwife of a woman!'

Patsy's mammy had a scar that ran from the corner of her right eye down to the right side of her top lip, where Peter had cut her with a Yale key, dragging it down into the flesh of her face. Then he had chased her through Bridgeton with a gun, and a taxi driver who intercepted him got the Queen's Award for Bravery. Peter was imprisoned. Patsy persuaded me to get my Mammy to bring Peter down to the Palaceum so she could see face to face if this really was the man who had screwed up her life.

That Saturday afternoon, Mammy and Peter sat in the lounge bar. Patsy told me to take Mammy into the toilets and, as we shut the door, she picked up a full bottle of Newcastle Brown Ale, calmly walked towards Peter and, before he could recognise her, swung the bottle up high in the air, then brought it down on the top of his head. It did not break.

'That's for every fucking punch you gave my mother!' she screamed, as he slumped off his seat, stunned. Her arm raised the bottle up again: *Thud!* She whacked him on the side of the head. It did not break.

'That's for getting my family put into care!'

Then she attacked with *real* violence. She had to be dragged off him. By this time, my Mammy had heard the commotion, come out of the toilet and stood horrified as Peter lay on the floor and Patsy screamed at her, 'Ye need tae get away from him! He will fucking kill you! You have nae idea what he did to my mammy!' All the emotions Patsy had held at bay with alcohol and men came out as she carried on screaming at my Mammy: 'You have nae idea! Ye need tae get away from him!' Peter was literally thrown out of the bar into the street in a heap. Back home, Mammy helped patch Peter's wounds and ignored everything Patsy had tried to tell her. That was my Mammy's way.

8
Training

Around this time, Mammy acquired a big smelly new dog called Major 2. I had never before heard of anyone buying a dog because, in Glasgow, they adopt you. The new dog was an Alsatian like the first Major, but he looked like a scabby lion. He loved my Mammy, but she grew to hate him. Major 2 would use his head to open the toilet door as she sat peeing. He would not leave her side. He would look at her with big doe eyes even as she took her shoe off to hit him on the head.

But she discovered he liked picking up tin cans, so she taught him to follow her into the local Asian corner shop in Darleith Street. While she chatted to the shopkeeper, Major 2 would steal his own food. It took her a week to get him to recognise the yellow label of the dog food brand he preferred then, as always, Mammy took it further. Major 2 was taught how to lift triangular tins because they contained her favourite: *Ye Olde Oak Ham*.

Often the shop owner, wee Aslim, would shout, 'Your dog is stealing from my shelves!'

But my Mammy would reply: 'It's not my dog, Asylum. I don't own a dog. You should call the Polis and have it arrested.'

'My name's Aslim,' the shopkeeper would reply limply.

I hated Mammy coming into the Palaceum but she would regularly ignore all my protests and march in for a drink with smelly Major 2. And sometimes Biff the cat trotting behind her. I suppose I was ashamed of her appearance. Gone was the bright-eyed, dark-haired, smiley woman I remembered from my childhood. Instead, standing there was a grey-haired, sometimes toothless woman. She only wore her false teeth if she happened to find them. She looked like what she was: an old, shabby, scarred, broken housewife; but she still kept her sense of humour.

One day, she came running into the Palaceum with Major 2 behind her. She pointed to the dog and shouted at me in front of the whole bar, 'Your dog has a light bulb stuck in its mouth and I cannae get it oot!'

I was about to shout back that it was *not my dog* when I realised the whole bar had fallen silent and was looking in amazement at Major 2. I looked over and, sure enough, that idiot shoplifting dog was standing there with, lodged tightly in its mouth, a big light bulb.

Glaswegians love nothing more than a bizarre problem to solve, so everyone tried, but the dog refused to let go of the light bulb. I was terrified it would burst in his mouth. Worse still, the stupid animal adored the attention and decided to play a game of chase round the pool table. I felt so embarrassed and wished my Mammy would just take Major 2 away but, of course, she did nothing of the kind. She took off one of her socks and dropped a snooker ball into it. She grabbed Major 2, turned him round, raised her arm and whacked him right on the bollocks with her weighted sock. The light bulb shot like a cannon from the howling dog's jaws and smashed on the toilet door. Almost every man in the room held his crotch in sympathy as the big dog howled in ear-piercing agony.

'See,' my Mammy said triumphantly, 'the daft bastard won't bite a light bulb again now, will he!'

She placed the snooker ball back on the baize table, turned on her heels and left Major 2 licking his wounds very publicly.

* * *

Things were going no better for me with the Storries. They still disapproved of me. By now, even the brothers' girlfriends were having a go.

'You don't have any eyelashes,' one of them declared to me in the Palaceum. 'If you put on some make-up and stop looking like a boy, maybe we would all take you more serious.'

I could never understand why black rings around my eyes would have made me look more intelligent and, anyway, Sean never once suggested I wear different clothes or make-up or wore longer hair: he liked me as I was. He and I were walking home one night, holding hands and kissing all the way up the road when Old George slowed his car down alongside us and stuck his head out the window:

'Fucking stop that kissing!' he screamed at Sean. 'Stop walking around holding hands! People will think you're a poof!'

I assumed maybe Old George saw any sort of expression of love as a sign of weakness. Eventually, though, the pressure became too much for us. Sean was still only 16 and I was only 18. We needed to escape the stifling Storrie family and just be together, so we decided to move down to Redcar. This made Old George so angry that he tried to bribe me.

'Have a wee holiday, hen, go see your pal then come home,' he said. 'I'll give you £30.'

I refused the cash.

I caught a train to Redcar one Saturday morning and Sean was due down the next day as he had promised to work the late shift at the Palaceum. When Maggie opened the door, we hugged like we had never been separated. I showed off my wee diamond ring and explained all about Sean. She told me that Uncle David Percy had been in contact with her after I left.

'He tried to get off with me, Janey; he tried to touch me and kiss my neck. I told him to fuck off and he ran out of the flat.'

I was horrified and desperate to tell her the whole story, but I didn't feel ready to tell anyone other than Sean. I think I was embarrassed.

'I hear,' she continued, 'that he's fucked off down to London.'

Thank God, I thought. I could look forward to Sean arriving tomorrow and Maggie meeting him for the first time. My two best pals in the world! We had arranged that Sean would get the train down but he wasn't sure when he could get away and I had no phone in Redcar, so it was a bit of a vague arrangement. I timed the connections from Glasgow and there were only two trains due in that day. So I sat on a bench, excited, at 3.00 p.m., waiting for the first train into Redcar's big Victorian railway station and watching every single passenger leave the old maroon and black carriages.

Sean wasn't there.

I waited for the next train and slowly my heart began to feel the creeping fear of rejection and desperation. *He wasn't going to come; it had all been a plan to get me out of his life.* I sat in my flowery dress – the only dress I owned – swinging my legs in my one pair of cheap plastic sandals, hoping against hope he would appear from that second train. *Any* fucking train. Just be here!

He wasn't on the second train.

I waited and waited. I finally gave up at 8.00 p.m.

I had been sitting there for five hours, slowly getting colder and more desperate. Maggie said nothing as I came back alone into her wee flat. It was as if she had never expected him to come either. I thought, *Is disappointment just mandatory in my life?* I cried myself to sleep that night, clutching my wee diamond ring.

At about eleven the next morning, I called the Palaceum from a public call box on Redcar seafront. It was pot luck who answered the phone. I knew if I got Young George, he would either lie to me or just shout, 'Fuck off!' and hang up. If I got Michael, then he would possibly tell me if Sean had left Glasgow and on what train – depending on his mood. As luck would have it, Old George picked up the receiver.

'George,' I said, trying not to let him hear the fear in my voice. 'It's Janey here. What time did Sean leave? ... Is he coming?'

'Shuggie is driving him doon – he should be there at two this afternoon,' George replied. 'Make sure you bring him home, Janey,' he added. 'I've gave him some money so youse two can have a wee holiday.'

I didn't hear anything more he said. My heart was too busy leaping in the air. *Sean was coming to me!*

And he did arrive that afternoon at two o'clock exactly. We hugged on the pavement and laughed all the way up to Maggie's flat. She was very much at ease in Sean's company and the three of us had a ball all the way through the summer of 1979, which was hot and sticky. We sat on the beach, swam in the cold grey sea under blue skies and just got to be 'us'. No one was judging or arguing with us any more. Sean and I were kissing in the street and staying out all night without worrying about getting up for work and Sean did not want to go home. But, after much deliberation and promising each other never to let anyone get in the way of our relationship, we did head back to Granda Davy Percy's flat in Glasgow.

I loved Sean so much, but his behaviour baffled me at times. I accepted he was very quiet, but he would sometimes just switch off and leave me feeling cold and unwanted. One night, he came home from the Palaceum and totally ignored me from the moment he came in.

'What happened?' I asked.

'Leave me alone,' he muttered.

He sat at the end of our bed and never uttered a word for about an hour.

I was babbling on and on, asking him if everything went OK at the bar. He eventually stood up and told me, 'I want this to end,' and left the flat.

I sat there crying my heart out; I had no idea what had just happened. Eventually, I fell asleep.

The next morning he arrived at the door and pleaded with me: 'I am sorry, Janey, I was just confused. I love you.'

Of course we fell into each other's arms. But he wouldn't talk about it or tell me what had happened. I was just happy he was back.

9

Homes and jobs

Back at my Mammy's home in Kenmore Street, Charlie had moved out, Uncle John had moved on and Uncle James had moved in again with his wife Crazy Katie Wallace and their kids Sammy and Jackie. They had been living on and off at our house for years, never able to keep their own home due to debt and Crazy Katie's penchant for Valium overdoses and general breakdowns. Sammy, whom I adored, was now getting into trouble glue-sniffing and staying off school. Jackie had learning difficulties and was just plodding along.

My sister Ann had just given birth to a baby girl Ann Margaret, who was very cute. Sean and I would baby-sit and loved looking after the wee girl, but Sean was always better at it than me because he had helped raise his own brother Paul who was now ten years old. Paul often stayed over with us at Granda Davy's, because he was not getting the attention he craved and needed at Toad Hall – Old George had no idea how to look after a wee boy who was too young to work in a bar.

Sean was working hard and all seemed fine, although his unpredictable mood swings were getting harder to deal with and he was still getting headaches regularly. One night in our bedroom, he shouted at me for no reason and, as I turned to argue back, he slapped me hard across the side of my head then turned away from me. I lifted our alarm clock and belted him on his back. He fell forward, then turned and jumped at me. I pushed him backwards and tried to punch him in the face. I felt his arms around my back as he wrestled me to the floor and pulled me round and then I saw his 'mad eyes'. The look in those eyes terrified me. I lay beneath his savage stare and did nothing. I was beaten. I could not believe this man who loved me had hurt me like that; I loved him so much and just wanted to understand why this had happened.

Whenever this happened again – and it did – he would break down in tears afterwards and beg my forgiveness and I always held him tight and promised to love him for ever. After a while, I could predict when his mood would change. He enjoyed the cash side and the organisational side of running the Palaceum bar, but having to communicate with people made him feel awkward. He was never one to socialise, hated people talking to him, hated having to chat in the bar and he would totally ignore customers who tried to start conversations. When someone asked a question he would simply stand me in front of the person and get me to chat to them as he sidled away. If he was confronted by a persistent chatterer, he would march away and later fly into a rage at me.

'Aye!' he'd say. 'Leave *me* with the fucking stupid people talking, will ye?'

I just learned to live with his moods.

* * *

Meanwhile, my brother Mij had got a job near the Palaceum, looking after an off licence owned by an Irish Catholic gangster called Tom. Mij had always loved being involved in anything illegal – it made him feel important. Unfortunately, he was never a good worker and, to cover for him, Mammy started looking after the wee shop part-time, with occasional help from Peter, who was still beating her. I was sick of the way Peter treated Mammy, so decided to get them both very drunk when they were in the off licence. Getting Mammy drunk was easy but Peter – always a clever wee fucker – was very suspicious of my offer of free booze. However, eventually, greed took over and he was soon so pissed he was staggering.

It was Mammy's job to clear the nightly takings, put them in a safe at the back of the off licence, lock up the shop, then take home the keys. That night, I pretended to put the takings in the safe for her – she saw me apparently do it – but I actually slipped the money into an inside pocket of Peter's donkey jacket, which was hanging up. Mammy never ever actually stayed overnight at Peter's house, so they said goodnight in the street. I laughed with them and joined in their drunken singing and watched Peter go into his flat on the other side of Kenmore Street. When Mammy was asleep, I called Tom and explained that Peter had stolen the takings and beaten up my Mammy. I gave him the address of Peter's flat and left the Irish boys to do their worst. They found the money but, disappointingly for me, Peter got off lightly. Mammy was aghast and came to tell Sean and me.

'Tom's mates have broken both Peter's arms! They said he fucking stole their money – he would never steal!'

'Did they find any money, Mammy?' I asked, quietly livid that he was still alive.

'Well, Tom said all the cash was there, but I cannae understand any of that coz you and I put it all in the safe, didn't we?'

'You saw me,' I answered. 'He must have stolen it, Mammy.'

Peter never spoke of the incident. When he came up to

Granda Davy Percy's house he didn't even talk to me. I smiled as I asked him how his arms were healing. He knew it was me, but said nothing and just smiled back.

* * *

It was not long before Sean and I outgrew Granda Davy Percy's house – we had started to buy furniture, a fridge, an electric fire and a bedside unit – and Old George offered us the chance to buy a flat above his pub in the rough Calton area of Glasgow. The neighbourhood was very Catholic and the pub was called the Nationalist Bar, but Old George told his son Philip, who managed the pub:

'If Rangers fans come in, shout, *Fuck the Pope!* If Celtic fans come in, shout, *Fuck the Queen!* If the Amish come in, wear black and switch off the TV. Just get their money.'

Old George owned the whole big four-storey red sand-stone building which stood on the corner of Green Street and the busy main London Road. It comprised the Nationalist Bar at ground level with two empty shops adjacent and then three floors above, three flats on each floor. The pub had survived a mysterious big fire in 1970, exactly ten years ago, and the building was basically sound and solid but badly needed repairs to the internal structure, facing sandstone and rooftop.

The Calton had once been a vibrant and busy area that led directly into Glasgow city centre but that part of the London Road was now a long, barren stretch of emptiness, seedy and run down. The Nationalist Bar's four storeys were dwarfed by the abandoned but still-standing six-storey Templeton's Carpet Factory across the London Road. It had been an amazingly beautiful building in its time though, by now, it was crumbling like the rest of the area. One entire side of the building had been built as a perfect replica of the side of the Doges' Palace in Venice, including tiles, turrets and scooped windows – the shiny gold and blue tiles glinted on those rare occasions when the sun shone on the Calton. Behind Templeton's was the once-sedate Glasgow Green which was now home to prostitutes, junkies and drunks. The houses of the community on both sides of the London Road had been razed to the ground, all the big majestic tenements had been dragged down and there were acres of wasteground beside Templeton's on one side of the road and on the other the isolated red sandstone building which housed the Nationalist Bar.

Outside, with the wind in the right direction, you could smell the fumes from the seething, hoppy, chemical mash in the Whisky Bond buildings across the Clyde. Inside, unlike the glittering Palaceum bar and disco, the Nationalist Bar smelled of years of piss and smoke. The old brown wood-panelled walls had ancient pictures of scary animals and the occasional painting of President John F. Kennedy.

'Why the pictures of Kennedy?' I asked.

'He was a Catholic.'

'OK, but why the scary animals?'

No one had an explanation.

The customers were a mixture of old, hardened drinkers, a few younger guys, ancient bikers and some mad old prostitutes who roamed the Glasgow Green selling their wares. The jukebox had black vinyl records by the Beatles and Elvis Presley, both of whom I hated, and Bobby Darin singing 'Mack The Knife', which I loved: it was the one song which had all the old men sitting in the pub singing along like extras out of Michael Jackson's video for 'Thriller'. It was a great song for bringing people to life, though it was a song about death.

Sean and I moved into our new flat, on the first floor.

The walls were plain brown and the curtains a horrible swirly orange. The fireplace in the living room had built-in wall-to-wall and ceiling-to-floor fake wood panelling. Old George had an obsession with wood panelling which defied logic; at Toad Hall, his hallways were all imitation wood panelling and it looked like a cheap mini bingo hall all the way upstairs. Here in our new flat, the extraordinary fireplace – which must have been specially built by a demented designer – had hideous wood-panelled shelving, and in between each shelf unit was a big leather bull's head with lights behind it so that the eyes lit up when you switched the fireplace on. These, I was told, were leftovers from a Steakhouse bankrupt sale which Sean's uncle had used to fit out the flat before we bought it. Old George had a penchant for 'obtaining' things at sales – they would first buy a carpet, then steal what they wanted and take it away hidden inside the rolled-up carpet.

The flat had a long hall, which was the norm with these big tenements, and Old George gave us fake leather hand-bag material to cover the floor, because he had bought it cheap at a sale. The fabric was brown and soon curled up at the edges and cracked all the way along the floor. I spent weeks tacking it down and gluing it. In that flat, my night-mares became worse and, for some reason, louder. Sometimes I lay awake listening to footsteps clomping up and down the hall and, when I got up to investigate, there was no one there but the hall was cold and I could see my breath as I gasped in the chill. There was also a strange smell like old people who had pissed on their clothing, or decomposed bodies – and the lights would flicker. I started to think it was haunted. One night I heard a noise, ran down the hall and, as I ran, the wardrobe doors burst open and piled-up newspapers came cascading out. I freaked.

Soon afterwards, I got my brushes out and painted a colourful mural along the whole hallway: it curled round the doors and swept into the living room. It was a beach scene, all blues and greens with birds and flowers which I liked, but it freaked out Sean and his family when they saw it.

I fought back with, 'Our floors are covered in fake leather handbag material!'

So Sean let my mural stay. His brother Philip Storrie managed the Nationalist Bar downstairs with wife Mary (Patsy Paton's sister); and another brother, Dick Storrie, lived in one of the other flats in the building with his girlfriend Maggie, who hated me on sight. I did try to be friendly but hers was an extension of the general Storrie family hatred of me. Dick despised everything I did or said, so Maggie felt she had to join in. Sean's brother Young George went even further in his hatred and in his attempts to split us up. I was walking down the main road in Shettleston one day, going to see my Mammy, when I was stopped by Mr Roberts, a wee bent-over man with a hacking cough.

'Janey,' he told me between coughs, 'my son Stuart says thanks for the wedding invite but he cannae make it coz he is living in England noo.'

I had been friends with Stuart, but I had no idea what Mr Roberts was talking about. He started coughing his lungs up and walked off waving goodbye with one hand as he held a handkerchief over his mouth with the other. That same day, my Aunt Rita came round to see me at my Mammy's.

'Are ye getting married?' she asked.

'No,' I replied.

'Ye never even invited me, did ye!' she shouted.

My Mammy asked in amazement: 'Whit's this aboot, Janey?'

'I don't know, Mammy.'

Aunt Rita held out a wee white card to me. It was a wedding invitation sent to Barra, my ex-boyfriend. In fancy, scrolled handwriting, it read:

Mr and Mrs Currie invite you
to the wedding of their daughter
Janey Currie to Mr Sean Storrie

'Barra's sister gave it me,' my Aunt Rita said. 'He wanted to let you know he couldn't make it coz he's in prison.'

'I don't know anything about this,' I replied, flummoxed.

I took the card home to show Sean.

'It's one of ma brothers,' he said immediately.

'Which one?'

'Don't know, but it's definitely a Storrie stunt.'

We found out that at least 20 wedding invitations had gone out to various friends and family. Sean and I managed to trace them all and let the intended guests know it was a hoax, but I felt so embarrassed. I remembered what Sean had told me early in our relationship.

'People will do things, but you've got to ignore them.'

The next day I sat with Frances, the barmaid at the Palaceum, a lovely girl, but a bit overwhelmed by Young George and easily influenced. She would iron his shirts and run errands for him in return for a bit of attention. After a few drinks, she told me that Young George had given her cash to get the cards, then traced all my relatives and ex-boyfriends and posted invitations.

'It's a good joke,' he had told Frances. 'Janey won't be annoyed.'

I confronted Young George at the bar in front of Old George and Sean. He denied everything, shouting at me and screaming at Sean for accusing him.

'Young George can be a bastard,' Old George said. 'Just ignore him.'

Sean and I did manage to laugh it off and, ironically, it gave us the courage to get married in reality. I can't remember Sean ever actually proposing to me; I think we just went ahead without him asking and without me agreeing. We set the date as the same one Young George had printed on his fake wedding invitations.

'I can never thank you enough,' I smugly told Young George one night in Toad Hall. 'I will be Janey Storrie and it is all thanks to you.'

'Ye are Janey Currie!' Young George started shouting. 'You'll never be Janey Storrie!'

'We are even keeping to the date you set,' I laughed at him.

'You'll never be part of ma family!' he screamed and then he spat at me. He always spat.

* * *

Sean was still working at the Palaceum in Shettleston and I had just landed a job as chambermaid at a big hotel in the city centre. Moving down to live in the Calton seemed like the new start we needed. I liked the Nationalist Bar even more now. It was a real mix of hard-drinking men with a smattering of drug takers. I had never seen heroin in Shettleston, but it had already arrived here in the Calton. When the Shah of Iran had been deposed in 1979 and replaced by the fundamentalist Ayatollah Khomeini, fleeing businessmen couldn't take their cash out of the country; instead, they converted it into heroin, which flooded into the West, including the streets of Glasgow's East End. The Nationalist Bar had always been a great place to buy stolen goods – the locals were very industrious thieves – and heroin addiction stoked the need to steal more.

But Sean and I settled in well. We started painting our new flat and organising our wedding. I could not wait to become Janey Storrie. Sean's moods had got better, although he was now sleeping for hours on the days when he was not at work – he would sleep through the night then keep sleeping until 6.00 p.m. or 7.00 p.m. the next evening. I had never known anyone that could sleep that long. I suggested he speak to the doctor about it.

'Do you think there is something fucking wrong with sleeping?' he barked at me. I shut up and never spoke of it again.

When he was sleeping he was not to be disturbed. That was one sure-fire way to get him into a rage; I had to wait until he awoke by himself and decided to get up. I learned to step quietly whenever he covered his head with the blankets.

For me, living in the Calton was also very different from Shettleston because there were no corner shops or local high street and it was much darker at night. There were no houses giving out light, a lot of the street lamps were broken and Glasgow Green opposite us had no lighting at all. A compensation for me was that Glasgow Green housed the People's Palace – the place I had visited and thought of as a fairytale castle when I was a wee kid. It was a fantastic redbrick museum which housed historic Socialist, Temperance and Suffragette Movement banners and had a 1930s shop, scenes of pre-war East End Glasgow and information on the tobacco barons – it was a glorious building with sweeping staircases and giant pillars going up. It didn't just contain fine art and imported Ming vases like most museums; the People's Palace celebrated the people of Glasgow; it was a very Socialist building and was the only place that had a card-carrying cat. Smudge the Cat had his own trade union card because he was employed as a mouse-catcher. He used to sit proudly on a tobacco baron's desk and unwary strangers used to think he was stuffed and part of the exhibit until he suddenly moved and shocked screams would ensue.

I loved wandering around the People's Palace, soaking up local history; and attached to the back of the People's Palace was the Winter Gardens, a giant botanic conservatory with amazing tropical flowers, banana trees and colourful, exotic plants, all incongruously thriving by the River Clyde. The Calton had once had many grand buildings like these, but most had been demolished by the time we arrived. Everything in the surrounding area had decayed and the ravages of heroin were beginning to make their impact.

It started slowly. Watching for signs and then recognising them was a weird process. Our norm became watching people we loved waste away. Some of the characters in the Nationalist Bar had been charismatic 'hard men' and conmen but, over a relatively short time, I saw them become beggars because of their addiction to heroin. Big John was one: a great friend of the Storrie family, who lived in the Nationalist Bar building. He had a smile to melt your heart and a great personality to boot. His shoplifting techniques were legendary. He would walk into the big stores in central Glasgow and leave openly carrying video players and electrical goods – staff just looked on, convinced he was management. He had been a boxer and keep-fit fanatic but then he hit heroin.

10

Death, heroin and hookers

I loved my new chambermaid job at the city-centre hotel, although it was really hard work and not very well paid; at nights, to make extra money, I had to go and help the Storries behind the bar at the Nationalist or at the Palaceum. I quickly became exhausted and was seeing less of Sean, but the flat was taking shape and our wedding plans were sailing along.

All was going well until one night when I went back to Mammy's flat after a late shift in the Palaceum. She told me a policeman had come to her door and broken the news that Uncle James had been killed as he crossed a railway line near us, coming back from Crazy Katie Wallace's; they were on one of their frequent separations. I was upset and cried for hours. Uncle James was a lovely gentle man who had been nothing but kind to me and I missed him sorely. Mammy was hysterical with grief and was convinced he had killed himself because he and Crazy Katie had separated. She vented her fury on Crazy Katie and told anyone who would listen that Katie had driven him to his death. Poor Sammy and Jackie were left fatherless at the ages of 13 and ten.

The week of Uncle James's funeral was difficult for me. Sean spent the days arguing with me and being very unsupportive. I left him at home one evening while I went

131

back to Shettleston alone to see Mammy. I managed to get a late-night bus back to the Calton and, on my return, found our whole flat in total darkness. I assumed Sean had gone up to Toad Hall. But, when I opened our bedroom door and switched on the light, I saw him lying in bed. He sat up and started mumbling:

'There's a worm in my beans,' he muttered. He was hallucinating. As I tried to speak to him, he started crying and held me tight as he blurted out: 'I've taken so many painkillers, Janey. I want to die.'

I jumped off the bed in a panic and picked up all the tablets that I could now see were lying on the floor, then I grabbed Sean and dragged him downstairs and into the street. We managed to get a taxi to the Royal Infirmary, where they took him into a side ward and stuck a thick brown rubber tube down his throat which made him vomit. His choking screams were horrible. I ran out of the room. Afterwards, I had to phone his dad. Old George just listened and then said, 'OK,' very matter-of-factly. He sent his son Stephen to the hospital and, when he arrived, I had to sit outside while the doctors spoke to the two brothers. Stephen came out and asked me:

'Why did he dae this? What did you dae tae him?'

'I was up at my Mammy's,' I pleaded. 'I was trying to help with my Uncle James's funeral. We hadn't even argued—'

'You fucking *must* huv upset him!' Stephen shouted at me.

I went into the ward and Sean looked at me then broke down in tears again: 'I'm sorry, Janey, I was really fed up and sad and I just wanted tae die.'

When he left the hospital it was decided that he should go home to Toad Hall to stay for an indefinite period. This lasted for two nights; he couldn't stand it; and then we were back together again. The suicide bid was never talked about. His depression continued. Just a few weeks afterwards, I lost my job at the hotel. The trade union told me not to do overtime. So I refused to do overtime. The management sacked me and five other girls for being insolent. Around the same time, Philip Storrie was in a car crash and could not manage the Nationalist Bar, so Old George came up with a plan to sort out both problems: he suggested Sean and I take over running the Nationalist Bar from Philip and his wife Mary, Patsy Paton's sister. As we already lived above the premises, it was ideal and we jumped at the chance – it meant we could get away from the Palaceum, make our own mark in the bar and work together again in our own building.

The rooftop had a fantastic monumental balustrade with round sculptured red stone pillars which supported a huge ornate balcony plinth all the way round the perimeter of the roof and housed a private garden; the views were awesome. On a clear day, you could see north all the way up to the Campsie hills over 20 miles away; they were the backdrop for 1960s council-estate housing schemes which took your eye straight up to the furthest snow-capped hill, like a pretty wee Scottish postcard with broken windows to spoil it for the Americans. Looking east, you could see Celtic football ground's floodlights peep above the trees that littered the view. To the west, you could see all the way to the city centre and beyond to the massive cranes of the main Clyde docks at least ten miles away. And, looking south, you could see the top of the Nelson's Column obelisk on Glasgow Green and the beautiful church spire of St Francis that marked Cumberland Street; but the monstrous high flats of the Gorbals blocked most of the view beyond.

It was a tough area in which to run a pub. A narrow footpath directly opposite the Nationalist Bar led straight across the Glasgow Green then, by St Andrews Suspension Bridge over the River Clyde, into the Gorbals which, by this time, had mostly been vacated by 'normal' people. Benny Lynch the boxer, Jimmy Boyle the murderer and a lot of major organised crime figures had been raised in the slums there. In the 1960s, the Cumbie gang from Cumberland Street in the Gorbals had eternally fought the Tongs gang from the Calton. The Tongs had been in decline for the last five or six years but, in Barrowfield, an area just east of the Calton where Celtic football ground stood, there were still terrible problems with open warfare between two deadly rival gangs called the Torch and the Spur. They divided up local streets into their territories. Young men regularly went to prison for knife attacks and murders; stabbings and razor slashings were a Glasgow tradition and it had long seemed nothing could break the feud between the two gangs in this small area. Young girls who were found dating boys from the other side had always been beaten for their 'treachery' and this warfare carried on into local bars. If a Torch or a Spur came in for a beer and saw a member of the opposing gang, you had to be careful as a fight could break out without warning over nothing.

However, as heroin took rapid and firmer control of the area, it ended the long-standing gang wars: Torch and Spur soon consolidated into one friendly needle-swapping commune. The flats above the Nationalist Bar quickly started to become drug dens as tenants became hooked on heroin. The rivalry between Torch and Spur was replaced by a bitter and violent rivalry between drug barons with addicts as their prey. 'The Railings' was where many addicts bought their drugs – a set of pedestrian railings by a road crossing right outside the main Gorbals Police Office. Big John, my favourite self-confident shoplifter and family friend, was by now desperately trying to sell anything from used jewellery to his old clothes just to get one fix. Within a few months, at least three young teenagers in the area had died and people started to wake up to what being a junkie really entailed.

* * *

For me, the good thing about living above the Nationalist Bar rather than at Grandpa Davy Percy's place was that I lived closer to my Dad. He started visiting me in the bar. I would also occasionally go up to Shettleston to see Mammy. Things were quieter for her now as my brother Mij, Cathy and the baby had moved out, my brother Vid was working away from home and, for the first time in her life, she had the whole place to herself. Peter even seemed to have calmed down a bit and there were no traumas or bruises visible. Perhaps I was just too wrapped up in my new life and my wedding plans to notice. Our wedding date was set for 27 September 1980. We were to get married in the new Catholic chapel of St Mark's and the reception would be held in the Palaceum bar where we first met.

Old George had trained Sean well at being what I called tight-fisted and what he called being economical. When we moved into our new flat above the Nationalist Bar, he controlled both our money and exactly where it went. I was given £20 a week to feed and clothe both of us.

'It's not enough,' I argued.

'But you don't need to buy me any clothes,' he explained. 'I've got three shirts, three pairs of trousers and one pair of shoes. Why would I need more? And no woman needs more than one dress and one pair of shoes.'

He was serious. I got my nylon wedding dress in a sale for £58 – plus a pair of white plastic shoes. It was not really what I wanted, but Sean could be pushed no further on the cash front. He borrowed a formal suit for the day from one of his brothers. My flowers were bought on the cheap from a local florist and Sean refused to buy a ring for himself as he said, 'I don't wear rings.' Mine was the cheapest plain gold band in the shop. I was hurt, but kept it hidden behind a smile. On the morning of my wedding, I was very nervous and getting more stressed by the minute. At one point, I needed white Kirby grips to hold in place a wee diamante tiara in my hair.

'Mammy, can't you just run to the shop for me?' I asked.

'I don't huv no money, Janey,' she replied, with a hurt tone in her voice.

'Oh, fucksake, Mammy!' I screamed at her. 'You *would* huv money if it wisnae fur the booze!'

'Don't get upset, Janey – no' today – don't fight with me,' she pleaded with soft, sad eyes and I apologised.

At that point, Dad came into the room in his best suit and smiled at me.

'You look lovely, Janey. Are you ready to go?'

'Yes, Dad.' I smiled back.

As we were walking down the stairs of my old family home in Kenmore Street, I suddenly stopped stock still. I looked at the window and the walls. I could see the wee Janey Currie I used to be, playing ball on the landing, I could hear all the childhood voices of my pals singing on the steps. I turned to Dad and said, 'I can't do it, Dad. I don't want to get married.'

I sat down on the dirty concrete stairs in my white nylon dress. Dad had a frantic look in his eyes as if to say *What's going on?* then he lifted me up and said in a totally calm, resigned voice, 'OK, Janey, let's go downstairs and tell his brother to let Sean know. I don't want you doing something you don't want to do.'

I stood for long seconds, took a breath, then put on a fake smile, held my bouquet of flowers tightly in my right hand and said, 'No, it's OK, Dad. I'm ready now. It was just a wee last-minute scary thing.'

He smiled and the colour went back into his cheeks. We climbed into Stephen Storrie's black Audi car with white wedding bands on the front and he drove us to the chapel. The service went well and, at 9.30 a.m. I became Mrs Janey Storrie. Afterwards, we posed for photos. The photographer kept saying, 'Give us a smile ... Give us a smile!'

But Sean remained stony-faced and gave him a *Fuck Off!* look. He hated being told what to do; he was like a petulant schoolboy. As I entered the Palaceum for the wedding reception, Young George spat on me and Sean's family never actually spoke to mine at all. Sean and I ate dinner and left the place by midday. We were driven in Stephen's Audi to a cheap bed and breakfast in Saltcoats on the Firth of Clyde, which was being lashed by freezing late-September wind and rain. By teatime, we were both bored and went to the local cinema to watch Dustin Hoffman in *Kramer Versus Kramer*, the Oscar-winning film about divorce.

Being married didn't change our relationship much. We just went back to the Nationalist Bar and carried on as normal. Sean took his role as pub manager seriously, although it didn't really need a manager – it needed customers who actually drank enough to pay the bills. But I liked the down-at-heel regulars, in particular the prostitutes – middle-aged women dressed in bri-nylon dresses with brightly painted red lips and a determination to face one more blow job before teatime. The hookers amazed me and ignited my imagination: they would often bring me gifts from the nearby Brigaitt flea market. These included a small glass vinegar bottle, ornaments and books. I may have left school at 16 but I loved reading and Dolly brought me a great selection including classics like *Moonfleet*, Flaubert's *Madame Bovary* and Robert Louis Stevenson's *Treasure Island* – I liked Stevenson's vivid descriptions. *Madame Bovary* also held a particular resonance for me: proof that bad marriages don't end happily – instead, you just die. Doris gave me stapled, A4 scripts of plays sold off by impoverished actors – including *The Threepenny Opera*. The world of the Calton was small and inward-looking but, in these books and plays, I could be part of a wider world out there. My horizons were widened by prostitutes. I had always assumed hookers were tall, blonde, young Hollywood babes – not short, dark, middle-aged women who smelled of cheap talcum powder and stale whisky.

'Men are all bastards, hen,' Doris would tell me as she stripped in the bar's toilet to change into a fresh flowery blouse. 'You gotta take whit ye can and then fuck off from them the first chance ye get!' The whiff of urine and wet armpits would hit me and Doris's black dyed hair and aspiring moustache made me wonder why men would pay her for sex.

'They want something that makes them feel naughty,' she would explain. 'I mean, I could look the spittin' image o' their own mammy but that widnae stop 'em!' She never seemed to mind me constantly quizzing her. *Why did men go to prostitutes? Why did men need sex so much they would go to such lengths?* I could never comprehend it.

Four of our customers – young guys from nearby Barrowfield – raped a prostitute and slashed her to shreds with the traditional Glasgow weapons of open razors; she almost bled to death, with so many gaping slits on her face it was hard to see any unslashed flesh. But she was 'only a prostitute', so the police made no effort to prosecute. When the full horror of the woman's injuries emerged in the press, a lawyer privately prosecuted the four guys. Our customers in the Nationalist Bar talked about nothing else, but it was difficult and uncomfortable for me to read about the trial daily in the paper. I had laughed with one of the guys, played cards with him in the bar; I had been his friend and here he was being charged with raping and slashing a woman to pieces. The general opinion was: 'She was a tart. She deserved it. How can ye be charged with raping a hooker?' The four young men were given long sentences but each had grassed on the other three, so this led to the killings of various brothers and friends as bloody revenge was taken by all four families – slashings and stabbings on the streets of Barrowfield which inevitably spilled over into arguments and fights in the pubs of the East End.

Sean and I were relatively safe from serious violence in the Nationalist Bar because of Old George's reputation. Everyone knew that, if you messed with any of the Storrie sons, you were in real trouble with George. But it wasn't the local hard men we were scared of – it was the daft drunk who had nothing left to lose who might hit you in the face with a pool cue or the random nutter who might lob a half brick at your head coz he was hearing voices. And, though we were mostly protected from serious crime, petty crime was rampant, with every other addict coming in and trying any trick to get cash for heroin. One ginger-haired man tried, 'Janey, Sean told me to tell you to give me £20 till he comes back. His car broke doon and he needs petrol, hen.'

'Fuck off!' I told him. 'That makes no sense and he doesn't even drive, ye dick!'

The bar had always been a one-stop shop for petty criminals and illegal goods, mostly stolen to order, but this increased as heroin took hold of the area and the amount of nicked electrical goods could have restocked Dixons anew almost every week. One benefit, though, was that I could forget about Sean's tight-fistedness because I was now being dressed by Glasgow's finest shoplifters. I remember snuggling up inside my first ever black leather coat, smelling the expensive hide and sliding my hand over the luxurious soft nap; the only downside was the size – it was on the large side and when I stropped around I looked like a cross between a Dalek and a member of the Gestapo. I didn't care, though: it was still very trendy.

Heroin was taking an ever-increasing toll all over the Calton; young guys were starting to look like walking skeletons, with those tell-tale gaunt jaws and that just-too-quick jiggy walk when they came back across the bridge from the Gorbals. Young girls who used to come into our bar for crisps and cola were now doing quick tricks and blow jobs to get money for their habit, taking over from the older prostitutes on Glasgow Green. There were prostitutes everywhere. I started being hassled by guys in cars even when I walked to the shops. While the outside world disintegrated, Sean and I just spent that whole year trying to keep the bar in profit, cleaning the toilets and painting our new flat.

My brother Mij and his family had now settled in the Gorbals and he became a frequent visitor to the Nationalist Bar. He was looking forward to his little daughter starting primary school and had settled down slightly, but he was still a great fantasist. If there was someone in the news who had been bitten by a shark, then he recalled how he had fought off that monstrous shark at the beach in Largs. He lived in a wee world of his own – one that protected him – but his partner Cathy was outgrowing his fantasy dreams and by now realised Mij might never get a real job.

Mammy was still fighting with Peter and one Monday teatime she arrived at our bar with a black bin bag that contained all her clothes. We only had one bedroom, but we let her sleep in the kitchen, which was quite big and contained the TV: it already had a pull-down bed in there for when young Paul stayed over.

'I need a break, Janey,' Mammy explained. 'Peter's being a right bastard but he won't come doon here in case you fucking tell him to beat it.'

After a few days with us, her mood brightened and she started to enjoy helping out behind the bar, meeting new people. I taught her how to pour a pint and top up the bottles; it felt weird, me showing my Mammy stuff about alcohol, but she loved it. She even managed to stay off the booze. I took her round all the local shops and introduced her to the neighbours; she in turn cooked me soup and then sat quietly and smoked, watching anything and everything on TV.

'Janey,' she asked one morning, 'can ye cut ma hair?'

'Are ye mad?' I laughed.

'Just do yer best.'

Her thick white hair was going yellow at the front, as if each cigarette had left a stain on her fringe; I stood there and cropped inch after inch off and, as the hair spun down to the ground, I started getting cocky and began to chop into it, making layers. The end result was amazing – she looked great! I went to the local chemist and bought a cheap dark brown hair dye and tinted the short hairdo I had created. She looked years younger. We both laughed as she pretended to be Judy Garland in my kitchen and danced around singing 'Easter Bonnet' into my soup ladle.

I was hoping that Dad would visit us and then maybe he and Mammy could get back together: I still had that same childish fantasy in my head. But, this time, Dad *did* arrive the following day and he took me aside. 'I need to tell you something. It's important.' He looked different and edgy. 'I've stopped drinking, Janey. I had such a bad time last week I felt I was going mad. I ended up in the Police Office screaming mad. It was the DTs. I have stopped drinking.'

'That's great, Da,' I shot back, pretending to believe him. I knew he would be drinking again at the weekend, though I had never heard him say those actual words before. *I've stopped drinking.* Not ever.

'*No,*' he insisted. 'I really *mean* I *huv* stopped. I am never gonnae drink again.'

I looked at him and saw his eyes were clear and he looked happy: 'That's really good, Dad, I hope you do it.'

Mammy and Dad decided to go out for a day in town. I dressed her in a fresh blouse, fixed her hair and wrapped her in my new black leather coat. She looked lovely but it felt strange. Here I was getting my Mammy ready for a date with my Dad. They set off around midday. I sat in the bar, playing my favourite Steely Dan songs on the jukebox and secretly smiled at the thought of them having a good day with each other. Around teatime, the bar door slammed open, banging off the wall. Mammy stood there glaring and angry.

'I hud to drink fuckin *coffee!*' she shouted at me. 'We sat an' talked in a *café* an' he didnae let me drink!' The leather coat was whipped off and she climbed up onto a bar stool demanding a half of lager. 'No drinking? He's no' my man any mare – he's a fucking weirdo. Janey, he talked aboot the meaning of life and shitey regrets and stuff. Fuck knows whit has happened tae him.'

I had thought this was what she had always wanted – a man who didn't drink and was good to his family. But I had been wrong. She sat there swigging down her lager, sucking on a fag and staring into the distance. As the week progressed, out of the blue, Mammy and Sean started sniping at each other. She had never been rude to Sean before. He mostly ignored her attacks and went downstairs to the bar; the only times he argued back were when she demanded that we watch what she wanted on telly. Sean always got his own way on that because it was important to him. Slowly, Mammy became quieter within herself. The only time she laughed and talked much was when she sat by the window at night and watched the prostitutes in London Road negotiate with men under the stark white street lights.

'Some of those hookers are as old as fuckin' *me*!' she'd laugh, then wrap a coat round herself, lift her skirt up and swagger round the living room, pouting: 'D'ye think I would get a tenner fur it?' She would howl with laughter. It was good to hear her laugh. Soon, she began talking about going home. I tried to talk to her about Peter, but she wouldn't. She left the Calton after eight days. She wanted to go home to him.

11

Down those streets

Sean and I were still trying our best to get customers into the bar, but no matter how many times you hoovered or tried to brush around the pool table, the place still looked like a dump and few new faces came in. The emptiness of the bar meant I played pool incessantly and read constantly – magazines, comics, classic literature, anything – and I organised our meals and washed our clothes and shopped for food to keep the boredom at bay. That summer was unusually hot and I would sit outside on the pavement watching the world go by. Each day, I would see a scattered procession of drug addicts quick-march on their tell-tale jiggy walk off across the Green to score at The Railings. Half an hour later, they would stumble back, dribbling, full of drugs, and meander across the busy London Road making me terrified they would get flattened by a bus or a speeding lorry. It was like the drunken men I had seen staggering up Kenmore Street on Friday and Saturday nights in my child-hood, only the drug had changed from alcohol to heroin.

By this time, most of Britain was gripped by Royal Wedding fever: Prince Charles and the virginal Lady Diana Spencer were creating a perfect template of wedded bliss for us all to follow. Five minutes down the London Road, in Bridgeton, there were street parties, cakes, happy children waving flags and balloons and the whole area was draped in red, white and blue Union flags to celebrate our Prince's wedding. In the Calton, though, there were no street parties, no flags, no festive bunting; people were not throwing themselves into it like other areas because the majority of people in the Calton were Catholics who were not by nature Royalists. The Royal Family were Protestants and one of the Queen's titles was Defender of the Faith – the Protestant Faith. Down those streets she was disliked as much as Prime Minister Margaret Thatcher.

I, though, *was* excited by the whole thing and sat glued to the Nationalist Bar's wee telly hanging above the pool table. I watched as the beautiful bride in her big crumpled cream dress headed towards St Paul's Cathedral in London. I loved it! I was in love with love and hoped they were going to be happy – even if only as happy as Sean and me. The bar only had three old customers that day. Just as Diana got out of her carriage at St Paul's and I waited to see what her dress looked like full length, one of them yelled out:

'Turn that fuckin' Orange bastard Prince off the telly so we can listen to the jukebox! … Give us "Mack The Knife"!'

I ran upstairs and spent the whole rest of the day following the live wedding coverage on our own TV. Sean stayed downstairs and looked after the bar alone. Despite his occasional angry and sometimes violent moods, he was usually loving and affectionate and always stood by me. One night in the bar, Sean told a big, hairy, middle-aged drunk guy he was not getting served any more booze.

'Ya specky bastard,' the man screamed at Sean, as he pulled him towards the door. 'I am gonna punch your fucking heed in!' I stood terrified by the cellar door. Sean was still only 19 years old. They both went out the side door and I ran out behind them. Sean stood in front of the man, slowly took his spectacles off then, without warning, suddenly kicked him hard in the stomach. The man fell forward and Sean jumped on him, raining blows on the guy's head. I became hysterical and managed to pull Sean off as other customers dragged the man away. Sean was spattered with the man's blood and shaking like a leaf. He went into the back shop and washed his hands. I ran in behind and put my arms around him.

He pushed me roughly off and yelled, 'Don't you *ever* fucking pull me off anyone again! Don't you *ever* hold my arms when I am fighting! Don't you *ever* fucking come near me when I am dealing with any of that!' As he screamed at me, spittle and blood were splattered over my face. 'Don't you *ever* fucking do any of that unless *you* want to fight him instead of me! Never – *ever* – be a witness! Do you fucking hear me? *Never* be a witness!'

He grabbed me by the neck and stared at me for what seemed like hours, his 'mad' eyes searing into mine, his fingers not moving but tightly pressing into my throat. I felt my breath slip away; I felt a pulse behind my eyes; I felt I was trying to scream but I couldn't. He let go slowly, then grabbed me round the shoulders and held me tight.

'Janey, I am sorry, I'm sorry, babes. But don't come near me when aw that happens, please.'

I stood there in our dirty back shop staring at the wallpaper, not breathing aloud or speaking, just looking at the floral pattern blur and magnify as the tears bloated over my eyes. Sean sat on the floor, looked up at me and then dropped his head onto his knees. I could hear him crying softly.

'I hate this, Janey. I hate this place. I hate fighting and I hate hurting you. You should just go home to your Mammy, hen, I am fucked ...'

But I wouldn't give up on him. He was only 19 and I realised it was hard trying to be a man in that world. The pressure I came under was different. To be married in the

East End and not have kids before you were 18 was seen as a sure sign of infertility. You were expected to get married, get pregnant (not necessarily in that order), get several children, then get depressed and practise putting make-up on black eyes.

'You no' pregnant yet?' Sean's aunt would regularly bark at me, like I had a defiant Protestant womb.

'I'm no' ready for weans,' I kept telling the many people who asked. Sean never wanted babies either; he reckoned we had to make some cash and live a wee bit first. I did get to be a surrogate mammy because we always had Sean's wee brother Paul Storrie, now a cheeky, funny young 13-year-old. We even took him on our first holiday together. We hired a boat and chugged up and down the River Thames. Paul loved getting to 'drive' the boat all the way up to Windsor. Seeing his smiling wee face as he fed the ducks and played on the banks of the Thames made my heart leap. At home, he never really got to be a wee boy much – he was driving cars and shifting big lorries for Old George.

When we got back to Glasgow, Paul was pulled in by the police as a witness in the trial of a Glasgow shopkeeper who was selling solvents to young kids. Paul had bought the glue for a glue- sniffing friend. The police insisted Old George attend a meeting at the local Police Office to discuss his son's upcoming court appearance. I had to be there too as Paul was staying with me and that legally made me involved. But I was really there to support Paul as he was terrified of what Old George would do to him for the trouble he had got himself into. We all sat crammed into an extremely small room at the London Road Police Office. Old George was dressed in his full formal suit with cashmere coat on top. It was stiflingly hot and he looked stressed. The atmosphere was dreadful.

Four detectives came into the room; Paul shrank behind me and gripped my hand. I held fast. Old George stood up, refusing to shake hands or exchange any pleasantries with the detectives, who tried but failed to introduce themselves.

'What the fuck am I doing here?' George shouted at them. 'He is not goin' to fucking court!'

'Maybe you should sit down and shut up,' a detective replied.

The room became oppressive; it was like trying to suck in air as you were being buried alive. The four policemen and Old George all stood their ground aggressively. Paul and I clenched each other's hands. One large detective sniggered as Old George dropped his shoulders. Then George turned to me, slipped off his big coat and, as soon as the warm woollen garment dropped onto my lap, he turned and punched the large detective square in the face. The five men fell over each other in the cramped room as Old George thrashed around punching anyone and anything that came near him.

'Calm down, for fucksake, George!' shouted one of the older detectives. 'It's OK, George! George! Calm down!'

It was over.

The fighting stopped.

The room was almost quiet.

Almost.

Two of the detectives stood holding their bloodied faces, swearing quietly.

Old George was standing in the middle of the room, his fists up high, jaw clenched and growling like a caged animal. He pushed his way past the men, walked to the door and almost wrenched it off its hinges, thumbing to us to follow him. Outside in the hallway, two startled young uniformed coppers tried to peer into the room but walked quickly off as soon as they saw the fierce look on Old George's face.

'You fucking bastards! If you want more, fucking come here right now!' George screamed, pointing to the floor in front of him. Paul and I just shuffled behind him as he made his way through the hall. 'My son is not going to court! That's the fucking end of it, OK?' he spat towards the men gathered in the hallway. No one moved, they just stood and watched us all march towards the outer door of the Police Office. As he reached the door, Old George turned, pointed at the desk officer and shouted: 'Tell those cunts no' to come near me again!'

Paul and I shuffled like mice behind him, terrified to speak. We both breathed quietly in case the noise of our exhaled nervousness upset him. When we reached the car park in front of the Police Office, Old George stopped and looked at the door of his big silver car. The window had been broken; inside, the radio had been ripped out.

'Oh my God. Please God, no!' I whispered to Paul. He just looked like a white-faced corpse. I held onto his hand even tighter and we stared at his father.

'*Aaagh!* That's fucking *it*! *No* fucking *way*!' Old George screamed at the top of his voice. He strode quickly back towards the Police Office.

Paul and I followed nervously. I don't know why we didn't just run for the hills at this point, but something made us stay with the old man. By the time Paul and I reached the front desk, Old George was already screaming at the desk officer:

'Who the fuck smashed my car, ye *bastards*?' The veins were jutting out in his neck and sweat was running down the side of his almost bald head. The young desk officer stood there docilely and asked politely 'What is your problem?' then said more firmly: 'And don't raise your voice to me.'

Old George pulled back his right arm and drove his fist straight into the young man's face. Blood spurted from his nose. I felt sick. Stinging bile forced its way up my throat. I grabbed Paul's shoulders, turned him round and we both fled back to the car park. We sat on a low wall and watched through the sliding glass front door of the Police Office as Old George flailed his arms about, pointing to his car as three policemen held their palms up towards him and shook their heads. We could hear his swearing and shouting, sometimes clearly, sometimes muffled, as the glass doors kept sliding open and shut whenever he paced too near the sensor as he ranted and swore.

Eventually, he was walked to the door by an elderly man wearing a suit.

Old George strode towards us, then shouted: 'Get in the fucking car!' We drove home in total silence. Old George stopped at the Nationalist Bar and spoke through gritted teeth to Paul as we were trying to manoeuvre ourselves out from the back seats: 'If you get into any more trouble, ya stupid wee bastard, I will fucking kick yer ass.'

Paul dropped his head and nodded. We walked away towards the bar and he finally let go of my hand. Paul needed help with his education and loads of comforting hugs. He did better at school once he was staying with us rather than at Toad Hall. We gave him some security and stability and Sean tried hard to keep him occupied during weekends. Paul's biggest problem was that he had a natural gift for getting caught; he was just innately unlucky. If anyone at school broke a window – even if Paul didn't do it – witnesses would remember seeing Paul among the crowd who *might* have done it.

* * *

That Christmas, Paul, Sean and I had great fun decorating the pub, putting up a tree and stringing lights all round the walls. We hoped for better business, but that allegedly festive week was abysmal. We fed Christmas dinner to the few punters who came, then sat silently round the pub's telly watching old films and eating hot chicken, occasionally pouring the odd pint for a desolate customer.

The New Year, though, held great promise. The Calton had been designated a 'regeneration area' – the wasteland across the London Road from the pub, barren and bleak with frost, had been designated for private homes. The blurb in the proposal described this heroin- and prostitute-infested stretch of road within the seedy, rundown Calton area as *Historic, set facing Glasgow's oldest park, central to the city centre. The area is fast becoming one of Glasgow's most sought-after residential communities.*

It was great news for us. The Nationalist Bar was soon bustling with burly workmen who liked a drink before, during and after work. The pool table started doing brisk business and our newly arrived *Space Invader* machine happily bleeped and gulped 10p pieces by the dozen. Sean and I were now getting on very well and planned a boating holiday. Paul chose the Norfolk Broads and we began saving hard for the trip.

When Mother's Day approached, Sean bought my Mammy a fancy big card and gave me an extra £5 to buy her something special. I got the card ready and rode the bus to Shettleston. I was excited to see her; she had never had a phone and I did miss her. I couldn't wait to catch up on what was going on in her life. When I arrived, she was at home, sitting quietly at her new electric fire.

'Hi, hen,' she welcomed me. 'Shut the door quick or that fucking daft dug will want in.'

'Mammy, the dug lives here; it will bark if ye don't let it in.'

'It is not *my* dug!' she shouted.

'OK, Mammy, here – Happy Mother's Day.' I handed her the card. She smiled at the picture of a big bunch of lilacs and opened the card up to read the words, smiling even wider when she took the £5 note and slipped it in her pocket.

'If Sean asks, tell him I bought ye chocolates,' I told her.

'Fucking chocolates! I don't eat chocolates. C'moan down to the pub with me and I'll get a coupla cans,' she said as she pulled on her woolly coat. I never got to spend the time I wanted with her. After she bought the cans, she turned round and told me, 'Tell Sean thanks. I'm off to see Peter an' I know ye don't want to come, so I'll maybe see ye next week.'

I felt a bit let down. I had wanted to be with her for a wee while longer. But she was right – I didn't want to see Peter. I watched her as she walked into the distance, following her red coat with my eyes until it finally disappeared as she turned a corner. Then I went and got the bus back to the Calton. I had only been away an hour.

Sean and Paul were sitting waiting for me; Paul had bought me a lovely card for Mother's Day. He had even bought me a Hall and Oates music tape. I felt better and decided that Mammy just wanted my cash; she had never even looked back to wave at me. I had my own life here with Sean and it wasn't that bad.

But, in my nightmares, dead people started floating through windows.

12

Each leaf and piece of debris

The world was changing around us. Fresh trees had been planted, grass verges were created and new fencing sprang up seemingly overnight. The Calton was looking better than ever. It made no difference to the locals, though. For each new tree, there were ten new heroin addicts. There was now hardly a building in the Calton that didn't have a 'user' living in it. The Nationalist Bar had at least three users living in the flats upstairs.

On the telly each day, Margaret Thatcher was banging on about Argentina. She was sending troops to the Falklands. The country was on edge. For more than a century, large swathes of the British Army had come from the poorest parts of Scotland. Glasgow was set to send lots of its own boys. I sat in the Nationalist Bar one Saturday afternoon, ignoring the news. I had more frightening thoughts. My sister Ann had just phoned to ask if I had seen our Mammy. No one had seen her for two days. She had told Ann she was going up towards Hamilton to fish with Peter – a two- or three-hour walk – and they were last seen walking along the banks of the River Clyde. I was really worried. Mammy had never spent a night out of her house before, apart from her stay in the asylum. She never stayed overnight with Peter; she always came back to her own home. There was no way she would just stay away and not let us know where she was.

'Maybe someone should ask Peter,' Sean suggested.

'He's nowhere to be found,' I explained. 'He's not answering the door.'

I spent all that weekend calling my sister for news. I went up to my Mammy's house and went across the road and banged on Peter's door for what seemed like hours, but it was no use. Neither of them was anywhere to be found. The police were contacted and they came down to the pub to question me.

'Fucking Peter will know where she is!' I snapped at them.

'Mr Greenshields says he has not seen her since they were up the Clyde,' the detective explained. 'He says she walked home in the dark.'

This was the first I knew that Peter had reappeared.

'Oh for fucksake!' I screamed at them. 'Drag the Clyde, coz he will have thrown her in! She would never walk home all the way from Hamilton herself!' They ignored me and left.

My brother Vid confronted Peter on the Sunday night. Peter stabbed him deep in the side with a six-inch boning knife and left him bleeding, he thought, to death. But Vid was rushed to the hospital and survived. On the Monday morning, I sat in my Mammy's house in Shettleston – the one I had grown up in, the one I was sexually abused in – and prayed she would walk through that front door. The house looked the same – the same burst couch – the same damp smell – the same filthy toilet. I knew if 9.00 a.m. came and went and she had not come to collect her Benefit Book then she was surely dead. Nothing but death would keep Mammy from her Monday Book.

I made tea in the wee kitchen. The old table's surface was encrusted with islands of white sugar that had hardened over time and turned brown where tea had been spilled over them, reminders of a dead woman's attempt at making tea while drunk. I looked in the sink and there was her cold half-drunk mug of tea. I lifted up the black-stained floral chipped mug and smelled her smoky taint. She constantly drank tea. She constantly smoked. I stared at the wallpaper. It never changed. It was always beige and splattered with stains and fat.

The room seemed so small now.

I looked at my watch.

It was 9.02 a.m.

No Mammy.

Nothing but silence.

I left my Mammy's home, hailed a cab and got back to the Nationalist Bar to open its doors at 11.00 a.m.

Sean held me tight.

'Don't assume anything … yet,' he told me.

By this time, my entire family had gathered back at Mammy's flat in Shettleston and was waiting for news, but I had my customers to serve here in the Nationalist Bar, in theory. In fact, we had no customers. By midday some had arrived. Sean kept telling me to go upstairs and wait for news, but I wanted to work. I put on the radio to distract myself and because one of the guys in the bar had friends in the British Army – he wanted to hear any reports of bad news from the Falklands. People were dying on the other side of the world. The radio newsreader said, 'The body of a woman from Glasgow has been found in the River Clyde today. It is confirmed she is Annie Currie, aged 47, from Shettleston.'

Minutes later, the phone calls started. They were too

late. A Radio Clyde newsreader had already told me my Mammy was dead. The bar spun out of focus. I could hear customers trying to ask Sean what was wrong.

'Her mum's just been found dead,' I heard Sean explain to the bewildered pool players. I ran outside and sat on the stairs by the pub. I didn't want to go up to Shettleston. I didn't want to go up to my Mammy's house. She wasn't there. She was dead. Sean tried to reason with me and get me to go upstairs to our flat. Instead, I ran alone across the busy London Road, past the Doges' Palace tiled on the side of the old Templeton's Carpet Factory, thrashed my way through the long grass, dragged my feet through all the tall spring daffodils and stood watching the River Clyde belt along on its way downstream. The dark bubbling water never stopped. I watched as each leaf and piece of debris floated past me. I had loved that river. On hot summer days, I had sat here. The Clyde had betrayed me. It had killed my Mammy. My head was exploding with anger and pain. *That bastard Peter killed my Mammy!* I sat on the grass and hugged my knees. Everything about that day hurt me. The beautiful smell of the spring flowers blooming all around me. The happy kids playing beside the water. I had no feeling except pain and fear. I walked back to the pub and let Sean take me upstairs. But nothing could take away from inside my head the image of Mammy's dead body being dragged from the river. *Was she in one piece? Was she dressed? Did she struggle?* Everything ran round and round and round in my head.

The police came to tell me that Peter had admitted he saw Mammy fall into the water, then walked home in the dark on his own.

'It's not illegal to watch someone fall in the water and not report it,' they explained offhandedly to me.

'He fucking tried to kill her before,' I tried to argue.

Nothing happened. Peter had given the police his statement. Annie Currie fell into the Clyde and died. End of story. She was an ordinary wee East End woman who meant nothing to them. The week passed in a blur. Her funeral was on the following Monday. I sat in the undertaker's and stared at her coffin. I was 21. Nothing made any sense to me. My Mammy was gone and my brother was very ill because Peter had stabbed him, yet the police let Peter go free. As far as Sean was concerned, dealing with Peter was not a Storrie problem; it was a Currie problem. Old George would certainly not 'take care' of Peter: that was up to my brothers. My Mammy was *their* kin.

When Vid was released from hospital after three days, we all tried to carry on with our lives. I don't know how the rest of my family dealt with it all. I went back to work. I simply went into the bar each day, poured pints, served customers and carried on with the routine. Sean and Paul rallied round and did their best to help me, but nothing mattered. I simply pretended it had never happened. Each day I got up and worked, sent Paul to school and opened the bar.

My Dad, of course, was devastated. He would phone me and try his best to come see me each week. He was still sober and remained off the drink despite the terrible time we were all going through. I never spoke to my brothers or sister about it; I never asked any more questions, I changed the records in the jukebox and told myself Mammy was still living in Shettleston and I would go see her soon. It was a comforting, good daydream.

My nightmares got worse and, in them, I started to run down hundreds and hundreds of spiral stairs as if I were looking for someone but couldn't find them. Down and down and down I would run, never getting to the bottom, never finding anyone, sometimes waking up feeling suffocated, gasping, barely able to breathe.

My nightmares might be understandable but the totally unexpected element was that, in the weeks after my Mammy's funeral, Sean fell apart. He threw temper tantrums and verbally attacked me; he screamed into my face and told me to leave. I could not even begin to make sense of it all. I was still fucked mentally after Mammy's death. In the middle of one night, I simply took my coat and walked out. I walked through the streets, just pacing with my head down. I didn't try to understand his mood, I just walked. It must have been about three hours later that I stopped and lifted my head up. I found I was actually way past the city centre. I had walked about six or seven miles. I was standing in the early hours of dawn, facing the River Clyde down at the old abandoned shipyards of Govan, where they had built the Queen Mary.

I sat on an old rusty dockside and rested. I was so tired. There were two old men sitting near me – old drunks who slept rough. The smell of piss was awful but I sat tight. They looked at me with sidelong glances but never spoke a word. I stayed there for hour upon hour, just sitting, thinking and trying to calm the noises and images in my head. Arguments, shouting, angry faces, my Mammy's coffin being slid into the black hearse, Sean ranting at me. It was like all these scenes were on film but they were all playing at once. Fear and anger and shouting and swearing all travelling through my head. It must have been late afternoon by the time I walked back to the Nationalist Bar. I don't know what I expected to say or what I expected to face but, when I stepped into the bar, Sean held me tight and pleaded his apologies to me.

I never spoke; I smiled at him and poured myself a Coca-Cola.

He was so upset.

'Seeing your Mammy's coffin brought it all back to me,' he said. 'My mammy dying. How I stopped speaking after she died.'

I stood looking down at him sitting there explaining how worried he had been, how he hated himself, and I sat down to let him hold my hand. He apologised. I accepted and, in my head, I wondered if Mammy was sitting in her wee pub drinking a beer and laughing.

The next day, I carried on serving drinks, looking after Paul and getting ready for our boating holiday in Norfolk. Paul was so excited. I personally didn't want to go anywhere near a river but we had it all booked and organised and Sean's brother Stephen and his wife Jackie were set to join us halfway through the holiday.

We travelled overnight on a sleeper train and arrived in Norwich early the next day. Paul scrambled into the wee boat and unpacked his bag quickly, sussing out the boat immediately. I was terrified of stepping on board. The sight of water made me uneasy, but I did not tell Sean or Paul. I stared into the water, imagining my Mammy sinking slowly beneath the murky surface. The image would not leave my head. Half the week I imagined she was still in Shettleston and the other half I watched the weeds for movement. The Norfolk Broads were awesome; the peacefulness was good for my soul. I spent loads of time painting the trees and views. After four days, Stephen and Jackie arrived with their little yappy dog in tow. We took the boat all the way across open Broads to Great Yarmouth and Paul spent the day at the funfair and on the beach. I read Voltaire's *Candide* which amazed me – Candide just got fucked at every turn. Everything was fucked and the philosopher-teacher said *Well, whatever is meant to be is meant to be* – I thought *Get fucked! Surely every single tragedy in your life isn't just meant to show you light at the end of some tunnel.* What a pile of trite shite!

Sean alternated between behaving like a bereaved son-in-law and a moody arsehole. I couldn't be bothered with either. It was a relief to get back to Glasgow the following week. At least I could concentrate on something that took my mind away from the pain. The pub kept Sean busy and out of my face for a while, though his sleeping patterns were getting worse and he sometimes never slept through the night: instead, he would stay awake and keep me awake too – arguing. It was OK for him – he would sleep all the next morning – but I had to open the bar. I resented his moodiness and almost every day would make plans to leave him.

But where would I go? Mammy wasn't there to go back to any more. Should I admit defeat and stay at my sister Ann's? Should I just kill him and hope I could get away with it? *No, that was stupid.* But what if he got really violent and killed me? It did happen. If anyone knew that it was me. *Men did kill their partners.*

I would sit in the bar and write everything down in a wee book I kept. One day, I poured out everything I felt about my Mammy's death, about all the injustice, all the fear, all the anger I kept hidden inside me. Sean's brother Philip found it under the till and read it aloud to the rest of the Storrie family. They all laughed.

Old George teased me: 'You gonnae kill Peter, are ye? You're gonnae write to the Prime Minister aboot yer wee Mammy? We all read it in yer book, Janey. Maybe Peter never killed her, coz I think he is a nice wee guy. Maybe I should get him to dig ma garden. I heard he wiz good with gardens.'

Old George seemed to enjoy torturing me. He behaved the same to his sons. If he found a weakness, he would pick at it like a scab until it bled. Old George had lost his wife; his sons had lost their own mother; but they were not averse to hurting me and laughing about my Mammy's death.

13
Redecorated

That same summer of 1982, Glasgow Council was cleaning parks and planning parties because Pope John Paul II was coming to the city. It was supposed to be a celebration, but it divided the city on vicious sectarian lines. Local pastor Jack Glass led protests against the arrival of the 'Antichrist' from Rome, proclaiming that the man had 'no right to set foot on a Protestant island'. I wanted to go to Bellahouston Park to see the Pope; I felt it was a great piece of history I could actually witness taking place. But I had to work that day as Old George had organised one of his regular trips to a sale and Sean had to go with him. Any sale was a big event in Old George's diary and I hated them as he often brought back hideous furniture or carpets and declared them cheap quality and worth putting in the bar. Even worse, they were often installed by the Storrie family's handyman, a skinny man not unlike an orang-utan, who was known only as The Gow. He was bald, with tufts of red hair on the side of his head and had thick curly red hair escaping out the top of his shirt. Everything he built had a tendency to fall apart, to the point that 'Gow-built' became a euphemism for rickety.

I had to watch the Pope on TV in the Nationalist Bar. All the Catholic customers wept as they watched the wrinkled wee white-robed man bless Glasgow. Sean came home late that night, filthy and carrying the brightest, cheapest orange carpet I had ever seen.

The new houses across the road from the Nationalist Bar were finally coming together and we had decided to revamp the pub in preparation for the new community that was about to descend on us. A plan was drawn up and Old George's mates were hauled in to start the work. One of George's mottoes was *Never pay a contractor – instead hire someone who is family or who spent time in prison with you.* We did not close the pub; George's mates merely built, painted and hammered around us, filling the place with sawdust, paint fumes and odd blokes fitting mirrors. George was clever. He paid them, then got the money back in booze bought over the bar.

Wee shrivelled Angus who came to reupholster our couches was 86 and looked 106. His body and gnarled hands were bent over his wee bag, his trousers kept falling down and I could not imagine a man who did not understand the concept of a belt being able to cover all our wall seating.

'I was the guy who upholstered the Queen Mary,' he mumbled while pulling up old pants and tweed trousers. 'You ask anybody up in Govan an' they will tell ye it wiz me.' He put a big handful of nails into his mouth and leaned onto the wooden backs of the seats as he stretched fake leather burgundy material (the same stuff we had on our bedroom floor) and deftly hammered in a perfect straight row of nails that he spat from his lips to his cracked palm as he went. He was agile and fit while he was working but, the minute he stopped, he lay on the floor and slept for 20 minutes at a time.

'I think that old man is gonnae die, Sean,' I whispered.

'It's the work that keeps him going.'

The job was finished in three days, the pale split beige plastic replaced by studded burgundy fake leather, all gleaming and new, and we changed the name of the pub from THE NATIONALIST BAR to THE WEAVERS INN. The new estate across the London Road was to be called Weavers Court and our pub would be the perfect cosy bar that added to that new community of would-be Yuppies. We had, though, to make a big decision about our current clientele, because some were either mad drunks or crazy fighting boys. This would not fare well with the new would-be Yuppies.

So, just before the first new owners moved into their new homes, we barred some of our old punters from the pub. It was a rotten feeling as they had stood by us in the past, but the world was moving on. Within months, couples and even families started to come over to the newly revamped WEAVERS INN. We started selling coffee and hot meals and the pool table was thrown out. We had more trendy music, cleaner toilets and there was not a drunken, brick-lobbing nutter to be seen. Sean and I dressed neatly and served quality wines. Thatcher's Britain had arrived in the Calton. Nobody was allowed to light a joint, prostitutes were moved on and shoplifters were now shown into the back shop for transactions.

* * *

The new clientele were a mixed bunch. Professional people working in offices and even well-heeled journalists became regulars. They loved our new-look bar and mixed well with the remaining 'safe' old customers we had left, including Big Malky, a good-hearted, friendly man who was part of a big East End family, but very well read and well educated; he had become a mature student then graduated into being one of the area's main social workers. On Sundays we hired musicians as the punters seemed to like that. Our main entertainment was Country and Western singers and a middle-aged man with a perm followed on the piano by a really old man called Will. They sang everything from the Stylistics to Dean Martin. It really was Butlins circa 1963, but it drew in crowds.

The pub's rebirth and its new clientele helped me focus on the good stuff; more cash was flowing in and eventually I stopped constantly thinking of Mammy. When times got bad I would just keep it in my head that she was up in Shettleston, sitting in her own wee pub. That was safe for me. Sean and I never discussed her. It was a closed subject.

When new customers asked me questions about my family, they were terribly shocked when I told them my Mammy had been found in the Clyde less than six months ago. I would just smile as I spoke of it all, trying to hide the fear in my voice, until one guy asked me, 'Did you not love your Mammy? You talk about it as if you were glad she died.'

It hit me like a brick. I had adopted this monotone, matter-of-fact attitude when I spoke of her death: 'My Mammy was found dead in the Clyde. Is that a lemonade you want in your vodka?'

The only time I could share grief was when Mij came over to see me. He and Cathy had now split up and he was looking after his wee girl Debbie on his own. Mij and I had grown closer as we grew older. Gone was the big fat bully and here now was a vulnerable young single parent. Mij and I would sit and he would cry buckets about the way he had treated Mammy.

'Janey, I was a bastard to her! I never even said ah wiz sorry!' he would weep.

I felt terrible for Mij, but it was no surprise Cathy had left him; he was difficult and made her life hell. She just couldn't take it any more. I often wished I had the guts to walk out on Sean; I would watch him smile at people and sneer at me and my heart would drop. His slaps around the head were now becoming low punches and terrifying rages. I no longer felt sorry when he had migraine headaches; instead I wished they were brain haemorrhages. I once went back up to Granda Davy Percy's house, just for a break and some breathing space.

'Do you miss your favourite Uncle?' Granda Davy asked me. 'He only just left. If you stay for supper, David will be back. He'll be glad to see you.'

I left quickly. I was annoyed at myself. I knew he was back home as he had made an appearance at Mammy's funeral.

Sometimes I would just walk out of the Weavers bar and go to my sister Ann's home, but it was hard for her because her marriage had just broken up too. She was left with two small children, a fair amount of debt and was not coping well with the separation; she was slowly coming apart. The last thing she needed was people banging on her door looking for me.

My only ally was Patsy Paton. She knew how Sean ticked and often let me stay over at her home when the shouting got too much for me. She would pick up the phone and dial the Weavers.

'Sean, fucking quit all this shit! Whit's going on in your head? Ye weren't brought up to hit women!'

She would hold me tight as I cried about Mammy and constantly reassured me that getting Sean out of my life was an option. The responsibility of running the Weavers always dragged me home; I didn't want to fail Sean; I didn't want to be a shit worker; I didn't want to be a failed wife; I didn't want his brothers to be right about me.

Occasionally, he and I could talk about his moods and he always promised never to hit me again.

'I am really sorry, Janey. I don't know whit goes through ma head. I wish I was dead, then this would all be over. Maybe you should leave me.'

Sean could make me feel so loved and so wanted; I would wake up in the night and watch him and gently kiss his face, careful not to waken him up. I loved him. I just didn't understand him.

* * *

We had a great Christmas that year; Sean was lovely and bought me a six-week-old, black-and-tortoiseshell kitten with a white belly which we named Twinkles. *Maybe it will all get better,* I thought. Dad came up to see me in the New Year: he was still off the drink and doing well.

'I bought myself a flat,' he explained, all pleased with himself. 'It's in Maryhill, near my work. Come up and see it? Maybe help me with decorating?'

I was really excited. Sean was not remotely interested. He still largely ignored Dad and would only answer in one-word sentences when spoken to. I felt terrible.

'I'm nice to your dad,' I'd tell him. 'Why can't you be nice to mine?'

'He never looked after you when you were a kid. He should have known you were being abused,' Sean would snap back.

'Does he know I'm being abused by you now?'

'Well, fucking tell him I hit ye. D'ye want *me* to tell him?'

'Dad didn't know Uncle David Percy was abusing me,' I tried to explain to Sean. 'Dad drank too much then. He didn't know what was going on.'

'And you're saying my hitting you is as bad as what your Uncle did? Well fucking leave me then!'

Sean stormed off. I cried in the back shop, waiting for him to get over his bad mood. It all went round in circles.

* * *

When I went up to see Dad's new flat, the wallpapering was perfect and the colours were all well suited. Pale beige walls with a lovely darker chestnut carpet and a vivid burgundy velvet suite – it was really good to see him happier. Dad, over time, started to ask Sean for advice and pull him slowly into being part of his family; and Sean slowly started to respect him for getting off the booze.

Sean had never got any praise from his own father. He would tell his dad how good things were going at the new Weavers Inn and Old George would just nod and walk away without reacting. Never any praise. Sean would sit with him and try to show him future plans we had for the development of the pub. But any ideas that weren't Old George's were immediately criticised and ridiculed. Even worse, Old George didn't like our new clientele.

'All these fucking poncey so-called journalists in suits. They don't spend enough money,' he would sneer. 'Talking fucking posh, thinking buying a Barratt flat across the London Road makes them a millionaire,' he would mutter under his breath. He had never trusted strangers. The old Nationalist Bar boys had been fine: he knew a looney when he saw one and could recognise a drunk and a fighter. These new folk in smart suits were hard to suss and they didn't know who he was, which was odd for him. Old George was very well known in the area, but not by these incomers.

The new homes were being built and bought as fast as possible. New couples were walking around, getting to know their new area, hoping to find a friendly face in the local pub and Sean and I were trying our best to provide the perfect place for them. Our trade expanded. We soon needed extra part-time staff and got increasingly busy at teatime. Sean and I could no longer eat together – we had to take turns to eat – one in the bar and one upstairs. We would meet, in passing, at the jukebox.

'Dinner's on the table, Janey … I made tea … It's in the pot … See you in an hour,' Sean would say as we passed and he handed the keys to me. With both his mind and body busy, Sean was now easy to be with most times. He loved chess and had set up regular chess competitions for the customers.

One night, I had to go up to Shettleston to pick up my cousin Sammy from his mammy, Crazy Katie Wallace. He and Katie had fallen out again and his wee sister Jackie was having more emotional and mental problems, so I had been asked if I could look after him for a while. I walked up the main road in Shettleston. It was raining hard and there were puddles all over the street. I was drawn to my Mammy's local. I opened the door and stood in the entrance of the wee snug bar. There was that same familiar smoky smell, her same old friends sitting in their corner with the same big dog at their feet. Two of the women smiled at me – sad smiles.

'Have ye seen ma Mammy?' I asked them.

The men at the bar turned round.

'Have ye seen ma Mammy?' I asked again.

The women sat staring at me.

I ran from the bar, slamming the door behind me. The wind and rain whipped the hair across my face as I splashed all the way up Kenmore Street. *She will be in our house*, I thought. *That's it! She will be there.* The hallway was

dark. *Fucking light bulb's gone again!* I ran up the stairs two
at a time, reaching my Mammy's door in no time. Suddenly
I put my palms on the red landing wall and tried to breathe.
The air is being sucked out of me. I looked at the door. No
name. It had been painted a different colour! *Who painted
our door?* It was no use. *I have to breathe properly.* My heart
was pounding and something was rushing through my
ears with a constant *boom-boom boom-boom*. My palms were
sticking to the red council-painted wall. I stared at my
name scraped into the old thick repainted plaster:

JANEY CURRIE – 1970

'Janey, fucking stop it, ye wee bastard!'

Mammy was standing there looking at me. She had just
climbed the stairs and was dripping wet, holding two plastic bags full of cans and butcher meat.

'Ye cannae write yer name in the wall!' she shouted.

I looked at the wall again. It had been redecorated and
my name had been filled in with red paint a few times since
1970 and I realised my Mammy was never going to come up
those stairs ever again with her plastic bags. I dropped to
my knees and hugged the pain inside me. Huge gulping
noises came out of my mouth; no tears, just cries. *She was
dead!* She wasn't in that house. I sat on the stairs for a few
hours, listening to the neighbours' televisions. Occasionally,
I slid over tight against the wall to let people pass me.

The journey back to the Weavers was horrible: the bus
was late, the cold rain soaked me and it was very late when
I reached the glowing lights. I walked straight through the
pub into the back shop and pulled off my coat.

'What's up?' Sean asked.

'My Mammy's dead, Sean … I looked for her, but she

wisnae anywhere. She's dead, Sean,' I sobbed. He held me tight and ignored customers shouting through for service. He stroked my head and sat us both down on the tiled floor.

'I'm so sorry, Janey,' he whispered. 'I will call Crazy Katie and get her to send Sammy down on his own.'

14
A biblical prophecy

Wee 18-year-old Sammy arrived the next day. He walked into the pub, his hair bleached yellowish, his clothes dirty. He was desperate for work and pleased to be out of Shettleston.

'Sammy, that hair needs cutting and dyed black again. Sean has some clothes we can dress you in.'

He was willing to be cleaned up as long as he had somewhere to stay. Sean treated him like another wee brother almost immediately and Sammy and wee Paul Storrie, who was still staying with us, hit it off straight away. Paul was five years younger than Sammy and still at school, but they became firm friends. Both of them 'checked out' girls at the Weavers. Paul was too young to get involved, but Sammy seemed able to chat up any woman in minutes. God knows how – a really lovely, intelligent guy but hardly a Hollywood stud to look at. He was about five foot seven inches tall, painfully thin with a rather big nose, big lips, his teeth needed some work and he seemed rather shy, but he had the biggest bluest eyes I had ever seen in anyone in my life. Maybe that was it.

Sammy and I had almost been brought up together at my home in Kenmore Street because he stayed with us every time his dad Uncle James ran out of money or his mammy Crazy Katie Wallace got into another emotional crisis. He had been very fond of my Mammy and missed her terribly; it was nice to talk to somebody who remembered her like I did.

'Yer ma wiz like my own mammy, Janey. I remember your Mammy trying to punch my mammy over the wee kitchen sink when she found out my mam hud left Jackie and me on oor ain all night.'

We both laughed at the thought of my Mammy attacking Crazy Katie Wallace in front of her kids.

Sammy soon started helping out behind the bar at the Weavers but, after a few weeks, he started disappearing for a few days and would come back without explanation. Sean would rip into him:

'Ye have to make a decent commitment to this job or leave, Sammy.'

But he was very insecure. He had been in trouble at school and had been glue-sniffing when he was younger. He was just a confused wee boy at heart. He had never had a stable family life and I knew working in the Weavers pub stifled him, though the customers liked him. He started to make an effort and started to fit in slowly. One day, he told me: 'When I wiz up in Shettleston seeing my mammy, I met big David Percy. He was asking for you.'

I froze.

'What did he say?'

'Well, I told him I wiz living here at the Weavers with you and he just asked how ye wur ...' Sammy looked at me oddly. 'You OK, Janey?'

'I fucking hate David Percy,' I spat out. 'He's a slimy bastard!'

Sammy never mentioned it again and never asked why.

Sean, Sammy and I continued to work hard in the Weavers. At lunchtime, new customers were coming in from the old Templeton's Carpet Factory, which had been renovated and was now a 'Business Centre' for new Thatcherite entrepreneurs. Computers were the future and all these healthy young shirt-and-tie men would stride into our bar to get cheap lager and fried foods. Yuppies were coming into the Weavers bar but, outside, the heroin deaths continued. It was sad to see grannies and grandads pushing prams and raising babies that their dead children had left behind. Our smartly dressed new customers who had moved into their fancy new flats in *one of Glasgow's most sought-after residential communities* were now fully aware of the area's problems: their houses and cars had been broken into; their valuables stolen; prostitution was everywhere; young girls were trawling the streets, bringing weird kerb crawlers with them; men in cars were slowing down, staring at any woman walking alone.

'You lookin' for business?' they'd shout out.

* * *

That New Year's Eve we got a call from Crazy Katie Wallace:

'Sean, is that you?' she croaked down the line.

'Aye, Katie, it's me. Ye want to speak to Sammy?'

'Naw, I just want tae die, Sean. I hate ma life. Will ye look after Sammy fur me?' she mumbled. 'I am really gonnae do it this time, Sean.'

Sammy had had a least four suicide calls from Crazy Katie that year.

'Look, Katie,' Sean replied quietly, hoping Sammy could not hear the conversation, 'you're only upsetting everybody with all this shite.'

She hung up.

Sean told Sammy about the call and Sammy got into a state about his mum. Crazy Katie had never been a supportive mother, always falling apart, always drifting; Sammy was more worried for his younger sister Jackie, who already had problems. She had had some learning difficulties but was now settling into a routine through a social-work programme.

The next day, Sammy went up to Shettleston to see his mum but, while he was still on his way, we got a call from the police. Katie Wallace had killed herself with sleeping tablets and gas in her boyfriend's flat.

Two days later, Sammy and I had to go and identify the body. We walked into town through the cold, slushy streets. New Year had just passed but Christmas decorations still hung forlornly from Glasgow's street lamps. Sammy sat on the steps of the City Morgue and hugged his knees, crying, his huge blue eyes spilling tears.

'Janey, I cannae go in there and look at her,' he wept.

'We will do it together,' I whispered.

Crazy Katie's body lay dead on the table, its waxy face looking very old, the hair bushy around its head. It really didn't look like her at all. At first, I thought it might not actually be her. But then I recognised her eyes and mouth. It was the first time I had seen a dead human body. Sammy collapsed. My heart broke. We were both really still kids and here we were both remembering dead mothers. We clung to each other in grief; I knew how hard it had hit him. She had never been the perfect mother but she was the only one he had.

We all rallied round and tried to help him through the funeral. We suggested bringing Jackie to stay with us but she did not want to. Sammy spoke to her social workers and the next month she was put into a social care home. Sammy told me he wanted to go home, but he had never had a single, stable home, so he just went back to Shettleston, where his friends were, and he stayed there while still working at the Weavers. But his mother's death set him back. His time-keeping became more erratic. A cupboard in our flat was filled entirely with bags and bags of Crazy Katie's clothing because Sammy didn't want to get rid of them but had no space to keep them at his new place in Shettleston.

It was inconvenient, but I had more personal worries. My brother Mij, who was living in the Gorbals, came over to see me more and more and I was worried about the weight he was visibly losing.

'Mij, what the fuck is going on?' I would ask. 'You are getting really skinny and looking ill.'

Eventually, I did scream at him the one obvious, scary question: 'Are you on smack, ya big arse? Are you fucking hitting up?'

He denied it.

But, without warning, I went to his home.

His flat was worse than our old home in Kenmore Street. There were clothes and pieces of food scattered around. My wee niece Debbie was sitting in by herself, when she should have been at school.

'Where is yer dad?' I asked her.

She smiled happily at me. 'He is over at his pal's hoose, Aunty Janey.'

I opened a drawer.

The first thing I found was needles.

Fucking needles.

Just lying there waiting to be found, waiting to be picked up by Debbie. *The big fucking idiot!* I grabbed Debbie and told her to show me where he was. She sang and skipped all the way along the road until we reached a house and a hallway that smelled of piss. She took me to a door. I banged on it until a scruffy man with a big Pit Bull Terrier answered. 'Whit the fuck do ye want?' he snarled.

'Is Mij here? Mij Currie?' I snarled back

Mij stumbled to the door, squinting his eyes. He looked shocked when he saw me standing there, holding Debbie's hand: 'Janey, hen! I, ah, meant to get hame in a minute. Debbie wiz just watching the cartoons, win't ye Debbie?' he said, looking pleadingly at his wee girl.

'Mij,' I told him. 'She is too young to be on her own. Tell me whit the fuck is going on or I will tell my Dad about all this.' I stood watching his face twitch. He slowly put both hands up to his mouth and mumbled something. I grabbed at his fingers and prised them off his mouth. 'Whit the fuck are you saying?'

'I huv been taking smack, Janey.' He buckled to the floor and started crying like a small child at my knees. 'I am sorry, Janey, I let everybody doon; just get me put away. I am no fit to be a da.'

His self-pity made me so angry I just walked out of the house swearing and shouting to myself. I raged as I walked quickly through Glasgow Green towards the Weavers. I spat and swore at the junkies I passed. They just staggered on, ignoring my rage. When I got back home, I made phone calls and arranged for Debbie to go stay with her mammy's sister but, eventually, she went back home to Mij and spent time living between them all. I was horrified. I was worried in case someone abused her. Eventually, I called Social Services. I knew they would call Debbie's mother's family and there would be some arrangement to get her better looked after. She eventually went to stay with her aunt, which worked out for a while although later she did end up in care. At the time, Mij was upset and angry. He came over to the Weavers one night and stood crying: 'Why did ye do that, Janey? That wean is my life.'

'She needs protecting, Mij, and ye cannae provide that if ye are fucked on smack, can ye?'

He walked out crying. I could deal with Mij's anger. I could not deal with her being abused.

And it was not just my own brother I was having problems with. Sean's brothers were becoming ever more difficult to deal with. Dick would come into the Weavers and antagonise me whenever he got a chance. One of his friends would sit at the bar and Dick would talk loudly to him: 'My dad George hates Janey an' we all hate her and she cannae huv kids!'

'Dick,' I would snap back. 'Just shut up. I don't fucking care if you like me. The minute you like me, I will change my personality ... And another thing – I just don't want kids right noo. I know it must confuse you – two people being together and one of 'em not pregnant, but I like having sex an' no kids, OK?'

Mentioning sex always shut him up. Mentioning sex was always the best defence in the Storrie family. If in doubt, talk about sex. For a bunch of so-called hard men they were easily embarrassed. There was always a strange undertone to Sean's family. I was never sure what it was and Sean always made sure I never asked. But, one night, he and I were woken up by a loud banging. A man whom I had never seen before stood at our door. He was tall, with very dark hair. He said something to Sean, then walked straight into our living room like he had been in the house all his life, leaving Sean and me behind in the hall.

'Who the fuck is that guy?' I asked.

Sean put a finger to his lips and went in to join the man. I watched the two of them climb up the hideous, bull-fronted, fake-wood, devil-worshipping fireplace I had always hated so much. Sean reached down into the gap behind the fake panelling and pulled out three long objects wrapped in cloth and tied up with string. I knew by the shape that they were rifles or shotguns.

'What the fuck is that?' I shouted as they walked past me in the hall.

'Keep her quiet, Sean,' the man told him in an English accent.

Sean carried the gun-shaped cloth-covered objects down the long hall, then downstairs and into the man's waiting car. I was shocked. Sean came back to bed as if nothing had happened.

'Sean, why did you not tell me there were guns behind that fireplace? Was it built just to hide guns?'

Sean lay quiet as I badgered him and then said: 'You never asked. So why do I have to tell ye everything?'

'Don't be fucking sleekit, Sean!' I shouted. 'Ye know whit I mean. Who the fuck wiz that Englishman an' why did ye give him guns an' why the fuck were they in oor house?'

He said nothing.

I lay in bed fuming.

'I want to fucking know! And I want to know *now*!'

So Sean explained to me how it worked. 'If you don't know, ye can never tell. And you can never be even suspected by my dad of being a grass.'

In the morning Sean left the pub without warning.

He was away for one whole day.

He was away for a second whole day.

I called his dad continually. Old George just kept telling me, 'Stay quiet, Janey. Sean will be home soon.'

I thought he had left me or had had one of his freaky moods and just disappeared. But, after two days away, he just turned up early on the morning of the third day to open the Weavers. I hugged him for a long time.

'Sean, I was so fucking worried, where were ye?' I begged.

'Don't ask me anything, Janey. Look, I got ye a wee present.'

He smiled as he produced a box of paints and some new brushes.

'Great! You are away for two fucking days an' ye bring me back paints? If I see on the telly about some big jewellery robbery an' all I got wiz these paints, you're dead!'

'Don't ever talk like that, Janey,' he snapped. 'I'm no' involved in anything dodgy. I am no' some fucking robber. Don't even start that shite! I might be George Storrie's son, but I'm no' a thief, OK?'

'Well, I think guns are dodgy an' you hid them in this hoose. So don't you start being all the perfect fucking citizen with me, Sean.'

He just laughed and held me tight.

'I was only at a sale for my dad. I'm sorry I never called,' he said.

* * *

Occasionally, some old customers would come into the Weavers and start talking about Sean's dad and his criminal connections but Sean would simply ignore or deny their claims. Sometimes, a local gangster would come in, resplendent in camel-hair coat and shiny coiffed hair. Most gangsters seemed to me to be failed actors and all the older, better-known thugs dressed like something out of *The Maltese Falcon*. I used to laugh under my breath and think, *They can't ALL pretend to be Humphrey Bogart*. They were smart and extremely polite in the kind of menacing way those dangerous men like to behave when around their viewing public. One gangster was a regular. He would order his Glenmorangie with ice and smile as his hand pushed several notes into mine, displaying a fine array of gold sovereigns on his fingers.

'Keep the change, sweetness,' he would slide out of the side of his mouth.

He was known locally as a 'drug baron', the aristocratic title now bestowed on lowlife dealers by the press.

One afternoon, Old George and I stood outside the Weavers watching other local drug barons drive around in their flashy BMWs.

'They are fucking bad luck, Janey,' Old George said venomously. 'Every penny earned from drugs is dirty money. Their kids will die. They will die. And bad luck will fucking land on all their families.'

It felt like a biblical prophecy ...

15

Sweet dreams are made of this

My Dad had been making great progress, was still off the booze and had found a nice girlfriend. He brought her into the Weavers one day to introduce us. She was called Mary and was everything my Mammy wasn't: blonde, well spoken and totally honest. She was a lovely woman with warm brown eyes and hair which framed an amazingly sensitive face; she was always well dressed and made sure she spent lots of time getting to know me. Her own husband had died a couple of years previously, after she had nursed him through a long illness. She had two grown-up kids of her own and worked as a care assistant dealing with people who suffered from Alzheimer's Disease. She was very much into crafts and I liked her instantly. But it was still weird to imagine my Dad loving another woman.

Mary would constantly ask Sean questions about his life, but he would hardly talk to her and merely grunted inaudible answers. I would sometimes go up to Dad's home to have tea with him and Mary, but Sean would never come and would go into one of his legendary huffs if I stayed away too long. After a few months, Dad and Mary decided to marry and sold their flat; they bought a great wee house up in Maryhill, near Dad's work, and were a very happy couple.

* * *

Sean and I went off on holiday alone for two weeks discovering Newquay and the surrounding area in Cornwall. The beaches were clean and surfers came from all over the world to take part in the Fistral Beach competitions. Sean and I sat in rose-covered garden cafés eating clotted cream teas, holding hands and being just us; it was great. Sean was amazing at times: his generosity could floor me. We spent mornings eating breakfast in bed from a big silver tea trolley that was wheeled into our room. Every day he brought me flowers. Every night he took me out to dinner. Laughing, kissing, holding me close to his face, he told me how much he loved me.

But the journey back from Newquay was tiring and Sean got more and more restless and argumentative as each mile dragged us closer to Glasgow. When we hit home, we found so many problems at the Weavers. Sean had left Young George in charge. Not only had he upset the regulars by smoking dope but he had screwed up Sean's uniquely weird but effective cash system. There was only one way to insert the cash takings into the ledger and that was Sean's way. He always got very upset if I dared to use a blue pen instead of a black one – or if I wrote too big – or if my figures strayed over the neat lines – or if I accidentally had to erase a figure and it looked messy ... To Sean's horror, when we got back, it looked as if Young George had taken a chunky crayon and drawn a dead zebra across the whole page.

'It's a fucking mess!' Sean screamed at me. 'He can't fucking count! He's upset everyone! I shouldn't huv gone on a fucking holiday!' He never confronted Young George. Instead, he shouted at me.

We were soon back in the old routine of veering towards complete disaster and/or divorce. There would be another night of silence; then a night of shouting, threats and me walking the night-time streets in the rain. It always happened, yet I was never prepared for my night-time flight. I always managed to take a jacket but never the shoes. I used to think I should prepare a packed bag with shoes, bra and some cash and hide it somewhere outside in the streets. Then I could run out, safe from prowling thieves and junkies, knowing I had shoes and cash to get me out of that street somehow. But I never did find the perfect hiding place so, on frequent nights, I would run from our home screaming, fear making me pound down all the steps in my bare feet, run through the wet puddles and feel every sharp stone cut into my feet, while Sean ran after me, hurriedly dressed in his jogging bottoms and a T-shirt, never able to catch me in time. Some nights, he'd only run down the stairs but not come right out the door because it was too wet outside. I would stay out freezing in the rain, in the orange-grey shadows of the sodium street lights, and I would walk around the streets and look through people's windows, watching them watching television in the warmth. I wondered *Do any of them ever run in the night?*

Eventually, I would huddle in some strange hallway or alleyway far away from my own street in case someone recognised me. I didn't want to be seen. I didn't want to be found. When daylight came, I would run on the balls of my feet straight back to the pub in time for opening. I would look up at the first-floor window to see if Sean was looking for me but he never was; he was sleeping. Eventually I would go up our stairway and knock on the door and hope he was missing me and was not still angry with me. Inside I was pleading *Please don't be angry with me. I'm really tired.* Often, when Sean opened the door, he was sleepy and staggered around trying to make sense of why I was out there. Then it would all come back to him.

'I am sorry, Janey,' he would say. 'Come to bed, babes.' Then he would hold me in his warm nakedness – he'd be naked at the door and wouldn't care – and even the pain in my feet would disappear. But I realised his mood swings were becoming more erratic. He was under pressure.

* * *

The Weavers *was* going great; we *were* making decent cash; but our success with the bar had only incited jealousy among the other Storrie brothers. They insisted Sean must be stealing from Old George. If Sean wasn't, then I was stealing; or Sammy was stealing. Old George had always made sure each son was at all the others' throats. He would spread whispered gossip from son to son, then sit back and watch the consequences. I once phoned him to complain about one of my sisters-in-law: when she came into the Weavers, she had argued with me in front of customers about leaving my big bin in the close. I rambled on and on to Old George about her as he encouraged me to get it all out of my system. Later, I discovered he had taped the whole conversation on his answering machine and had played it straight back to the woman. She came storming into the bar the next day, repeating the cruel and careless comments I had blabbed to Old George. That night, Sean spent an age screaming at me for talking about people behind their backs and told me to never ever trust his father.

Sean was trying to talk him into repurchasing all the flats above the Weavers and turning them into bed and breakfast rooms. Old George owned most of the flats but we needed to own all nine outright to make the plan more financially viable. Sean explained that each bed could house an unemployed homeless person and the government would pay us £40 a week to house each of them.

188

'Multiply that £40 per week by the 34 beds we would accommodate between all the flats,' he explained.

Old George's elderly business cronies advised him that Sean's idea was ingenious but this only served to make him oppose the idea; none of his sons was allowed to be smarter than him. Still, the idea was sensible and the plan did start moving along.

* * *

We had good fun in the Weavers in between the shouting. We already had chess nights and now we started a five-a-side football team – ladies included. I made good friends with some of the new regulars and started to employ some of them part-time to help with our increasing workload. One was Gordon. He had just moved into one of the smaller one-bedroom flats on the other side of the London Road; it was quite characterless, but Gordon did a lot to make it homely because he was gay and therefore knew how to use soft furnishings. He was enormous fun. At last, I had someone to share my love of 1970s music! He had a huge collection of everything from Steely Dan to Supertramp to early David Bowie and T Rex. I loved it! He was also good with Sean; he understood his quirky ways and was happy to have found friendly faces in this new part of town he had moved to. Gay Gordon loved to throw parties and, when he heard our fourth wedding anniversary was imminent, suggested:

'You should throw a fancy dress party!'

Sean dressed as a Mississippi Gambler in a dandy waistcoat and cowboy hat while I got to be Cinderella in a silver sticky-out dress and a silver bodice. Our regulars took the party to heart and everyone turned out in awesome costumes. Archie The Architect came dressed as a priest, Sandra The Social Worker dressed as Little Bo-Peep, Jack The Janitor and his wife dressed as a Frenchman and his French maid. And even Old George turned up dressed as Fidel Castro in a green military uniform with a beret and black beard, sucking on a big cigar. He surprised us all by bringing along Sandra, an ex-girlfriend of his son Michael – the same Sandra who had grown up at the bottom of Kenmore Street – the wee, blonde girl with the cute dimples and *Children of the Damned* blond brothers. Sandra had by now fucked virtually the entire Storrie family including Michael, Young George and now Old George. She was still very blonde and very pretty but was also very clearly trouble. She came dressed as a hooker but I didn't realise this immediately, as she often wore similar clothing around the streets in her everyday life.

Despite this strange reappearance by Sandra, the night was magical. Sean and I cut a big fourth anniversary cake that our customers had bought and we all danced to the sounds of Madonna, Tears For Fears and U2. It was good to see Sean enjoy himself. He had never really made an effort to make friends with anyone before. The next day, he rounded up 40 of our hungover partygoers and loaded them onto a bus bound for Germany on a pre-arranged trip to the Munich Beer Festival. While he was away, my sister Ann, Gay Gordon and I ran the Weavers. Finally, I could count the cash, do the books and lock the door – all by myself. It was the most peaceful five days I had had for ages and I loved it.

'For all his faults, though,' I told my sister Ann, 'it's good when Sean's with me because I can help him through his demons. When he feels down or he has a migraine, I can understand him.'

'Just enjoy him being away,' Ann replied.

A couple of days later, Old George popped in with Sandra again in tow – to check I was OK, he said. Sandra sat and purred over him like a cat, which made me feel very uncomfortable. She was the ex-girlfriend of two of his sons and was quite childlike in her manner and speech. She had broken up Michael's relationship with his long-time girlfriend Mags and I thought Sandra was just a gold-digger. I had preferred Patsy Paton – she was great fun and had been more than a match for Old George. It soon became clear my antagonism to Sandra caused problems for Old George. Whenever we met, I would be snide to Sandra. In return, Sandra would complain to Old George that I was not showing her the respect she was due as his girlfriend and insisted he told me off. Old George would try to keep the peace.

'Get off Sandra's back,' he once told me. 'She's only got the intelligence of a wee girl.'

'Then,' I snapped back, 'you shouldnae be sleeping with her, George!'

Sandra had by now started calling herself 'Mrs Sandra Storrie'.

Eventually, after five days away, the Munich tour bus arrived back. I waited patiently for the hiss as the doors swung open, then ran out and hugged Sean so tightly in the street. He had made new friends on the trip and, after that, started enjoying his job more. He was sure his dad would be well proud of his progress. He was still only 23 years old and desperately trying to prove himself worthy of being the son Old George wanted. He never drank alcohol, never smoked and hated drugs. He never got into trouble with the police. He was always working, always making progress with the pub. Yet, still, Old George never gave him any praise. That was the way he was. If you got anything wrong, then all your mistakes were told in great detail to all the other family members, with the intent of making you look the fool you were; but your successes were never mentioned. Sean wanted a pat on the back, he wanted his dad to be proud. The irony was that I was not even recognised as existing. I worked all the hours God sent and Sean never bothered to praise me either. We both worked hard. We worked every day including Christmas Eve, Christmas Day and New Year's Eve. We only closed on New Year's Day and then only because it was illegal to open.

* * *

Each year ended with the Storrie New Year Party, when all Old George's seven sons and their respective partners and families gathered in Toad Hall just before the midnight bells of Hogmanay. No one was ever in party mood; it was a gathering of a bunch of people who never actually got on with each other. Some of the sons would disappear into a side room for a quick smoke of weed, some would sit awkwardly with their father and, in between, sat, stood and meandered various sisters-in-law, wives and girlfriends while little grandchildren ran around. I never got on with any of them because we really had nothing in common to talk about. I enjoyed playing with Dick's two lovely wee kids but his girlfriend Maggie would sneer at me and make biting comments any chance she got.

'You an' Sean still no' huving any kids yet?'

'We want to wait until we're able to afford them,' I replied, looking at her lovely wee daughter.

'Ye saying we cannae afford oor kids?' she snapped back.

'No Maggie,' I replied, feeling the tension mounting, 'I'm sayin' I will huv kids when I want to – OK?'

'Maybe ye cannae huv weans, an' ye just don't want to say,' she persisted.

I got up and walked into the living room. The telly was blaring the obligatory New Year bagpipe music. Old George sat quietly in his seat. It was a sad time for him as this was the time of year his wife had died of heart disease in this very house just after she had moved in ten years ago. She came to Toad Hall, spent one night in it and died in her bed. I offered Old George some tea and lit one of his favourite cigars.

'Steak pie nearly ready?' he asked. It is traditional to have a big steak pie and potato dinner at 'the bells' in Scotland.

'I don't know, George, the other women are doing that,' I answered gently. 'I'm just standing about annoying people like I normally do.'

He laughed and told me to sit down. The bells were about to start. The Storrie family all gathered in the big room, some sitting on the floor, others on their mammies' knees, a few on the arms of chairs and the rest on the floral sofas.

Bong! Bong! Bong! Bong! Bong! Bong! Bong! Bong! Bong! Bong! Bong! Bong!

'Happy New Year! Welcome to 1985!' the tartan-clad man shouted on the telly. Loud cheers rang out on the screen, in the street outside Toad Hall and in living rooms across Scotland. But, in the Storrie living room, each person shook hands in silence and immediately disappeared back to their steak pies and potato, to their hash, to their kids. I got up and walked into the dining room, where I sat alone and wished I could see my Mammy again.

After a while, Sean came in. 'What you thinking aboot?' he said.

'Nothing ... You?'

'I miss my mammy,' he told me. 'She died at New Year.'

'I know,' I said and held him tight. 'I miss my Mammy as well.'

All seven sons sat together with their father at the big table in the dining room where all Sean's late mum's best furniture and crockery was kept. The women all sat together in the kitchen, eating on their knees or at the wee pine table. In the dining room, Sean lifted his plate and walked towards the kitchen.

'Where are ye going?' Young George asked him.

'I want to sit with Janey an' eat my New Year dinner,' Sean replied. Not looking back, he left the room and came into the kitchen. We sat together, eating in silence.

Suddenly, Young George stormed into the kitchen. 'All us sons eat together! The wumen sit in here! Fuckin' get back in there, ya bastard!'

'No,' replied Sean. 'We don't talk to each other. We don't even fucking like each other.' He kept eating his steak pie.

Young George stood waiting for Sean to pick up his plate and return to the dining room.

'Fuck off!' said Sean, scooping up a forkful of peas. 'I'm not going.'

I watched as the two brothers glared at each other across the brightly lit kitchen. Sean suddenly dropped his cutlery with a loud clatter. He stood up and turned to me.

'Janey, get yer bag,' he said very quietly. 'We are leaving.' Then he started shouting: 'Fuck you, George! Fuck yer big family dinner! Janey is *my* family – OK?'

Within minutes, we were out of Toad Hall and into the cold air of a Glasgow street, walking towards our car.

'Sean,' I tried to reason with him, 'you shouldn't huv

done that. It was a family thing. He only wanted you all to sit and eat with yer dad.'

'Why?' he shouted at me. 'Why? We are not a fucking family any other day of the fucking year!' We drove home in total silence.

* * *

On 2 January, Sean and I opened up for another new year at the Weavers. The locals were all there in their droves. The bar was busy; we cooked sausages and chips for the businessmen; we kept our daily vigil for heroin users trying to sneak into the toilets to have a fix. We had decided to try and pull our fraying relationship together. He knew his temper and behaviour were getting out of hand and agreed to seek counselling for his mood swings. But he was not good at discussing his feelings. All his life, he had been encouraged and trained by Old George to trust no one and to tell no one about himself, his business or the family business. He was naturally defensive and our lady therapist had problems from the beginning. Sean had refused to go through his family doctor, so the therapy was all paid for privately and Sean's natural thriftiness soon persuaded him to stop paying good money to argue with a strange woman when he could do it with me for free.

That summer, we decided to go together again to Newquay, where we had been so happy before. One night, as we sat together on the beach, Sean surprised me by saying, 'Janey, come off the pill and we will try, eh? If you don't get pregnant in six months, then go back on it and we can try another time. It just means that it was not meant to happen. It's just like havin' a wee gamble.'

'I am not sure,' I replied. 'I still worry about us. What if

I have a baby and you go fucking mental again? I can hardly run out into the street with a small child.'

'I promise,' he begged me, 'I will never hit ye again, never threaten ye again. Trust me, Janey.'

After two weeks in Cornwall, we headed home. That same week, my Dad and Mary got married. It was a lovely affair at the local registry office. Sean and I went along to join Mij, Vid and Ann in the reception room; it was good to see all my family together.

The following Saturday was the day of Live Aid, when Bob Geldof pulled together the biggest rock concert in history. Sean had borrowed a big-screen TV and we threw a party to celebrate the event. I got up that morning to clean the bar and Gay Gordon was waiting downstairs for me.

'Good morning, dance partner,' he said, holding two doughnuts and some fresh milk. He liked to dance with me in the morning.

'I don't feel well,' I muttered. I felt sick and weak.

It took us 20 minutes to get the pub clean and then we sat down to breakfast, playing the jukebox full blast. By the time Annie Lennox was belting out 'Sweet dreams are made of this', I was on my knees and vomiting in time to the drumbeat. I sat with my head against the cool tiles of the toilet, looking down into the bowl, hoping the wave of nausea would pass. Doughnuts look horrible when they have been freshly puked.

Gay Gordon popped his head round the toilet door. *'Pregnant!'* he shouted at the top of his voice.

'Fuck off, poofy!' I moaned. 'I am not pregnant!' I wiped my mouth with our cheap, hard toilet paper.

Then it hit me. *Fucking hell – I COULD be pregnant.* I had stopped taking the pill for two days in Cornwall. I had secretly hoped that, after six years of being on it, I would still be protected. I really didn't want a baby. *But surely it was not physically possible?* It was only *two* Saturdays ago that I had started having unprotected sex and then only for two nights. Not six months. Only two fucking nights! *It could not be possible.* I told Sean as soon as he came downstairs.

'Go get a test at the doctor's,' he replied with a wide smile.

I made the call. The appointment was set for Monday. Sean was excited. I was scared. That Saturday, when Live Aid performed to the world, I danced with Gay Gordon, sang with the customers and cheered as Freddie Mercury and Queen took to the stage. Outside, I looked happy. Inside, I was nauseous and terrified. We raised about £1,000 for the Feed the World charity and everyone cried as the Cars sang 'Who's Gonna Drive You Home?' with images of poor starving children on the big TV projection screen. Bob Geldof swore at the nation – 'Get out of the fuckin' pubs! Get your hand in your fuckin' pockets!' – and I vomited up pig meat and bile from two sausage rolls. Sean spent the weekend staring at my stomach as we lay in bed at night. He never spoke. He just stroked the wee roll of fat I had always seemed to have.

Monday came soon enough. I woke, vomited and pissed into a bottle for Dr Cameron. It was just a few simple questions and the handing over of a urine sample.

'Have you told Old George yet?' Dr Cameron asked. He had been the Storrie family doctor for years.

'Told him what?' I replied, quite annoyed. 'That I vomit too much? No I huv not and you aren't sure I am pregnant yet.'

All Tuesday night, I vomited constantly.

'Fucking hell!' I cried, sitting and sweating on the toilet

floor. 'I hope I'm not pregnant if this is what fucking happens!' I tried to stop Twinkles the cat from crawling over me as I puked.

Wednesday arrived.

Sean and I waited on tenterhooks for news to come. I had wanted to buy a home test kit. Sean hadn't.

'I'm no' sure they can be trusted,' he had told me. 'And they cost money. The doctor is free and is more exact.'

We went downstairs to the bar to call Dr Cameron, as we had never had a phone in our flat.

'Nope, sorry, Mrs Storrie,' Dr Cameron's lovely wee wife chirped over the line. 'It is negative. Maybe next time, eh?'

I breathed a big sigh of relief.

'To be honest, Sean, I'm glad,' I told him. 'I wisnae ready tae have a baby. We aren't really settled and I'm scared of being a mammy. I must just have some bad bug. That's why I am so sick. We don't even know if we should be together, do we, Sean? We do get a bit fucked up, eh?'

Sean sat with his eyes looking straight ahead: 'Yeah, but I really wanted a wee girl an' to be a good daddy.' He smiled sadly.

'I don't like weans, really, Sean. We should work on getting ourselves stable an' we huv all the new rooms above the pub to get going soon.' I smiled and slid along the fake leather seat to hug him.

The phone rang.

'Hi, Weavers Inn ...' Sean answered. There was a pause. 'Hang on, I'll just get her.'

Sean held the phone out to me. I listened to what the woman on the other end of the line said, then she hung up. Sean gave me a quizzical look.

'What is it?' he asked.

'They made a mistake ... I *am* pregnant ... Oh fucking hell! I am gonna vomit!' I blurted out and ran to the toilet. For quite a while after that, we both sat on the floor of the ladies' toilet, me throwing up into the bowl and Sean smiling happily as he held my curly black hair back so the puke didn't hit it as it came out of my mouth.

'I hope she doesn't have your curly hair, Janey,' he laughed. 'It gets so tuggy.'

'I am having a boy,' I spluttered between spews.

'Nope, only girls cause this much trouble,' he insisted. Sean was over the moon. He phoned his dad and told him within minutes.

'That's great news,' Old George agreed. 'That'll put to bed all the rumours she can't huv weans, Sean.'

'Did naebody think it might have been me with dodgy sperm?' Sean shot back. 'Why is it always the woman's fault?'

'Ye kidding?' asked Old George. 'With oor sperm? I had seven of you, didn't I?'

My own Dad and Mary had just come back from their honeymoon and came straight down to see us and hear the good news.

The vomiting didn't get any better. Whenever customers were congratulating Sean, I was busy holding onto the sides of a toilet pan and trying desperately to hold down any saliva I had swallowed. Food was not an option. Everything came back up again. Within two weeks, I had lost nearly a stone in weight and that wee roll of fat I used to try to get rid of was gone to be replaced by a sunken, white, flabby, sick tummy. Everyone in the bar had a story to tell or a remedy to ease morning sickness. I couldn't give a fuck what they thought as this wasn't morning sickness; this was 24/7 sickness and I didn't believe anyone could suffer this much and live through it. I had never been this sick since I was 14 and had mumps and nearly died. Sean got very frustrated. His building plans were falling into place and his workload was doubling and all I could do was vomit in time to the jukebox. By five weeks into the pregnancy, I was shattered, had lost even more weight and could hardly stand. I lay in bed one morning listening to Sean complain about my lack of work.

'For fucksake, Janey, my mammy had seven of us and she managed to make breakfast every morning. What the fuck is wrong with ye?'

He was shouting and being a moody unreasonable bastard, but I couldn't even summon up enough strength to argue. I felt this overwhelming blackness creep over me. I was vaguely aware of hearing the door slam as he left. The coldness wrapped itself around me. I couldn't swallow. I could hardly breathe. I thought *I am going to die!* and that felt good. The relief of not feeling like I was on the brink of another vomit was wonderful. Only the icy darkness creeping through my veins made me aware I was still alive. Four hours later, I am told, Sean came upstairs again.

He felt my head, screamed out loud and called an ambulance.

I was very cold and totally unconscious.

He thought I was dead.

* * *

I woke up two days later in hospital.

'You have been in a coma,' I heard them telling me.

They told me the pregnancy was killing me. I had 'hyperemesis gravidarum' – I thought those must be the Latin words for *vomiting too much* and *hating being pregnant*.

'There is no real reason why it happens,' they told me, 'and no real cure.'

I felt terrible, like I had let Sean down; I couldn't even carry his baby safely. While I had been unconscious, they advised him to sign a form to 'terminate' the baby. He had refused. He told them it was not his decision; he did not want to make that choice for me.

So, when I came out of the coma, the obstetrician advised me to 'terminate' the baby:

'This is not ordinary morning sickness,' he explained to me. 'You may not survive the nine months without proper nourishment if you cannot keep food down properly and, in those circumstances, the baby would certainly die anyway.'

I refused to give the baby up, so they devised a plan to feed me through a drip if the illness persisted. Over the next nine months, I was fed through a drip every three days at the hospital and I was regularly admitted as an in-patient when it all got too much. I was constantly weak, lost weight but still had a fat tummy. They told me the baby was fine. They said it was me who was dying.

* * *

I never gave up work at the Weavers. Every minute I felt stable enough, I would get behind the bar and do a shift.

Patsy Paton was also pregnant. She had another partner now, but never told us who he was and it was not our business to ask. I was happy for her, as was Old George. Despite their falling out they had remained friends. Patsy was a picture of health during her pregnancy and she did her best to help support me whenever I was very ill.

As if things were not hectic enough, when I was six or seven months pregnant, the building plans were passed and we moved from our flat to the one next door in a single day. Twinkles the cat was completely confused, running backwards and forwards not knowing where she was supposed to live. I was not sad to leave as I had never really settled in that spooky old flat. I liked our new corner flat immediately. It had loads more light coming in and the rooms were bigger and seemed more welcoming. We planned to have a separate baby room, just off the kitchen, in a recess.

Being organised, Sean had done research on all the guys he wanted to house in the proposed new 'bed and breakfast'. Lots of young guys we knew and some of George's older mates were more than happy to take up the offer. The newspapers, if they had known, would have called us 'slum landlords', but that was not the case. Our idea was to take revenue from the Government for housing unemployed, homeless individuals but – unlike other unscrupulous landlords – we intended to treat them well and genuinely look after them. No junkies would live in our building. There would only be one buzzer – ours – so everyone had to go through Sean or me to get access to the hallway. Sean planned a clean towel/bed linen service, heating and hot water, comfortably furnished rooms, a weekly cleaning service to keep the rooms tidy and in-house service 24 hours a day to anyone needing help. After all, we lived there with them.

By this time, the overhaul of the building had actually captured Old George's imagination because he realised we were able to renovate the whole place without closing the money-making Weavers bar. He and Sean started going to sales and bought up loads of hospital beds with rubber mattresses, carpets torn from hotels that had gone bankrupt and bedside cabinets en masse. The renovation wasn't serious structural work; it was scrubbing, cleaning, painting, furnishing and minor repairs. The Storrie family's regular, orang-utan-like carpenter/handyman The Gow was called in to help and even my brother Vid was employed to carry out general painting and decorating.

One Friday, when my brother was helping and The Gow was hanging over the bath washing out some paint-brushes, Vid saw a waistline of blue satin material peeping out of the top of The Gow's trousers. It was obvious he was wearing women's knickers and it was obvious where he had got them. Ever since Sammy's mammy Crazy Katie Wallace had killed herself about two years before, bags of her clothing had been stored in our flat.

'This is weird as fuck,' Vid told me. 'The Gow is wear-ing Crazy Katie's clothes!'

'You're fuckin' jokin'!' I told him. 'How d'ye know they're Katie's knickers?'

'Well, they're no' fuckin' yours,' he replied, 'and there's a big bag of Crazy Katie's clothes lying there.'

Every Friday evening, The Gow came down to the bar to get his pay from me. This particular evening, he'd washed and brushed himself up because he thought it would make him irresistible to the opposite sex. Sometimes he'd wear a cravat and an acrylic sweater and stand, skinny and bald with bits of red hair sticking out, leaning against the Weavers' bar to attract girls. But, this particular night, when the door opened, Vid and I saw he was wearing a woman's grey jumper with a butterfly design. He either didn't know it was a woman's jumper or he knew but didn't care. Vid just laughed out loud: 'What the fuck are you wearing, Gow? That's Aunt Katie's top and you've got her knickers on too, ya weirdo! Get those fuckin' clothes off!'

'There's nothing wrong wi' it,' The Gow replied.

'Except,' I pointed out, 'they're Sammy's mammy's clothes and she killed herself with gas and pills. Do you really think he wants to be reminded of his dead mammy by looking at you wearing her clothes? Get them off, ye psycho.'

'I'm no' wearin' her knickers!' he insisted.

'C'mere,' Vid said and pulled down the waistband of The Gow's trousers to reveal the top of some blue satin knickers.

'Ya weirdo!' I screamed. 'Get them clothes off!'

We had to strip him and throw all Katie's clothes out or he would have kept walking about in them and reminding Sammy of his dead mammy.

* * *

I had a strange and difficult pregnancy.

Patsy Paton gave birth to a lovely wee girl just eight weeks before my due date. It was her second child; her first son Andrew was already a teenager.

'It's scary, but you just get through it,' Patsy tried to reassure me. 'After all the fucking illness you've had, the birth itself will be a relief.'

But I was still petrified.

I used to stay working late in the bar, lugging my huge vomit-inducing foetus around inside me as I poured beers. The smell of Guinness brought on sickness every time. My nausea, occasional hospital visits and the ongoing building work had worn Sean thin.

In a way, I still didn't really believe I was actually going to have a baby. I thought I might just remain a huge vomit machine until I was ancient and die years from now, huge and still pregnant. But I really was looking forward to having a boy for Sean; I would talk to the bump and call him 'ma wee boy' in the hope, if I repeated it enough, that any female genes would immediately transform into male ones. When the baby finally came, I was lying in a hospital bed praying that, whatever the hell it was, it would bloody well come out quicker.

I was three days in labour.

Doctors fretted.

Sean paced.

My Dad cried.

I screamed.

My baby decided to stay put.

The pain was unbearable.

I hated this baby now. I'd been dangerously ill during the pregnancy and now it was trying to kill me again.

Eventually I was given drugs and a large, very manly doctor from Australia decided to pull the stubborn child out with forceps. I was trussed like a chicken and watched sharp blades and big metal tongs being passed around as if I were the meal at some scary picnic. Sean and Paul sat outside. The baby arrived silent but with a very angry face as if annoyed we had interrupted its mission to kill me.

It was – of course – a girl.

'Happy birthday,' I whispered as they lay her on my chest. She stared at me as if she knew who I was. She looked so alert it scared me a bit. Then Paul suddenly burst into the room with Sean right behind him.

'Mr Storrie,' the nurse told Paul, 'you have a daughter!' and gave the baby to him.

'Actually,' Sean laughed with relief, 'she's *my* baby,' and scooped her out of Paul's arms.

Paul was sent outside to wait, but he was so excited he kept popping his head back in to watch us. Sean came round to my bedside holding the baby. He leaned over.

'Janey, you should see the blood on the floor. I feel faint.'

The nurse – a friendly dark-haired lassie – immediately leaned over and, with one hand, scooped the baby out of Sean's arms while putting her knee behind Sean's back and easing him down onto the floor where he lost consciousness.

'Sean!' I shouted out. 'You only held her for a minute and you almost killed her! Ye big idiot!'

After that, things got a bit hazy and I too passed out. My blood pressure had dropped severely; I was rushed to intensive care and spent the night unconscious. But I had managed to get the evil baby out of my body.

* * *

The next three days passed quickly and it was wonderful to get home. On my first day free from the hospital, I went back to work. Sean and Paul took the baby upstairs and I served behind the bar. It really was good to get my body back. I could eat and not be sick; I could drink and keep it all down. It had been like having car sickness for nine months. The male customers were amazed to see me back at work while Sean looked after our daughter; they didn't believe a man could look after a tiny baby. Their women had spent years convincing them they didn't know where their own shirts were and raising their eyes heavenwards at men's inability to work a washing machine. But Sean was better at domesticity than me every time. I was good with the baby but equally desperate to get my own life back. The women in the Weavers poured scorn on my attitude.

'A baby needs its mother!' I was told over and over again.

Sean was looked on as a freak; this man who fed and washed his own baby. But he was obsessed by our wee child. We would both lie awake and occasionally get up and go into the next room to lie on the floor and stare at her as she slept in her lace-fringed crib. She had a shock of black sticky-up hair and a fat wee face. In fact, she looked the spitting image of Paul. I had no breast milk because of my illness and watched her guzzle from the array of bottles that now cluttered up our kitchen. Sean could feed and change her better than me. He showed me how to sterilise all her stuff and how to dress her easily without being scared to snap her fragile, twig-like arms. It worried me that she slept loads. But Sean would laugh and assure me that, when she wanted feeding, she would let me know. I did go in every half hour, convinced she was lying dead in the cot.

We needed a name for her. Whenever Gay Gordon took her for a walk in the new pram, Sean and I sat in the back shop thinking up possibilities.

One day, with the big deep fryer behind me, Sean stood up and pointed to the electric socket: 'Ashley Electronics. That's it!'

I looked at him. I looked at the electric socket. I looked back at him.

'Ashley Electronics,' he explained. 'I like that name. Ashley Jane Storrie. That's it ... I love it ... What about you?'

'Ashley is good,' I agreed. 'But not Electronics.'

Meanwhile, the new bed and breakfast system was in full swing. The tenants all registered as being there but mostly lived elsewhere and screwed the DHSS for cash; we had no responsibility for any of them, as we could not force 34 men to come home to their flats. Every week, the tenants came to pick up the unemployment cheques that had arrived for them and their rent was paid to us monthly by the Government. I was kept busy not only with Ashley but with overseeing the laundry rota – towels, sheets and bed linen for the boys who did live upstairs. We employed a cleaner to tidy the rooms weekly. The entire building was a hive of activity; rooms were still being cleared out and painted as young guys dragged their possessions up the ancient staircase in black council rubbish sacks. These new 'real' tenants were a mixed bunch. Sammy took one room himself; Sean's cousin Stephen moved in. The Gow took a room up the top. And there was Old Wullie Kerr whom I had never met before and who, in typical Storrie fashion, was introduced to me on the stairs by Sean with a curt, 'Janey! Old Wullie – he's living here now.'

Old Wullie was a retired safe-cracker who had done time in prison with Old George. He later became a black-smith for Glasgow Council; he didn't shoe horses, he fixed the metal fences all round Glasgow and used to make things for Old George – like garage gates and 'specialist' welding jobs. He was very tall – about six foot – and I named him *The Ribena Man* because he had a purple face from drinking so much. He didn't talk much; he just used to mutter, 'Ttt ... ttt ... ttt ... shush, ya cunt!' under his breath, like a verbal tick.

His big dog Sara was the palest, blondest Alsatian I had ever seen – more the colour of a Golden Retriever – and she had had her tail cut off, but Old Wullie would never tell anyone why. Old Wullie and Sara took over one bedroom in the three-roomed flat on the same floor as us.

All these incoming tenants meant Ashley now had a huge group of new people to fuss over her and Old Wullie expanded his conversational repertoire when Ashley was around to include: 'Ttt ... ttt ... ttt ... Hello ...' Sammy had been a father to two kids and he was a great help to have round, but young Paul was much more confident in handling her; and my Dad and stepmum Mary were always free to take her round to their place when we got too busy at the Weavers. Ashley was an easy baby; slept loads, ate well and would sit staring in amusement at Twinkles the cat.

The cat became very protective of Ashley and it worried me in case she might get smothered in her bed. But there was no chance of that – whenever Ashley cried or even moved in her cot, Twinkles would trot into my bedroom, bat her damp leathery paws into my face and *miaow* loudly. She was the ultimate baby alarm.

One night I sat preparing to bath Ashley myself without Sean there to supervise me. I was very nervous and opened our baby book to read the instructions. The pink plastic baby bath was sitting on the floor with towels spread around. Wee Ashley sat naked on my knee. The book said *Close all doors to keep out draughts.* So I got up quickly, still holding Ashley, and slammed the living-room door. There was an ear-piercing *miaooow!* I had jammed Twinkles' tail in the door. I dropped Ashley into the bath and dragged the cat from the door, trying to comfort her. Then I heard a splashing sound and realised what I'd done. I turned and looked down into the bath to see Ashley flailing her chubby wee arms around, trying to understand why she had been dropped into water and no one was holding her. She wasn't crying, just startled. I was horrified. I had dropped my own daughter into a bath so I could tend to a cat.

Once I went to the local supermarket. Trying to manoeuvre the pram round the cramped wee store was too difficult, so I parked it beside the tall Asian storekeeper at the till as I hurriedly got my groceries. It was not until I was halfway home carrying the heavy bags that I realised I'd left Ashley behind. When I walked back in, the Asian man was still standing by the till, looking slightly confused, holding Ashley.

Motherhood did not come naturally to me. Sean was a calming influence and much better at dealing with this curious wee creature than me. I was scared of everything. If Ashley was crawling around behind Twinkles on the floor, I would be busy hoovering and bleaching every surface, convinced she would get a disease. The dirt of my own childhood still haunted me.

'Janey,' Sean would reassure me as I wiped the floors with disinfectant yet again, 'she needs to catch *some* germs to build up resistance.' But Twinkles had started to pee all over the corners of Ashley's bedroom; it was getting too much and we sadly had to give the cat away. Ashley was upset but accepted it had to go.

She loved life in the Weavers. All that constant attention. Every man and woman in the bar wanted to sit and chat to her. She could talk from a really early age, I guess due to the level of stimulation she received. As she approached her first birthday, she would mumble, 'Daddy look, me sing.' A little later, she would reach up with her arms to Sammy. 'Ups-a-daisy,' she would say. We were all amazed by her chatter but she absolutely refused to walk or even attempt it. She was carried upstairs like a wee princess by all the boys and maybe she assumed that she would never have to walk.

We were a close-knit group – the tenants and us. Stephen was Sean's cousin. Paul and Sammy were Ashley's 'uncles'. One of the other lads, Andy, was great friends with Sammy, so Ashley grew up believing she owned the whole building and everyone was related to her. When she decided to walk, she would run upstairs and demand that one of the boys read to her or play dolls or dance and sing with her. They were great with her and I trusted them all. I didn't worry about men being with her; I didn't think every man was a child-abuser. My Dad wasn't; my brothers weren't. One man was – my Uncle David Percy. And my Granda Davy Percy was a bit dodgy. But my Uncle John had been lovely; I had adored being with him; he had a lively sparkly character, was the coolest old dude in the world and never once looked at me weirdly. So why should every man be the sort of man who would look at children and want to have sex with them?

As she grew to understand what she was being told, I taught Ashley to be careful of being near and speaking to strangers but she had little concept of 'stranger' as she knew everyone who came into her world of the Weavers and the building above it. She became very confident telling wee drunk but affectionate men that she didn't want a kiss or a hug; she would explain very clearly that she only kissed her Daddy and her family. There was more danger of her being picked up by a stranger in the street than being molested by a relative or a Weavers regular.

She loved her grandad Old George. When he came down to see us, she would climb all over him, hug him and say right into his face, 'I love you, Grandad!' as she squashed her chubby wee fists into his cheeks. 'Now,' she would add, 'now you have to say you love me too, Grandad!' then her wee face would frown as Old George looked very uncomfortable. He would just hug her close. This was not a man who spoke of love in public. He would hug her close and try to avoid saying the three words.

'Ashley,' I would interrupt before she demanded his love out loud again, 'you know Grandad loves you. Now come on and get ready for bed ...'

'I love you too, Ashley,' Old George would sometimes say in a gentle, low voice as he put her onto the floor.

'See,' Ashley would squeal, 'I knew you could say it, Grandad!' and she would jump back up to hug him tight.

I tried to bring her up speaking politely. I hated my own East End dialect and accent. So Ashley was taught to pronounce the words 'head' and 'bread' instead of the local Glaswegian 'heed' and 'breed'. But this just ended up confusing her totally. One afternoon, I held her in my arms as we looked out of our window at the rain – it was Glasgow, after all – and I asked without thinking: 'Can ye see whit's oot the windae?' Then I immediately corrected myself: 'Sorry, Ashley, the word is *window* not *windae*. Mummy was silly talking like that.'

The next day, as I carried her down the street, her wee woolly hat blew off and I said to her: 'It's very windy today.'

'No, Mummy,' she corrected me. 'It's very *window*.'

Sean adored her, but his behaviour was still erratic. When Ashley was out of the way, he would start picking on me, even throwing an occasional slap at me. I would sit quietly wishing him dead because then I thought all my problems would be solved. When he got angry, he would tell me, 'Don't ever take my baby! If you want to leave me, then you go alone! I am telling you, Janey, if you take my daughter away from me, I will hunt you down. Take the money – you can fucking take the lot of it – but don't you ever take Ashley!'

I knew I could never take her away from him. Not because I was scared, but because she adored him as much as he loved her. I accepted Sean would never be the husband I needed but I knew he would always be the father she wanted. I never wanted to separate them; I remembered vividly being separated from my own father when I was a child. It had broken my heart.

* * *

Locally, I had friends who came round for tea with their own chubby wee kids. Donna was one of them. Her daughter Kara was only a bit older than Ashley. Donna was a heroin addict but a great mother to that wee blonde girl she carried everywhere. She and I would sit just like any other two mothers, chatting and watching their babies play on the floor.

'Ashley is getting big, Janey,' Donna told me, smiling happily once as Ashley climbed onto her knee. 'I'm gonnae get off the smack and be there more for my ain wee wean.'

Soon afterwards, Donna's mother came round to the Weavers to beg me not to buy any children's clothes from Donna. 'I buy everything for wee Kara but Donna tries to sell all the good stuff to buy drugs.'

'She has never tried to sell me anything,' I replied honestly.

It didn't surprise me that Donna sold her child's clothes to feed her heroin habit, nor that Donna's mother had come round to plead with me. It was a sad fact of life in the area that, increasingly, young mothers were selling clothes off their own children's backs and sometimes even selling themselves.

George's prophecy was coming true: *Drug dealers are fucking bad luck, Janey. Their kids will die, they will die and bad luck will fucking land on all their families.*

One local drug dealer's wee boy climbed into an abandoned car, which somehow caught fire; he couldn't get out and was burnt to death. Locals shrugged their shoulders and said, 'That's what happens when you sell drugs to weans.'

Two brothers of another local drug dealer died and then his child was killed in a car accident. A third dealer who, unlike most, never took drugs himself, lost his daughter and mother to cancer within weeks of each other. It was as if a vengeful God were striking down the entire families of wrongdoers, as if a list had been kept somewhere by Fate and names were slowly being ticked off one by one.

Even Glasgow crime 'godfather' Arthur Thompson's daughter Margaret died from a drugs overdose. Drug addicts were dying and the count was getting higher. Each death became less of a shock. I half expected my brother Mij to be the next one found dead in some flat somewhere. He would often come over to the Weavers from the Gorbals with exaggerated tales of lost Giro cheques and stolen wallets, in the hope I would bail him out. Heroin addiction makes people the best improvisers in the universe and he was playing out the whole Glasgow drug image thing; he even got two Pit Bull Terriers called Rocky and Tyson.

Sammy was as horrified as I was by what was happening. 'That fucker,' he said, naming a local drug baron, 'drives about in his big BMW, living in a council house; he goes to Spain every other week with his wife and it's all financed by kids dying in the street.' Sammy hated heroin. So did I.

But I had no moral problems about running a pub. Alcohol and spirits were legal, therefore I was doing nothing wrong but sometimes I wondered if maybe watching all these people slowly destroy their lives with the booze I sold them made me as bad as the drug dealers. I used to watch the women in the Weavers letting themselves go wild on booze. Some very respectable, professional, married woman would start getting loud and falling about or, in some cases, get pissed-drunk and end up shagging Sammy.

There was a hidden corner of the bar which I could only see because of a well-placed security mirror and sometimes I'd see Sammy snogging some local woman or getting her tits out. One woman I liked worked at the Stock Exchange in Glasgow and she would arrive in her business suit, stay all night and, by the end of the evening, she'd be so pissed-drunk she would pee down her tights, slide off her chair and have to be carried home. 'Ooh! Whit?' she'd slur, slightly surprised.

I never understood why people wanted to drink vodka late at night in a bar, but then I never drank and never fancied getting drunk. Alcohol to me was only a method of losing control and I hated the thought of losing control. I had watched my Dad and my Mammy lose control – him falling all over the house, looking nothing like the man I admired, her banging her head and incapable of even fighting Peter off as she, in my mind's eye, struggled with him that horrible night on the bank of the River Clyde. They found high levels of alcohol in her system when they checked the dead body; maybe if she had been sober she would still be alive. So I hated booze, but didn't mind selling it. And it had the advantage of attracting eccentric and interesting clientele.

One couple were very keen on listening to Country and Western music. 'Wild Bill' was a thin, tall man in his late sixties with a middle-class Glasgow accent and grey-white shoulder-length hair. He always wore a Wild West stetson hat and dressed in full, black cowboy gear – not just in our bar but in his everyday life. He actually had a 'Red Indian' squaw who called herself Sioux. Well, she wasn't a real Red Indian. She spoke with a Glasgow council-estate accent and wore traditional Sioux clothes around the streets in her daily life – loose-fitting animal-hide clothes with Indian beads round her neck. It always amazed me how this man who liked to dress up as a cowboy had found a woman in Glasgow who, just by luck, liked to dress up as an Indian. She was maybe a wee bit retarded: she looked like she'd maybe made baskets as a teenager or had a gene missing and she had the strangest mouth I'd ever seen. She had inexplicable teeth. When she smiled, her lips parted and her gums looked as if they were made of dark yellow plastic while her teeth had layers of lighter yellow plaque on them. She had jet-black hair plaited into Red Indian ponytails with big ribbons on them and she also had a slight black moustache, which was quite disconcerting.

You couldn't hold a conversation with her. I'd say, 'That's a lovely dress you've got on.'

She'd reply, 'Uhwhuhehe,' and just laugh and I'd think *Right. Wild Bill has found a backward Indian called Sioux. In Glasgow.* I wondered if she might actually live in a wigwam somewhere in Maryhill, near where my Dad had bought a flat.

In 1891 and 1904, the real Buffalo Bill Cody had come to Glasgow with his Wild West Show featuring 100 Red Indians plus cowboys, Mexicans, Bedouins, Cossacks, Argentinian gauchos, Japanese cavalry, buffalo, elk, horses, a group of African tribesmen, six performing Burmese elephants, Annie Oakley wearing tartan and a man on a bicycle who did stunts. They were all based in the big army barracks at Maryhill and about seven or eight of Wild Bill's Sioux Indians stayed on in Glasgow and married Scottish women. In my childhood, we had sung the local nursery rhyme:

> *Buffalo Bill from Maryhill*
> *Disnae work and never will*

It seemed that, perhaps, their descendants still roamed the streets of Glasgow.

16

Que sera sera

When Ashley turned three, Sean developed various worrying ailments, like flu, food poisoning and the migraine headaches he'd had all his life but much worse. He got very thin and weak. Lots of people thought he had AIDS; this was, after all, the East End of Glasgow in 1989. It was really hard on me, as I had to work double shifts to make up his hours; I became exhausted trying to do everything in the Weavers and looking after the flats day to day. Ashley was juggled between my Dad and my sister Ann. Eventually, after months of worsening illness, Sean went into hospital for a lumbar puncture to drain spinal fluid and he also had a brain scan. The hospital tested him and assured him he did not have AIDS, but the scan revealed he had had a brain haemorrhage. I felt terribly guilty; I had wished him dead so many times.

Sean became even more ill, so weak that he could hardly walk or talk at all; it was as if he were turning into a vegetable. Ashley understood what was happening and was stricken with fear. She was a real daddy's girl and did not want him to stay in hospital. She once refused to leave his bedside and screamed as she was dragged off by the nurses. My Dad visited Sean daily. Old George never went once; I explained what was wrong with Sean by phone and he never asked again, not even for any progress reports. As I did not drive, while Sean was ill, Sammy drove me to the cash-and-carry warehouse to buy goods for the Weavers.

But, one night, Sean's brother Stephen drove me because he wanted to borrow Sean's car afterwards. When we got to the till, I pulled out Old George's cheque book and signed a cheque for the alcohol and food.

'Is that my da's cheque book?' Stephen asked me suspiciously.

'Aye,' I said irritably. 'It's the same cheque book I've been signing for the last seven years. Why?'

'Does my da know you sign his cheques?' Stephen asked, even more suspicious.

'Aye he fucking knows!' I snapped back. 'OK? It is his pub. I have worked there for the last nine years. We use his cheque book. We give him the books to check. What is your fucking problem? D'ye think if I wanted to steal with your da's cheque book I would buy booze and fags when I don't drink or smoke? Oh and, by the way, booze and fags happen to be what we sell in the fucking pub. Ye think that's a coincidence?'

The till girl carried on putting goods in bags without looking at us; she knew me because I came in and signed a cheque every other week.

Sean had just come out of hospital two days before and was lying at home in bed, trying to do all the books and deal with the cashflow while he struggled with his brain and lung disorders. His speech was slow and he felt constantly confused.

The next afternoon, Old George came to see him at the Weavers, although he had never visited him in hospital. Sean dragged himself out of bed and went downstairs with me. There were just the three of us plus Sammy and Paul and a few old men down the far end of the bar.

'Why is she using my cheque book?' Old George snapped at Sean.

'Janey always signs the cheques, Da. She's always done the cash-and-carry run with Sammy. Who d'ye think runs this place? I've been away for six weeks.'

'I don't like it!' Old George snarled back.

'Well, big fucking deal,' replied Sean. 'Here – I'll tell ye whit, Da, why don't ye give the cheque book to your junkie sons and I'll take the thieving wife away? That's it. Here – take the fucking pub keys!' He slammed the keys onto the bar. 'Sammy, Paul, Janey – upstairs!' Sean boomed. 'I need you to bring doon all my da's paperwork and all of the fucking accounts and any other shite that belongs to him.'

Old George stood firm; he was as white as a sheet and gritted his teeth so loud they could almost hear it at the other end of the bar. He always literally gritted his teeth when he was angry. Sammy, Paul and I bolted out of the door and ran upstairs. Sean followed us slowly.

'Sean,' I tried to placate him when we were all upstairs. 'Be careful. Old George is angry.'

'Well, fuck him!' Sean screamed as he packed files and folders into a big box. 'This is all shite, Janey! You have been helping with his paperwork for years, running his fucking bar, counting all the cash in the machines, dealing with licences and – suddenly – you are stealing by using a cheque book at the fucking cash and carry?' He slowly walked downstairs again and dramatically slammed the bar door open, carrying a big cardboard whisky box. Old George had not moved. Bemused customers were patiently standing at the bar waiting to be served. I walked in slowly behind Sean.

'I will go serve the –' I started to say as I stepped behind the bar.

'No!' Sean shouted at me. 'Don't fucking serve anyone!

You are a thief, remember? Let *him* fucking serve *his* customers!' Sean banged the box down in front of his dad. 'Here you are – all your accounts for the flats above, the bank details, the council reports Janey got for the grant we are trying to get for the building, the takings from the Weavers and any other shite I have that we do for you. Take these and yer pub keys and don't fucking ever even speak to me again!' Sean walked straight back out of the door and went upstairs again. I was left in the bar, rooted to the spot. The customers just looked at me as if to say *Are we ever going to get served?*

Old George stood there, rock solid, like one of those faces on Mount Rushmore, and stared at me with that chilling look in his eyes which used to freak me out – like he just didn't care what happened to me or to himself. I knew Old George would do anything; he'd be willing to throw everything away; it was the sort of stare a cat gives a mouse or a bird just before it jumps.

Eventually, after a terrifyingly long silence, Old George spoke: 'This is all your fault!' he growled.

'My fault?' I tried to reason with him. 'Why? All I did was go to get stock for the bar. You know I've signed your cheque book for years, George. You've even been there in the cash and carry with me when I signed it. I don't understand the problem.'

There was a moment of total silence, then ...

'Tell him to come back doon here!' Old George commanded.

I walked slowly towards the door but, as I opened it, I turned and said to him, 'No, tell him yourself.' I slammed the door dramatically behind me then leapt, terrified, and ran upstairs, glancing over my shoulder to see if he was chasing me. Sean was sitting quietly in our living room.

He was entirely calm.

He said nothing.

I said nothing.

I paced the floor, worried. Ashley was in her room playing with her toys.

Downstairs, customers were waiting to be served, but I could hear nothing, separated from them by the concrete floor.

There was a knock at the door. Ashley ran out of her room into the hallway to answer it.

'It's Grandad!' she shouted, excited at seeing him. 'Lift me up, Grandad! Lift me up!'

George lifted her up into his arms as he came towards us through the hall. Sean stood up as his father entered the living room and pulled Ashley out of George's arms into his own.

'Grandad was holding me, Daddy!' she shouted angrily.

George stood there filling up the living room with his brooding presence. He very rarely came into our living room but, when he did, it was as if he filled up the whole room with ... George-ness. He was about six foot tall and very broad. Toad Hall had big rooms; our rooms were small. I had rarely seen him in small rooms, so he seemed even more imposing now. There was silence. Neither Sean nor Old George was going to raise his voice in front of Ashley. Both were distracted by her persistent chatter as she ran around her beloved Granda's legs wittering. She was totally unaware of any antagonism in the air. Old George spoke first.

'Sean, I am sorry,' he said quietly.

'Don't apologise to *me*,' Sean answered. 'I wasn't the one you called a thief.'

'What's a thief?' Ashley asked, turning her face up to look at her granda.

'Come on, chatty girl,' I interrupted nervously. 'Go into your room, Ashley, and get some drawings to show Grandad.' And off she happily trotted.

Old George smiled his best big charming grin at me. 'Janey, I shouldn't huv said any of that. Now, you both go down and run the bar for me, eh?'

'Janey will go down if she wants,' Sean said firmly. 'But I am staying here. I am ill.' He turned his back on his father as Ashley came through the door with a big piece of paper.

'I drew a dead rainbow. It fell into the street.' She had seen diesel spill from a taxi on the wet street, its spectrum of colours spreading and shimmering in the daylight.

The drama was over – for the moment.

* * *

Over the next few weeks, Sean went back to work slowly. He had recovered as well as he could but had been told that, for the rest of his life, he would need to take tablets for sarcoidosis (a disease which causes inflammation of the body's tissues) and a nasal spray for diabetes insipidus (an inability to recycle the water in the kidneys). He was very subdued and overly anxious at the same time, which made his temper even worse. He had always had an inner need for small details to be perfect, but now it got totally out of control.

We used to have a company who delivered all the laundry and tea towels for the Weavers and the flats; they would hand me a small receipt which I had to punch two holes in and put into Sean's laundry accounts folder. One day, I punched the slip and clipped it in as normal, Sean arrived, opened the laundry ringbinder – and immediately rammed it flat, full force into my face.

'Look! It's all out of fucking line!' he started screaming at me. 'They're all up and doon! The receipts have tae line up perfectly! You have tae punch the holes in exactly the right place or they don't look neat! It's a fucking mess!'

I looked at the bundle of receipts and one or two were indeed sticking out ever so slightly. I watched Sean unclip the receipts and trim them with the very sharp blade of a Stanley knife and a ruler so they all sat perfectly in line in the folder. He did it in total silence.

In the bar, he also started to shout at staff if the beer bottles in the chiller cabinet were not all standing with the labels facing front-out in a regimented fashion. Even if I had made sure they all faced front, he would pull the chiller out and make tiny adjustments to ensure they looked 100 per cent perfect. Tiny pedantic issues started to dominate his life. In the bar, the glass-cleaning cloths had to be folded in a very particular way. In our bedroom, the sash windows had to be raised to a certain level and no more – he marked the wood with a pencil to show how high it should be. I had no idea what had made him get so picky, but I worried more and more about his health and how he would cope on our forthcoming holiday.

This year, we had long planned to take Ashley for a visit to Disney World in Florida. It was to be our holiday of a lifetime. Sean assured me he would be fit enough to go and the doctor gave him the all-clear. Ashley became increasingly excited about her big visit to meet Mickey Mouse but I was even more excited. I had dreamt about Disneyland ever since I was a wee girl. I had seen that big magic castle and those flying Dumbo elephants on television in the early 1960s and the anticipation of seeing them for real burned inside me. I had always dreamt of escaping to Sleeping Beauty's castle.

When the ferry finally took me across to the Magic Kingdom and that beautiful pink castle appeared on the horizon, I had tears in my eyes. I completely forgot about Ashley as I stood there holding onto the boat rail, transfixed by the image. I was 28. Ashley was three. We went into Mickey's home and walked around with all the other tourists. As we entered Mickey's bright bedroom, Ashley shouted loudly, 'Look, Mickey and Minnie sleep together here!'

An overweight American man leaned over and drawled: 'No, honey, we would know if they were married. They would have had a wedding.'

Ashley smiled innocently up at the man: 'But they must sleep here like boyfriend and girlfriend,' she explained, 'coz Minnie's shoes are there on the floor ...' And, sure enough, there on the floor beside Mickey's big red bed were, indeed, a pair of Minnie's black high-heel shoes. The fat American stood with his hands outstretched towards the bed and a *What can I say?* expression on his face.

* * *

When we returned to Glasgow, I would stand at the bar of the Weavers and look out through the front window at the glamorous Doges' Palace tiling on the side of the old Carpet Factory – bright glinting tiles, Venetian turrets and scooped windows – which bore no relation to the seediness into which the Calton had fallen. Ashley loved that exotic building almost as much as the People's Palace behind it. She knew every single exhibit at the People's Palace and would wander round chatting to people about the Glasgow tobacco barons, Billy Connolly's big banana boots, the wee 1950s newsagents that was recreated within the museum and she would play with Smudge the Cat, the only card-carrying trade union membershipped cat in Britain, who always followed her around. Ashley became so well known to the staff that she was allowed to walk around as though she owned the place.

'I am the Princess of the Palace,' she told me. 'Tommy Security Man told me so!'

We would often catch her chatting to Americans, Canadians, anyone and everyone about the various exhibits. We kept warning her about talking to strangers but she would tell people firmly, if they got a bit too close, 'I'm not allowed to be picked up or touched!'

The area around the Weavers was dangerous, full of drug dealers and kerb crawlers looking for hookers. I had complained to the local community police about young schoolgirls aged 14 or 15 being allowed to stand outside the bar selling themselves as Ashley played in her wee sandpit by the side of the pub. I would only send her out to play if one of our boys – our tenants – sat out there with her and she hated having a minder:

'I can watch myself, Mummy – I can!'

Then she would sulk as she dug holes in the sand and would insist her minder stand away from her or sit on the low fence at the side of the pub as she played on her own. She was incredibly independent. She hated anyone tying her shoes or helping her over the fence between the pub and the sandpit at the side of the building.

'Do it myself! Do it myself!' she would repeat so often that it became her catchphrase with the regulars.

Sean and I decided she would not eat sweets as our own teeth had become rotten to the core like many Scottish kids raised from cradle to grave on a diet of sugar and fizzy drinks. This proved a hard exercise as almost every customer in the bar started bringing Ashley sweets as a gift. We eventually took the deceitful step of telling everyone she was a diabetic and, as Sean's dad had diabetes, the scam worked. She knew she was not ill, but learned to refuse sugary snacks, never really complained about it and ate loads of fruit instead. Sean was very strict about this sugar thing but inevitably Old George always felt he knew better and hated Sean making any of his own rules, so Ashley's diabetic grandad vehemently insisted that she would eat sweets when she was with him.

'Grandad Storrie tried to give me chocolate again,' Ashley would explain to me afterwards with her 'serious' face. 'I told him *no*, but he said it was allowed. I never ate it, Mummy – look – I hid it safely in my pocket.'

Gay Gordon also adored Ashley and was always there to keep her happy. Through him, she developed an early love of musicals. A gay man in the Calton was relatively rare, so he relished his role as her personal tutor of Doris Day hits. She would often run into the crowded Weavers bar, climb on a stool and belt out 'Que Sera Sera'.

Gay Gordon would stand behind her like some crazed Mrs Worthington, as she sang her heart out, copied dance moves she had seen on TV, then bowed to her always-appreciative audience. Up in our living room, she would sing and dance along even more uninhibitedly with 'The Deadwood Stage' and every other song in her favourite VHS musicals.

It reminded me of my Mammy, clearing back the furniture so she could be Judy Garland for at least one rainy afternoon.

* * *

One day, when Sean and I were out walking with her and had almost got back home, Ashley ran ahead of us towards the Weavers. She was wearing a wee waxed blue shooting jacket and a pair of dungarees. She turned the final corner before we did and, as soon as we got round the corner, we saw she was standing up against the white fence with her hands tucked behind her back, looking straight ahead at a stranger parked in his car by the nearby kerb.

'That man asked me the time, Daddy!' she shouted, her wee finger pointing at the guy. 'I don't know him, Daddy!'

Sean immediately ran to the car and wrenched the door open as the man frantically tried to hold it shut and start the engine at the same time.

'What the fuck are you doing?' Sean screamed. 'She can't tell the fucking time! She's only three!' He rammed his fist into the man's face through the open window.

'I thought I knew her,' the man spluttered from his bloodied mouth.

I ran after Ashley, who was by now climbing over the wee fence and running up the grass incline away from the Weavers with her coat over her head.

'Daddy! No, no! No, Daddy!' she was crying.

'Ashley,' I said, grabbing her. 'It's OK, baby, come here.' I held her close. She buried her head into my shoulder, crying for her daddy, but looking back at what he was doing. She didn't want to look but couldn't stop herself. Sean had now dragged the guy from the car and was kicking him in the head and body. Our new barman had seen all the commotion through the window of the Weavers and he now came running out to join Sean in his attack on the stranger.

'I'm sorry ... I only spoke to her!' the man was trying

to shout between blows and kicks. He tried to clamber back into his car.

'Let him go! Let him go!' I yelled.

Sean booted the man in the face and his nose burst – blood went everywhere – and the stunned stranger half-sat, half-fell back into the driver's seat. He drove away frantically, semi-conscious, blood spattered all over his windscreen.

I stayed with Ashley at the top of the grassy incline. Sean sat on the fence with his head in his hands trying to get his breath back. As he looked up, two community police came running over.

'Sean,' one asked. 'What the fuck happened?'

'That guy asked Ashley the time, for fucksake,' Sean told them. 'There's no way a child of that age can tell the time ...'

'He was a fucking pervert!' I told them.

'Fucking jail me!' Sean snapped at the policemen. 'I hope you got his number. Find him and get him to charge me! I'll go to court.'

'No, Sean,' said the other policeman gently. 'You did the right thing. I would have done the same.'

Sean broke down in tears.

Ashley was still sitting on the wee grassy hill, with her coat pulled over her head, her eyes peeking out and watching, her knees hugged up to her chin. Sean and I walked up the slope to her.

'I am sorry, Ashley,' Sean said softly, 'I hate you seeing that, but he was a bad man; I was so scared he would hurt you.' He didn't pick her up or hold her because he had the man's blood on his hands and all over his clothes. But Ashley hugged his neck. She had her wee serious face on:

'I think he was bad too, Daddy, but you kicked him in

the head and he was all blood. If you kill him, the policemen will take you away. That's what happens if you kill
people.'

'Ashley,' he tried to explain, 'I will never kill anyone.
But bad people can hurt wee children. You need to know
that there are bad men and women who take wee kids
away from their parents. I was very angry at him.'

* * *

Ashley loved living in the Calton; so did I. But we had to
accept there was danger everywhere and children went
missing all over the UK, not just in the East End of Glasgow.

The building we lived in was safe as Ashley knew
everyone there and it was a great commune for her to grow
up in. On the rooftop, which we used as our private garden,
she had a paddling pool and all her outdoor toys. The
views were still awesome and I could still see the high flats
which dominated the Gorbals' shopping centre across the
river, but I knew the area was now awash with heroin
addicts hanging around dealing at The Railings right
outside the main Police Office.

That roof was our sanctuary from the city, but the
whole building did need an overhaul and we had been
trying desperately to get a council grant to renovate it.
Glasgow City Council was a Labour Party stronghold but,
when we begged for help through their much-publicised
regeneration scheme, they never even replied to our letters.
Sean was an out-and-proud Tory and the Labour Council's
attitude got right up his nose. Two of our local district
councillors regularly drank in the Weavers but, no matter
how many times we tried to raise the issue with them, they
just turned the argument around to blame the then Prime
Minister Margaret Thatcher for everything from light bulbs

not working in the street to Celtic getting beaten in the Scottish Cup Final. We even housed a Labour councillor upstairs – eventually, he screwed us for the rent and had to be evicted. He left the place so dirty we had to get an agency in to clean it.

After several months, we did finally get a letter from the city council informing us that not only would our building not get an improvement grant but they wanted to demolish it. It was too old and they had decided they wanted to put up new housing on the surrounding land. We were devastated. We argued our case in person but the council sent out an engineer to do a 'core test' in our pub cellar to prove the building was sinking and needed to be demolished. The Storrie family lawyer, a Lithuanian called Mr Bovey, told us we had no choice but to let them go ahead.

Monday morning saw a funny wee man called Nick the Greek and his entourage appear with huge yellow machines to dig up the floor of our dark, damp beer cellar. He couldn't pronounce the name 'Storrie' – he kept calling me 'Mrs String' – but he kept me updated on all the stuff that was going on downstairs:

'Mrs String, we are now dig *this* much ...'

He never took one drink and his team spent the whole week digging and drilling and driving us mental with the noise and inconvenience. Eventually they got the core test they wanted – a huge cylindrical hulk of earth of various colours. They cleaned up the insect-infested Victorian cellar and went away to do an investigation on the core back at the council laboratory. The results came back within the week. Our building was one of the most solid, safe, well-built tenements they had ever come across.

We still didn't feel comfortable as we suspected the

council would come back with a new strategy to get us out. One of Sean's uncles dealt in property; he told us that our land was ear-marked for very profitable development and Glasgow City Council was completely corrupt. One of our regular customers, Archie the Architect, worked for the council and he confirmed that people within the council had decided we were going to be harassed until we agreed to the demolition.

'Sean,' he explained. 'You need to keep on your toes, pal. They will try everything to get you out, believe you me.'

So Sean came up with an idea.

'Why deal with the corrupt Labour politicians in Glasgow?' he said. 'Let's deal with the people we voted in at Westminster.' He held a meeting at the Weavers for all the tenants in our threatened building. 'OK,' he explained to them, 'this is what we need to do. If you want to stay here in this building, you have to join the Conservative Party Association.'

The place fell silent. This was like asking Catholics to dress up as Orangemen.

'The Labour Party won't listen to us, so let's try to get beyond them. I will pay your subscriptions, we will go to some meetings and Janey will do the talking.'

'Fuck off, Sean!' one of the young guys shouted out. 'I'm no' becomin' a Tory. My da would turn in his grave!'

'Look,' explained Sean. 'It's just political prostitution. You don't huv to like them to fuck them. There's corruption everywhere and this is a long shot, but it's worth a try. If we can take this issue all the way to London, then we can bypass Glasgow City Council.'

Unfortunately, it turned out there was no local Conservative Association to join. Almost no one apart from

Sean had ever voted for the Tories in the Calton. We had to join the Cathcart Conservative Association away on the other side of the city. But we recruited 25 members in one week and at least another 18 the following week. We attended all the Conservative Association functions we could. There were Burns Suppers, raffle nights, charity balls and even days out for the Young Tories which we effectively were. All those elderly middle-class people making tea and sandwiches in the Cathcart must have been horrified to see a bunch of slang-jabbering, dope-smelling, totally mad East Enders sitting in on their meetings. They could make no sense of it at all; but they knew we were recruiting lots of new fee-paying members for them.

Four months after joining, I was invited to the 1989 Scottish Conservative Party Conference in Perth. I was so excited and the people I met were so genuinely nice to me and actually listened to what I told them about my area, that I got caught up in it all and became very vocal about the drug problem, the prostitution and general issues surrounding my community. I even got to meet the head honcho. I was nervous as hell beforehand and felt I should at least look the part, so I dressed from head to toe in shoplifted clothes and smart shoes with a matching handbag. Most people there had stylists; I had thieves with attitude and all my sizes written on the back of their hands when they stole for me. The Conservative Party leader, Prime Minister Margaret Thatcher, spoke to me with very intense eyes and said she was informed that I had recruited all these East End Glaswegians to the Conservative Party.

'You should represent the Calton area, Mrs Storrie,' she told me. 'Politics needs more women like you.'

I thought: *Fuck that! I couldn't be a politician. I want to be liked too much.*

By the end of that year, we received a phone call from a Scottish Conservative MP at Westminster assuring us our building would not be demolished. Our tenants were happy they no longer had to eat cucumber sandwiches and I threw away my floral dresses. The MP later turned out to be homosexual and got thrown out of the Party.

17
Glasgow smiles

At night, my bad dreams were still there. Some nights I had to stay awake because I was frightened the nightmares could actually take me straight to my death. The worst dreams, though, were not the ones where I was attacked, chased and slashed by demons but the ones where I met my Mammy and she was laughing, chatting and stroking my head. I got to chat with her and tell her how much I missed her. I hugged her and even Major my dog came into these dreams and let me stroke his wiry coat. When I awoke, the grief was horrendous. I had to confront the pain of separation all over again and that pain would stay with me all day. I would stomp around the Weavers, my head all foggy with images of my Mammy, her eyes twinkling, laughing with me. I didn't want 'glimpses' of her, I hated smelling her near me in my dreams, touching her soft face, hearing her grainy voice and then, in the morning, having to face the fact she was dead. I preferred no contact. I didn't want to feel that terrible emptiness and pain anew again. I wanted to sleep like Ashley.

She giggled in her sleep; she was beautiful to watch; she snuggled into her teddy bear and would whisper a breath that blew the fur gently on her wee soft toy. Maybe she was dreaming of being in Hollywood because, at three years of age, she told me, 'Mummy, I am going to be a movie star.'

Watching all those musicals with Gay Gordon and having my Mammy's DNA must have given her the notion. My own hopes of acting had not waned. There was an advert in a local newspaper for extras to appear in a small independent Glasgow film called *Alabama*. I went to the auditions. Sean could not look after Ashley that day – he was off at a car auction with Old George. So, on a horrible rainy Glasgow day, Ashley and I took a bus to the city centre and entered a spacious West End flat. The young director bent down to Ashley and shook her hand.

'Hello, what's your name then?'

'I am Ashley Storrie. I am three and I can talk really well, don't you think? I am going to be a film star when I grow up.'

I was embarrassed and smiled down at her. 'Ashley,' I said gently, pointing to the bright red sofas across the office, 'can you sit over there till I talk to this man, please?'

'What's your name, sir?' she quickly asked the director.

'I am Thomas.'

'Mum, please, can I sit with Thomas and look through that camera when he films you?' She was putting on the charm.

'You know,' he said, 'we need a wee girl for a speaking part, Janey. Can Ashley audition for it?'

Great! I thought. *I'm being upstaged by my own toddler!*

'Mum, can I please?' she pleaded. 'Please?'

Within minutes, she was standing in front of the camera, confidently delivering the words Thomas had asked her to say.

'I am stuck!' she shouted, with a cardboard box on her head. 'Help me! I am stuck!' The scene was set in a hospital emergency ward and Ashley was supposed to have a tea urn stuck on her head.

She got a speaking part. I was not cast. She couldn't wait to get back to the pub to tell all the boys she was in a real movie.

'Daddy! I got a part in a movie and I get to talk!' she yelled as she ran into the bar.

I had to escort her to the film set the following Saturday. Her movie debut went very well; she let the director place a huge metal tea urn over her head; she held the bottom; she shouted out her lines in one take.

After that, in the Weavers, she would come down on Saturday evenings, grab the mike and sing karaoke songs for the customers. My wee girl would belt out the words to 'Pearl's A Singer' in her pyjamas and, later, plead to be allowed to sing one more song before Sammy took her up for bedtime.

The bar was always full now and Sean and I were busier than ever with the run-up to Christmas but the tension between us was increasing. I just wished my Mammy was around. *Would she have helped me or just insisted men needed special treatment?* She gave her man so many concessions that it ended with her being found dead in the Clyde.

My sister Ann had finally found a good new man and got married that year. She looked radiant walking down the aisle with Big Brian, a lovely young guy who clearly adored her. Brian was a kind and happy soul; I would watch him cuddle Ann and laugh with her and, within months, she was expecting their first child. Her two kids from her first marriage were very excited. In some ways, I was jealous of her happiness. I wondered if she knew what a bastard Sean could be when I was alone with him. *Were all men bastards behind closed doors?* I secretly believed they were. I would stand behind the bar, play loud music and stare out of the window, pondering who I might have been if I had not become his wife.

* * *

One day, I had a great idea while pondering; I decided to write a nativity play for the pub. I set it in the Calton today – 1989. The Virgin Mary would be working as a counter assistant in the local Fine Fare supermarket and Joseph would be a woodworker on a Youth Training Scheme. Mary's family would be Catholic and Joseph's family would be Protestants. I sat and wrote a script for the short play, included a few funny lines, appointed Archie the Architect as narrator, cast a few customers as actors and set the performance for the evening of Christmas Day. The *Glasgow Evening Times* heard about my plans and asked the opinion of Pastor Jack Glass, who declared my play was 'the Devil's work' and slated me for bringing divisive sectarianism into the beauty of the nativity story. I just laughed and told the *Evening Times*: 'How many Glasgow pubs do *you* know that, on Christmas night, will be discussing the birth of Christ?'

Despite or perhaps because of the newspaper coverage, it was a huge success. Complete strangers came from miles away to see it. *I had written a play that worked!* I was so happy that I had finally got to do something creative.

* * *

New Year 1990 came with a bang. Literally. The biggest firework display we had ever seen was organised to celebrate the start of Glasgow's year as 'European City of Culture'. All it meant to me was facing a whole year ahead of 3.00 a.m. extended licensing hours and late shifts. Sean and I were still doggedly trying to make things work between us, after almost ten years of marriage, so we were constantly under stress even without this certain strain of longer hours.

Old George and Sandra were now a full-time couple and, when they visited the Weavers, she would talk condescendingly to me. She was, after all, the boss's girlfriend – he owned the whole building – so she quietly explained to me, 'You have tae show me some respect, Janey.'

In some ways, I did feel sorry for Sandra. In the Storrie family, there was a tendency for the boys to fuck women, then pass them on to their father. She had dated two of his sons – Young George and Michael – and now she was firmly ensconced with the patriarch in the family home but, in practice, she was treated by one and all as some cheap concubine. I believe Old George did have genuine feelings for her. She had had various breakdowns and had been admitted to the local mental hospital for short spells. He did care for her as a person. But I could never really hold a lengthy conversation with her because she only had two mental starting points: she was either full of Valium or in a screaming mood. And the dogs didn't help.

Old George kept his two Alsatians – Brindle, the evil black vicious one, and Junior, the blond passive happy one – in a dog pound at the back of Toad Hall and Sandra owned two literally shitty Yorkshire Terriers – the kind of wee bitey dogs that tremble and demand ribbons in their hair. I hated them. They had never been house-trained properly, so they pissed and shat randomly on any and every surface they could find. Toad Hall was a grand house, but it stank of dog piss.

Sean also hated Sandra with a passion because she would make eccentric comments when he was trying to talk business with his dad. If money was being discussed, I would always leave the room, but Sandra sat there and even managed to bring squirrels into the conversation during one of Sean's attempts to engage Old George in details of a complicated financial business venture. Whenever we left Toad Hall, Sean's temper would have reached boiling point.

I had resigned myself to the fact that our marriage was unlikely to last. Sean's violence against me had escalated. One night, when I was asleep, he came noisily into the bedroom; I woke up, complained and snapped at him. He jumped on the bed and held me down, the fingers of his right hand tightly closing round my throat. I could hardly breathe and was starting to see bright white lights pulsating behind my pupils. I kicked him hard in the crotch and he jumped off me.

'*Oooh! Fuck!*' he screamed.

He left, slamming our bedroom door behind him. It went very quiet. I panicked and quietly lifted up the sash window in our bedroom. I looked out and, still wearing my cotton pyjamas, lifted my leg very carefully through the wooden frame, brushing my calf against the hard sandstone surround, and climbed out onto the foot-wide stone ledge which ran round the building. It was drizzling with rain. I was terrified to look down. I slowly edged my way along the side of the building and tapped on Sammy's window. I had to be quick. If Sean came back into our bedroom and realised I'd gone out onto the ledge, I had no idea how he might react. Sammy opened his window, surprised.

'Just let me in, you fucker,' I told him.

I jumped into his room with no explanation because I had to make it out of his bedroom, down the hall and through his front door before Sean opened our front door which was right next to Sammy's in the main landing. My heart was thumping; I felt I had to get out of that building. *Sean is going to kill me! Why else would he grab my throat? Maybe he has gone to get a knife? He will be back with it soon.* I was so scared; I just scuttled down all the stairs, threw open the front door and ran through the streets in my pyjamas and bare feet, splashing through puddles as the dark sky rained down on me. No shoes again. I always seemed to be running away down empty streets in the rain. *My bare feet will do for now. At least I am still alive.*

When I stopped running I was far enough away, sitting in the dark rain beside an old graveyard. I was worried people passing in the street might see me and realise I was half naked and barefoot. *Maybe they will think I am a loony or something and report me to the police. Maybe if my Mammy had run away from Peter like this she would still be alive.* Then I realised that I was being irrational. Sean had not threatened to kill me at all. Yet something inside me had now blown up. I was now so fucking angry with Sean. Angry with myself. Angry with that bastard Peter. *I am going to go home right now. I am going to confront Sean. I am going to tell him how scared he has made me. And, after that, I will never have to run barefoot in the street again.* I was so full of burning hatred and boiling fury that I stamped in my bare feet all the way back through the puddles. As I turned the final corner to see our building, Sean was standing there in the street. My pyjamas were by now soaked through and the constant silver rain was blowing all around him. I could not tell from his face if he was angry or sorry. But I didn't care.

'I am fucking sick of being scared,' I told him, loud and fast. 'I am fucking sick of you making me run in the rain … Look!' I pointed at the pretty wee windows of the Barratt homes opposite; bright warm lights twinkled behind peach curtains. 'Do those people run in the night?'

'Where the hell did you go?' Sean asked me in a genuinely concerned voice. 'I went to the kitchen and when I came back, you were gone.' He stood there in the rain, his shirt soaked through, with his arms outstretched towards me. 'What the fuck is going on with us, Janey?'

'I thought you were gonna kill me,' I explained, still angry. 'You keep frightening me. You might just totally lose it one night and you might really kill me.'

Sammy hung out the first-floor window: 'Is she OK, Sean?'

'Yeah, Sammy,' Sean shouted back. 'It's OK. I upset her.'

'Fucking upset me?' I screamed. 'Fucking upset me? You had your fucking hands around my fucking throat!'

Peach curtains twitched in the Barratt houses.

'Come upstairs, Janey,' he pleaded, looking defeated.

'Fuck off!' I screamed back. 'Fuck off!'

'If you thought I was capable of killing you, why did you leave Ashley with me?'

'I know you would never hurt her,' I whispered half to myself, exhausted. I walked towards him but shrugged off his attempt to hold me. We went back upstairs and sat in our living room. I shivered. Sean got me a towel. Sammy, who had been looking after Ashley while she slept, went into the kitchen to make us some tea. Sean got up and stood over me.

'Janey, I am sorry. What makes ye think I am gonna fucking kill you? Whit makes ye think that?'

'Well,' I hissed at him, 'are you telling me that men don't kill their partners? Are you telling me – *me* – that they don't do that, that this fucking constant bullying is OK? You fucking – fucking – really scare me.'

Whenever Sean hit me ... afterwards, when we talked about it ... he always admitted it was his fault; he never blamed me; he never said, 'You made me hit you'; he always took the blame. We talked through the night. Sean sat quietly trying hard to explain his fears, his uncontrollable angers, how hard it was being him, being Old George's son; and all the time my heart was split in two for this man who loved me but who made me scared. I wanted to leave the room. I wanted to leave him.

'Sean, this is the last time I go through all this. If you hit me one more time I am going to the Polis. I am taking that child who's sleeping in there and I will get so far away from you that you will never see her again.' I was adamant. I meant every word. That night, I slept with Sean wrapped around me like he was clinging to a lifebuoy in stormy, dangerous seas.

Early the next morning, Ashley came running into our bedroom. She jumped up onto the bed and hugged Sean: 'Wake up, Daddy, I love you – look, it's snowing!' she squealed. I lay there watching her kiss his head and drag him out of the warmth of sleep to go look through the window with her at the cold white world outside.

'So, Ashley,' he laughed. 'Who is gonna build a snowman?'

'I am, Daddy! I am! I am going to build a snow-daddy – a snowman that looks *just* like you!' she giggled.

I rubbed my swollen feet and said sarcastically to her, 'Make sure it has no mouth. At least then it will be a snow-daddy that can't shout at Mummy.'

Sean looked over her head and, mouthing the word *Sorry*, put his hand out to me: 'Come and see all the snow, Janey.'

I watched Ashley play happily in the snow and buried my fears until the next time.

* * *

It was hard trying to bring her up with a good attitude. She was surrounded by uncles – Sean's brothers – who often verbally attacked each other in front of her.

'Yer daddy's a bastard,' Young George told her.

'Mummy,' she asked me later, 'why does Uncle George say bad words and call my Daddy bad names?'

I tried to be polite about the arse. 'Never mind, babes, just ignore him.'

* * *

Around that time, we were hosting regular party nights at the Weavers and even had 'Safe Sex Nights' where we invited all the HIV awareness groups to come along and distribute their information. Ashley was, of course, around while this happened and there were colourful balloons everywhere. All the customers would play games with condoms and learn about safe sex from the local authorities' Scottish AIDS Monitors who came along to leave pamphlets. HIV was by now not only affecting the gay community but also heterosexual heroin addicts who shared needles; and other sexual activities had made a surge in the crossover of HIV a real threat to everyone. At one of our safe sex nights, there was a competition where you had to run with a cucumber and put a condom on it; whoever could get the condom over the cucumber first won. We let Ashley compete in the race but she didn't really understand what it was about.

She had been told by us what HIV was: we had had to explain to her why it was dangerous to touch any needles she found lying in the streets outside the bar and about the danger of coming into contact with other people's blood. I had kept it simple, brief and in very general terms but she was very intelligent and asked a host of questions which I tried to answer honestly so, in her head, the one thing she was certain of was that it spelt certain death. She was surrounded by addicts and many were HIV positive.

Sean had rented out the wee shops we owned next to the Weavers to the Calton Athletic Support Group, an amazing and innovative drug rehabilitation group fronted by Davey who used to live in one of our flats upstairs. He was not only clean and off smack himself, he was now managing to get other addicts off heroin with his own drug-free therapy. His ethos was to build self-confidence through group support, keep fit and self-worth. He had addicts running marathons, playing football and signing up for various educational programmes such as confidence building, health awareness and nutrition. Families were reunited, marriages were saved, young men and women were again walking with their heads held high instead of dying in squalor in the Calton.

It was astonishing and heartening to watch young people walk into those wee shops which had lain empty for years. They would walk in looking like skeletons, with that junkie schlonky walk, hunched over, dragging their feet and then, six months later, they'd be standing outside in the sunshine in their shorts and buff six-packs looking fantastic and girls would look at them in a way they'd not had girls look at them in a long, long time. Not all addicts were successful but many did stay clean and it felt good to have this positivity around and beside us. The odd thing about addicts is that they do repair very quickly. When ex-addicts came into the Weavers, they were virtually bouncing on the balls of their feet instead of sidling up saying, 'Janey – you wanna buy a cat?' which was something an addict did say to me; he had it in his pocket.

But Davey was not the only person involved in

running the Calton Athletic Support Group. One other, well-dressed, man often came to the pub to collect shop keys for their meetings. I knew Old George disliked this man and, one evening, when I was sitting with Ashley waiting for Old George to arrive at the Weavers, I looked through a window and the neatly dressed man was standing in the street outside.

'Oh fuck!' I said without thinking. 'All I need is Old George to walk in now!'

'Who is that man?' Ashley asked. I grabbed our fat bunch of keys and muttered, 'He's someone who was locked up in prison for killing another man and he smeared his own shit up the cell wall.' I ran towards the door and looked out to see if Old George had parked his car yet. It was OK: there was no car yet, but he was due at any time. I did not want to talk to the man.

'Ashley,' I said quickly, 'go give these keys to him for me.'

She happily trotted off and approached the well-dressed man, who smiled down at her. 'Hello,' she said brightly. 'Are you the man who killed someone and spread jobbies up the walls?'

I gasped, but I heard the man laugh: 'Yes I am. How did you know that? Are you Mij's niece? You sound a lot like the wee girl he told me about. Do you have an uncle called Jim?'

'Yes, I am Ashley Storrie. What is your name?'

'I am Jimmy Boyle.'

He looked over her head at me and smiled through the window. I did not smile back.

* * *

It was around this time I bought Sammy a large gold sovereign ring set in a very distinctive diamond-cut mounting which he wore on the very recognisable skinny middle finger of his right hand. Sammy liked decorative jewellery although ironically, in Glasgow's East End, the more showy jewellery you wore the poorer you actually were. Sammy wore gold chains round his neck and had a tiny new girlfriend called Sarah, who was blonde, pretty, very intelligent, in her mid-twenties and worked in one of the local 'massage parlours' which doubled as sex salons to get round the letter of the complicated British and Scottish sex laws. In the 1980s, massage parlours arrived as an everyday front for prostitution. There had been shebeens – drinking dens – before where, sometimes, sex went on but the women in them weren't really prostitutes – they were just women who would fuck men for drink. These new massage parlours were run as businesses and often financed by newly rich drug dealers with their large cash incomes. Their status symbols were owning a gold sovereign ring, a Pit Bull Terrier, a blonde girlfriend, a large BMW and a massage parlour named after something classy from a Harold Robbins novel. Sammy had no problem with Sarah's job and neither did I; she was a good friend to me and Ashley loved her company. One day, when the two of them came back from a trip playing on the swings in the park, Sarah mentioned she was going off to do 'a shift at work'.

'What *is* your job, Sarah?' Ashley asked, as Sarah changed into her white nurse-style uniform. Sarah and I locked eyes and a slight pause followed until Sarah said very casually, 'I'm a hairdresser, honey.'

Ashley looked surprised: 'Then why don't you ever cut *my* hair?' she asked. 'I need my hair cut, sure I do, don't I, Mum?'

'Sarah is too busy, Ashley,' I laughed nervously. 'That's why I don't like to ask her.'

Sarah would stay the night with Sammy then come downstairs into the bar each morning and we would have a coffee together before we each started our shift, albeit in very different jobs. One day, inevitably, I asked, 'Don't you mind having sex all day with strange men? Doesn't it feel weird?'

'Well,' she explained, 'I make great money and I could never go back to working a 40-hour week for shit cash.'

'Yeah, but fucking strange men all day?'

'The sex is easy and, you know, sometimes it's really good,' Sarah said, her big brown eyes twinkling over the mug of coffee.

'What's it *really* like?' I asked, as I pulled the bar stool closer and watched her put on her lipstick. She turned her face and looked in my eyes. 'Janey, all you do is just shut your fucking eyes and imagine every £10 note and £20 note being dropped into your purse. You lie back, smile and take it any way you have to and – as they pull their dicks out of you – you visualise all the stuff you can buy.'

* * *

My brother Mij's girlfriend was also a 'working girl'; like Mij, she was on heroin. He came over to the Weavers to see me one night, looking very upset; I took him upstairs to chat and, as he stood in my kitchen, he told me, 'Janey, it's all fucked … Ma hale life is fucked!'

Then he started to cry. I pulled out one of the chairs for him to sit down. It had been so long since I saw anyone, other than Sean, cry. I was incapable of dealing with it. I tried not to show my own feeling of inadequacy.

'What's wrong, Mij?' I asked, standing over him as he slowly lowered his head into his hands. All his previous visits with fake tales of lost Giro cheques and stolen wallets rushed through my mind. 'If this is another one of your scams to get cash you can fuck right off!'

'I am HIV positive,' he blurted out through his tears.

I stood there in shock, not knowing how to react.

'I got tested and they told me last week.'

I looked down at him, hugging his chest with his skinny arms.

'I am gonna die with fucking AIDS!' he suddenly shouted. '*Me!* I'm gonna die!'

I still didn't fully believe him. Mij had always been a drama queen; he lied so much you were never certain what was the truth. He still occasionally reminisced about the times he fought the big shark off the coast of Ayrshire and tamed the wild lion from Glasgow Zoo. But he explained the whole medical procedure and testing routine to me. He told me he had shared needles with a guy who recently found out he had HIV. I started to believe him and it all looked so bleak.

'Mummy,' Ashley's voice said. I turned round. She was standing in the doorway. 'What's wrong with Uncle Mij, Mummy?'

She had always loved her Uncle Mij; he was so childlike and so silly and had always been a great playmate; they would do crawling races on the floor and he would do all the funny voices when she was watching cartoons and would tell her bizarrely mental stories about rainbows and butterflies.

'He's just a wee bit upset, honey,' I told her. 'Uncle Mij just needs to sit with me for a while.'

'He said he has AIDS, Mummy. I heard him shouting. Does he have AIDS, Mummy? Will he die next week?' She sat down on a chair and big tears started plopping from her eyelashes.

I remembered reading in a magazine about how

doctors had been afraid of the first AIDS patients and they used to feed them under the doors, because they didn't quite know what disease they were facing.

'It's just something between us, Ashley,' I tried to explain. 'Uncle Mij wants us to keep it a wee secret until he's ready to tell everyone himself.'

A few weeks later, Mij phoned up and she asked him, 'Are you not dead yet?' Death wasn't terrifying to her; it was just something that happened in the Calton.

'No, I'm no' dead yet,' Mij told her. But he was mentally devastated by his HIV; the only thing that kept him going in the next few weeks was that his Pit Bull terrier Tyson had just had pups. Mij loved his dogs – Tyson and Rocky – more than any person in the world. I took Ashley over to see the puppies when he felt up for a visit.

'Uncle Mij, can I hold one?' she asked excitedly, as if they were new toys; she'd never seen a puppy before.

As Ashley fussed over the puppies, I asked him: 'How are you?' It was a question I asked every time I saw him, but I never had any idea what his answer would be on any given day. Today, he replied, 'The doctors are all bastards, Janey ... They don't give a fuck aboot me ... I'm just another junkie wi' AIDS ...'

Dealing with him was hard. Mij had always blamed everyone else for his problems. It had been Cathy's fault she left him. It was wee Debbie's fault she got into trouble. It was never Mij's responsibility. The world hated him and it was the entire world's fault he was screwed. I loved him, but his self-pitying and destructive behaviour had always frustrated me, even in this situation.

'I fuckin' hate it,' he muttered. 'The doctors don't treat me right ... I've gotta get injections ... They're all bastards ... It's no' fair ...'

When he was a wee boy, he used to batter his head against the wall until he blacked out just to get attention.

Later that same week, I took Ashley up to see my sister Ann. Unlike Mij, she was doing well. She lived in a comfortable jumble of toys and clothes and collectable nick-nacks and her life seemed to have turned a corner and be sailing in the right direction. I had not yet told her about Mij's illness. Ann and I sat watching TV while Ashley sat on the floor happily playing with her doll when a programme came on about dogs. 'Look, Ashley,' I said. 'There are puppies on the TV. You never told Aunty Ann what Uncle Mij has now.'

'Uncle Mij has AIDS,' she said matter-of-factly. Then her wee hand went up to her mouth because she realised she told *the BIG secret*, so she turned away from the television and smiled up at us, adding: 'Oh, and he has puppies as well ...'

Ann's mouth had opened. She looked at me in horror. I felt awful.

'I am sorry, Mummy,' Ashley said. 'I didn't mean to tell the secret.'

'It's OK, honey,' I said, bending down to stroke her wee head. 'That was a big secret for you to keep all on your own and it's my fault.'

'Mij has AIDS?' Ann almost shouted.

'I'm sorry, Ann, he just told me last week. Well, he has HIV which isn't really AIDS, so let's not worry too much.'

But now the secret was out and we all tried to make sense of Mij's illness and his lifestyle. My Dad tried hard to help, but his generation had never had to understand heroin or HIV. I felt sorry for Dad; his life had been turning out just fine with Mary, his new wife. Now this had happened. We all tried to cope with Mij's increasing dramas; life went on; and the late hours we opened the Weavers during Glasgow's year as European 'City of Culture' put Sean and me under even more strain. How I hated the bar that year!

* * *

One wet Saturday, I took a trip back to Shettleston to meet my other brother Vid in his favourite local bar. I hopped off the bus and ran through the rain – it inevitably rained when I went home. It always felt slightly weird going back because these streets looked the same and nothing had really changed in the area, but I had changed. I had played in these streets, grew up running round them and cycling along them on my bike and now I felt alien. The only people I knew left here were my brother, grandad and Aunt Rita. With my Mammy gone, the area felt empty. I went to Vid's bar and, when I pushed the door open, the smell of cigarette smoke punched me in the face. You would think after running a bar I would have got used to that oppressive smoky stench, but it still made me flinch. I looked around the bar and strange men looked back, staring over their shoulders or turning completely around to see me. I recognised none of them. A barmaid looked over at me and smiled. I think she knew me from school.

'I'm looking for my brother Vid.'

'David?'

'Yeah, has he been in?'

'Sorry, I huvnae seen him, hen.'

I was angry; Vid had told me to meet him here in this bar. I stepped back out of the pub into the rain. It was getting dark. The old church where I used to attend Brownies stood opposite. I loved that church. It looked so comforting. Looking at it, I thought *I want to go up to my Mammy's house, just to see it again, just to check it is still there. Maybe she'll be standing at the window looking out.* Then I realised I was being daft. I shrugged off the leaking pain in my soul as I flagged down a taxi to take me back to my real home in the Calton. By the time I got back, it was dark and the Weavers was getting busy, the karaoke was in full swing and Ashley was standing in her pink stripy housecoat behind the bar waiting for Sean to take her off to see Old George.

'I'm going to Granda's home to see him,' Ashley explained to me, her wee head bobbing about as she chatted eagerly. 'He is going to play his piano for me and I am going to sing Doris Day. He promised that on the phone.' Her hair was wrapped up in five bunches, bright-coloured rubber bands gripping them, making the hair wiggle-wiggle as she moved. She looked like some pop singer from Bananarama or Culture Club, her blonde spiky hair standing up on end at straight angles to her head.

'Who put all those funny pony-tails in your hair?' I asked, smiling.

'Sammy did it for me! He helped me do it and gave me a mirror to watch myself and he says I am beautiful,' she enthused, stroking her mad hair.

I kissed her on the cheek and started work behind the bar as she went off to Toad Hall with Sean. Saturday nights at the Weavers were always hectic nowadays. When the phone behind the bar rang this particular night, I barely heard it over Old Wullie singing 'Love Is A Many Splendoured Thing' with Sara his big tailless Alsatian at his feet howling along in time to the rhythm.

'Hello?' I shouted into the receiver with my left hand over my ear.

'Janey!' the voice yelled. I could hear the sound of another bar in the background.

'Yeah, this is Janey! Who's that?'

'Is that you, Sweet Pea?' the voice yelled.

I froze inside. The only person who ever called me Sweet Pea was my Uncle David Percy.

'Janey! Were ye lookin' fur me today? A guy tells me ye were in the bar up Shettleston looking fur me!'

Behind me, Old Wullie's voice trembled at the high notes as he sang:

For l-o-o-ove is a many sple-e-e-ndoured thing ...

Cold fear gripped me inside. Why was he calling me? I took a deep breath.

'No, I wasn't looking for you!' I paused. 'Why the fuck would I?' I shouted. 'Did ye think I wanted sex?' I paused again. *'Or am I too big fur ye now?'* I screamed.

The customers at the bar behind me went quiet. Old Wullie had finished the song and they had heard every word. I slammed the phone down with a bang. It fell out of the vertical cradle which was mounted onto a pillar behind the bar. Shaking inside, I picked it up and slammed it into the cradle again with even more anger but it fell out again. Angry at the inanimate object, I just threw the receiver into mid-air and watched the spiral cord twist and turn as it finally unravelled and crashed to the floor.

'My Uncle called,' I announced to our customers as if in a trance. 'He used to sexually abuse me as a child. I hate him.' I turned to face Old Wullie: 'Lager, Wullie?' He simply looked at me and nodded with an almost angry look in his eyes, as if he understood why I'd said the words. I grabbed the beer tap and pulled him a pint. I could feel some of the customers watching me carefully as I kept my head down and averted my eyes. I think they were more stunned than uncomfortable; they were just a random bunch of ordinary, good people who had gone out for the night; the last thing they expected or needed was me throwing my problems in their faces. I felt suddenly guilty and stupid.

'Good song, Wullie,' I muttered uncomfortably, holding his beer out to him, feeling the first tears dripping over my eyelashes.

Why had he called? I had not spoken to that bastard in years. *Of course I wasn't looking for him.* I was looking for my brother Vid. *What made him think I was looking for him?*

'You OK?' I didn't hear the words at first. 'You OK, Janey?' Weavers regular Big Malky was speaking to me.

'No, not really.'

I walked into the back shop. Sammy followed me.

'Sammy, that was ...' I gulped; I found I could not speak.

'I know all about it, Janey,' Sammy said as he put his arms around me. 'You told me, remember?'

But I couldn't remember telling him anything. Maybe Sean had told him.

'I know, Sammy,' I eventually replied. 'I'm sorry. Give me two minutes to get myself together and I will be OK. Go watch the bar for me, eh?' I sniffed, trying hard to fix my mascara. By telling the customers, I felt I had unleashed something. I had spoken to Sammy, Paul and Sean about the abuse, but not anyone outside this safe wee inner circle. Now I had confronted the abuser himself with the knowledge that I had not forgotten what he had done. Now my Uncle David Percy would know I was not going to bury away what had happened. I had no idea how all this made me feel. One minute I was elated: *I have said it to him!* The next moment, I felt like a bad girl: *I am causing trouble!* It was out now, but I didn't know what the consequences would be.

Sean came home at about 10.30 p.m. with a sleeping Ashley draped over his shoulder. He went straight upstairs and put her to bed. I told him all about the phone call. He was surprised but glad I had brought it out into the open. He was ready for any confrontation that resulted; I wasn't.

'Well, maybe it's time you did tell your Dad all about it, Janey. Why do you have to carry the whole of this fucking emotional bundle and none of them know anything?'

'I cannae tell him, Sean; he disnae know and it'd really hurt him. He was an alcoholic back then; it wisnae his fault.' As I spoke, I could feel the panic rise inside me at the thought of the whole thing becoming unravelled.

'It wisnae yer fault either, Janey,' Sean said gently, putting his arm round me.

I sat quietly thinking about it all and decided not to say anything to my family. *Not yet*, I thought. *Not yet*.

18

*'Janey, shut
the door, eh?'*

Glasgow's year as European City of Culture was too much for us all. We had to be open from 11.00 each morning until 3.00 the next morning. Sean decided that I should take Ashley on holiday alone, as he could not possibly get cover for both him and me for all the extra working hours. So, one evening, Ashley and I caught the overnight train down to Torquay in south-west England. She was *so* excited we were going away on our own; it was a great adventure. She begged me to let her sleep on the top bunk and I finally gave in to her four-year-old demands; within minutes the train jolted and she came flying off the bunk and landed on her head on the train floor.

I screamed.

I thought she was dead.

'Mummy,' she laughed, rubbing the back of her head. 'Did you see me fly?'

I always felt so inadequate when she was my sole responsibility. When Sean was there he always seemed to know what to do and say. It was like I didn't function properly when he wasn't with me. Torquay, though, was good for me because I was alone with her, my confidence soared and I made all the decisions about where we went and how much money we spent. We seemed to spend the whole week swimming and beachcombing, walking for hours along the seafront. When we arrived home by train the following Saturday at Glasgow Central, Ashley ran into Sean's arms as soon as she saw him.

'Daddy!' she shrieked into his face. 'I've got shells in my bag for you! *Special* shells that whisper!'

Sean was so happy to see us. He hugged Ashley so hard she pushed him away.

'Daddy, you are squeezing me too hard!'

'Sorry, babes, go strap yourself into the car; I want to chat to Mummy.' He held the car door open for her and threw our bags into the boot. I could see something frightening in his eyes. My mouth went dry.

'What is it, Sean?' I panicked: 'Is it Mij or my Dad?'

Sean leaned against the boot of the car and held my face gently between the palms of his hands. 'Janey, Donna from up the road died two nights ago: it was heroin.'

She had been such a lovely young woman and her wee daughter Kara was just getting ready to start school that year – she was almost the same age as Ashley. *Is everyone going to die from it?* I thought.

As soon as I got to the Calton, I went up the road to Donna's home. She had lived on a very nice council estate where the houses had verandas. Her open coffin was lying on a trestle table in a candlelit bedroom cloaked in semi-darkness, with flowery curtains pulled tight. She lay there like a wee angel looking about ten years old in that wooden box. Her blonde hair was spread out all over the beautiful soft white silk lining. I stood there for long minutes and prayed. I had never really prayed before, because I didn't have a religion. I suppose I just stood there and whispered hopes and fears to a God I didn't believe in, thinking: *Such a waste of a life!* The tears started to squeeze through my tightly closed eyelids. I heard low voices and looked over to the shadowy corner of the gloomy, candle-lit room. As my eyes grew accustomed to the darkness, I saw Donna's sister and older brother Kieron both sitting there heating up a small spoonful of heroin over a Holy Candle that had been lit for her Mass.

'Janey, shut the door, eh?' Kieron said quietly. 'This is the stuff she overdosed on. She left it an' it's good an' I'm sure she wid want us to huv it.' He had his trousers pulled down to his knees; Donna's sister had the left leg of her jeans rolled up. The two of them turned away from me and started to split the gear into two syringes. I watched as Donna's sister sat quietly injecting brown fluid into the back of her left leg while Kieron pushed the needle slowly into a vein at the top of his right leg where it joined his groin.

It was the same week the fair came to town.

19

Trains and floats and pains

Glasgow Fair is a traditional celebration left over from when all the shipyard and factory workers got two weeks off work; during 'Fair Fortnight', they used to take their whole big scabby families to other parts of Scotland, usually 'doon the watter' to Rothesay on the Isle of Bute in the Firth of Clyde. That year, Glasgow Fair was a community project to celebrate the City of Culture year. A big-top tent was set up on Glasgow Green near the Templeton Carpet Factory, just opposite the Weavers. There were big swinging boats, loads of activity tents, a mirrored German Spiegeltent where musicians played, stilt walkers and loads of entertainment to cheer up local people.

The Weavers entered a float in the fair parade, which followed a circular five-mile route starting and finishing at Glasgow Green. We borrowed the float from Sean's relatives who were Gadgies. Our float was amazing. It was a long, flat-floored lorry with a big kiddie ride filled with lots of fibreglass Disney cartoon characters – Mickey Mouse, Donald Duck and big glittery Goofys – on which our customers sat wearing fancy dress; but the moulded children's characters were all too small for adults, so everyone had to contort their bodies to sit on them. Our regular Country and Western crowd were there, including 'Wild Bill Hickok' and 'Sioux' wearing full Western outfits, which made me smile because they weren't in fancy dress at all – this was their everyday garb. They shopped at Safeway supermarkets, went to the cinema and got on the bus wearing their cowboy and Indian outfits. They hadn't known we were going to be wearing fancy dress that day; they had just turned up dressed as normal.

There was an extraordinary assortment of outfits. My face was painted as Minnie Mouse; one middle-aged guy was dressed as a baby; a few of the female customers dressed as Hawaiian Hoola girls with grass skirts, bare midriffs and garlands on their heads; Gay Gordon – of course – was dressed as a woman with fake breasts, fishnet tights, high heels, a blonde wig, blue eye shadow and lipstick that went up round his nose. He had turned into a particularly grumpy version of Bette Midler: he was hanging off the back of our lorry, carrying a handbag, swigging gin, spitting it at passing children and shouting out, 'Feck off! Don't! I'm a lady! Don't speak to me like that!'

Every community group in the area had decorated lorries, small cars and even ice-cream vans to enter the parade. Music blared, dancers boogied the length of several streets, kiddies for miles around had brightly painted faces, the atmosphere was great. The parade took three hours to make it out of the Green and a mile up to the Gallowgate. As the parade passed along Duke Street, only a few blocks from the Weavers, Wild Bill Hickok and Sioux started yelling and whooping and pulled out their Wild West revolvers, firing them wildly into the air.

Bang! Bang!

Bang!

Bang bang!

They couldn't have chosen a worse place. It was right outside Mills' Bar which was a known haunt of nutters, a place where real bullets had been flying recently. At the sound of gunfire, local kids started screaming and ducking in fear as their parents tried to shove them down onto the pavement; dogs started barking, babies were picked up out of prams and policemen desperately started running over, yelling through their megaphones, 'Stop the parade! Stop the parade!'

Then two police horses bolted and ran amok into the crowds. Policemen tried to calm their whinnying beasts. Miraculously, there were no injuries, but the parade was halted and Wild Bill Hickok and Sioux were removed from the float by pissed-off police.

'What the fuck is going on here?' a white-shirted officer shouted at my Minnie Mouse face. 'Are you in charge of this fucking float?'

'Fucking hell!' Minnie Mouse screamed back at the man in the flat police cap. 'How wiz I to know he had a fucking gun wi' blanks in it? I never knew he wiz gonna fire his pistols. He thinks he's a real fucking cowboy!'

The copper stood and looked in disbelief as Wild Bill Hickok took his revolver back and simply put it into his holster saying, 'Sorry,' rather sheepishly. Sioux took her gun back, put it under her squaw costume and smiled sweetly while telling the policeman, 'He's a *real* cowboy, ye know.'

The man just looked at her in stunned silence, turned to look at me and raised a single eyebrow. I stepped back up on the lorry then turned and shouted down: 'He's hardly fucking Arthur Thompson! He's wearing a cowboy hat and she's dressed as a squaw!'

The float moved on and the rest of the parade went without a hitch: Wild Bill Hickok and Sioux clapped their hands instead of firing their guns. They looked a little disappointed. Later that day, the Weavers won second prize for best float; we lost out to a West Indian Calypso theme lorry from the Gorbals Community Centre. Sammy accepted the trophy for us but was too embarrassed to say anything. He was often very shy, though he always seemed to hit it off spectacularly with women.

* * *

Later that summer, Sammy had visits from some of the many children he had had by various women, particularly one woman called Betty. He was very affectionate with his kids, but none of us was sure exactly how many he had; he was very private about his various relationships. We guessed he had about seven kids by three different mothers but none of the women had ever stayed very long with him though obviously long enough to procreate. He, of course, paid no financial support to the mothers, though if he had some spare money, he would buy them bits and pieces. Betty seemed resigned to the fact Sammy was not up to committing to their relationship or to any of the wee kids he fathered.

'The weans annoy him when they cry,' she tried to explain to me. 'He's no' very good at changing nappies and stuff – an' to be honest, Janey, I like it this way. He can be a real bastard to live with.'

All this baffled me: Sammy was great with Ashley. He was placid, happy, easy-going and never seemed to throw a temper. Sarah, his then-current girlfriend, accepted that he had other women and kids outside their relationship; it never seemed to faze her. They never had any kids together because she was too busy making money as a prostitute and he was too busy smoking dope or working in the bar. He did tell me once that he wished he had made more of an effort to be with his own kids because he seemed to have more of a bond with Ashley than with any of them. He was just innately very secretive and shortly after my conversation with Betty I discovered another of his secrets.

We had a few press photographers regularly drinking in the Weavers; they would sit and drink too much while their drivers tried to encourage them to get on to the next job. Sometimes they had glamorous young model girls with them who used to sit dead bored at the side of the bar with big pouting lips waiting for the guy to drink up and get his arse moving to the shoot at the Winter Gardens or the People's Palace. I became really friendly with these photographers and one of them – Ray Beltrami, the brother of Arthur Thompson's long-time lawyer, Joe Beltrami – used to come to the Weavers before opening hours to get a drink. I would go down from our flat and let him in, then go back upstairs to our flat to get ready for opening. When I came back down, Ray would always have listed every single drink he had taken and he paid before he set off for his first assignment. Before long, Ray and a few of the other photographers would ask me to let them use Ashley as the token child in whichever particular 'photo opportunity' picture they had to take that day. So she ended up in newspapers quite a lot as the wee girl who sat in the police car as the mascot for Glasgow Fair ... or the child who met Desperate Dan at the launch of some new Marks & Spencer food range ... or the wee girl who met Wet Wet Wet as they prepared for their free concert on Glasgow Green. Before the year was out, she was offered professional modelling jobs through an agency and appeared as a bridesmaid in live bridalwear shows and children's clothing adverts in the newspapers. Ashley loved it, enjoyed the work and we kept her money in trust for her until she would be 14 or 15 and big enough to spend it. One day, Ray Beltrami showed me some of his latest shots.

'They're going to be on the front page of the *Daily Record* tomorrow!' he told me with justified pride.

One picture showed a young woman stretching her arm into the open passenger window of a car while a man injected her with heroin. The picture was particularly evocative as it was taken at The Railings right outside the Gorbals Police Office, in full view of passers-by walking to the shops. It was a shocking photo that highlighted the problems of drug dealers operating under the police's nose in broad daylight. But it was another of Ray's pictures that caught my attention. The photo showed a guy called Big Danny, a well-known heroin dealer, chatting to another young man in a black puffer jacket and blue jeans, his face hidden in shadow. From the way the guy in the black jacket stood, I knew it was Sammy.

The man not only looked like Sammy and had Sammy's hair, he also stood with his left hand in his back pocket, which was a distinctive Sammy trait. And he wore the gold sovereign ring I had given Sammy – in its very distinctive crown setting – on the recognisable skinny middle finger of his right hand, which was pointing out, making the ring clearly visible. I felt cold fear grip me. *What was Sammy doing chatting with this drug-dealing bastard?* He knew I hated Big Danny and he had never in any conversation with me mentioned he had been meeting him. Sammy never went over to the Gorbals – he had no reason to. He bought his hash from a guy in Parkhead, near Celtic Park football ground, in the opposite direction.

Ray Beltrami did not recognise Sammy because he had snatched his wide shot from the side, at a distance and the face was obscured; there were also lots of other people and details in the shot. He realised I had recognised the man in the photo but just accepted that I naturally would, as it was taken in the Gorbals and I lived in the Calton.

'When did you take the photo?' I asked.

'Yesterday.'

When Sammy arrived to take me shopping in his car later that day, I sat in the front seat quietly.

'Sammy,' I asked nonchalantly, 'where were you at lunchtime yesterday?'

'Errmm … sleeping, I think,' he replied casually. 'Why? Was the pub busy?'

'So you were nowhere near the fucking dealers in the Gorbals then?' I blurted out.

'Oh, aye!' he said, still casually. 'I wiz talking to Big Danny over at The Railings.' Then he added, 'How the fuck did you know that?'

'My brother Mij saw you,' I lied.

'Well, he should huv came and spoke to me, the big bastard,' Sammy snapped at me as he turned the car into the main road. 'Coz it was Mij I was looking fur – he owes me £20. I asked Big Danny if he had seen him, coz he would see him before anybody wid, bein' a dealer an' all.'

I sat quiet for a while.

Sammy was silent, too.

Finally he spoke. 'I lent Mij cash last week, when you told him you couldn't.'

'Why, Sammy?' I asked, my mind genuinely confused. 'Why lend him money? He is a fucking junkie, Sammy; he never pays me back, he won't pay you back and it all goes up his arm!'

We sat next to each other in silence all the way to the supermarket, as I tried hard to believe his story. But I knew the one certainty in life is that junkies lie.

Later, I tried to talk to Sean about it, but he was not really listening.

* * *

He and I had been fine for almost a whole year but then suddenly, one night, 'You fucking don't listen to me!' he screamed into my face. 'This is not how ye fucking defrost a fridge! Look – there is still ice in there, ya daft cow! There are still little slivers of ice at the back!'

He pulled me by the shoulder and dragged me from the bar to the back shop, holding the neck of my jumper so tight with his fist that it started to choke me.

'Sean,' I stammered, 'I cannae I cannae b-breathe ...'

He stopped, dropped his hands, said nothing and walked out the room.

I realised Sammy had been standing quietly in the corner watching us.

'I huv had enough, Sammy,' I said. 'I cannae do this any more. He's just a big bastard!' I cried as I ran out of the door and upstairs. Ashley was sleeping peacefully. I sat on her bed and stroked her wee head.

When Sean came upstairs that night, he just gave me a dirty look as he came to bed. Next morning, as he slept, I packed a bag and lifted Ashley up quietly, got her dressed, grabbed her folded buggy and left the house as silently as possible. This time I had decided to leave for real and had prepared everything – I had clothes, credit cards and cash. As I pushed her quickly towards the railway station, Ashley swung her legs happily in the buggy: 'Where are we going, Mummy?'

'Don't really know, baby,' I said, more to myself than to her, 'but I am really gonna go this time.'

The station was busy. I bought Ashley a doll to play

with on the journey and we jumped on the first train I saw. It was bound for Stranraer, a town on the south-west coast of Scotland that was the sailing point for ferries to Northern Ireland. Ashley was dressing and undressing her doll as the train rumbled along. 'Why are we going without Daddy?' she asked, looking confused.

'I don't want us to go back to Daddy, Ashley. I want us to go away for a while and we can see him again maybe in a few weeks. I need to be away from him and I need you to be a big girl about this.' I tried to explain as best I could. She suddenly stopped playing with the doll, looked up at me and started screaming.

'I want my daddy!' she howled.

People started looking over at us.

'This is not my mummy!' Ashley screamed hysterically. 'Somebody take me to my daddy! This is not my mummy! My home is the Weavers Inn pub in Glasgow! Help me! I am being taken away!'

I had to get her off the train at the next stop, trying to shut her up and confused about which town we were in: it turned out we actually were in Stranraer.

'Ashley, stop it,' I pleaded as I dragged her off with the buggy behind me. 'It's OK. I promise I will take you home tomorrow. I promise, now stop that noise. Ashley, stop shouting!'

She was inconsolable and sat crying on a bench in the station. She wouldn't get off that bench.

'Mummy, please, I want my Daddy!' she cried over and over. 'Mummy, please, I want my Daddy! Mummy, please, I want my Daddy! Mummy, please, please, I want my Daddy!'

I decided to stay in Stranraer overnight. I was tired and needed to think a bit. We checked into a wee hotel near the station where the owner had a blue, red and green parrot called Sugar sitting on a perch behind the bar. This seemed to take Ashley's mind off things for a while. She started to chat-chat-chat to the parrot in the lounge while I had a cup of tea and decided to call Sean and let him know we were OK.

'Janey, where are ye?' he asked as soon as he heard my voice. He sounded frantic. 'I woke up an' ye were both gone. Is Ashley OK?'

'We are fine,' I said flatly. 'I'm just fucking fed up with you an' the shit ye put me through. I'm gonna stay here tonight an' we'll both be home in the morning.'

'Will ye come home just now?' he pleaded. 'I am sorry; please come home.'

'Ah cannae. I'm in Stranraer. We got on a —'

'Whit the fuck are ye doing in Stranraer?' he interrupted.

'Sean, I just jumped on a train. Listen, I will be home. The wee wean cannae live without ye. I will come home tomorrow. I am fucking tired oot an' she has been crying fur ye.' As soon as I said it, I regretted saying that last bit as I knew it would wound him to know she was upset.

'Put her on, please,' he asked. It sounded as if he was crying.

'Hello, Daddy, I miss you lots and Mummy said you were not nice today and I have made friends with a parrot called Sugar ...' She felt she had to give out every piece of information she could in one sentence. 'I am coming home in the morning time and I love you too. Here's Mummy to talk to you and be nice to her then she will come back, Daddy. Say you are sorry to her and she will come back.' She held her hand over the mouthpiece and said to me: 'Daddy says he is sorry he was angry and please go home in the morning.' Her wee face looked up at me with Sean's soft brown eyes staring into mine. Ashley had Sean's eyes when they were reassuring but, in her eyes, I had never seen anger, madness and death. Sean could look at me and make me feel I was safe, but he could also turn his head slightly and look at me with eyes I knew had seen things that frightened me. Ashley held the phone out to me. As she stood behind me, I heard her whispering to herself: 'He is sorry; he is sorry; he is sorry.'

My heart felt like it would crumble.

'Janey,' Sean spoke between tears. 'Please, I am sorry. Tell me you will be home, eh?'

'Yes, Sean, tomorrow, I promise.' I hung up while he was still talking.

Ashley slept badly that night; she woke up about three times asking for Sean and falling back asleep in a sweat. That was when I knew that, whatever happened, I could never take her away from him and knew I could never live without her. I sat up in that damp, floral-wallpapered hotel room in Stranraer, watching the daylight slowly creep between a gap in the floral curtains and realised this was going to be my life until Ashley was at least 16. *Only another twelve years to go.* I smiled sadly to myself as I made another pot of musty tea and ate damp shortbread from the hospitality tray on the bedside table. Ashley would be going to school next year and I needed to get myself together.

20

Ashley's education

We looked at local state schools, but Sean was adamant Ashley would be privately educated. We left it to the family lawyer, Mr Bovey, to investigate which school would suit her, as neither Sean nor I knew anything about private education at all. Mr Bovey was a Lithuanian with glassy blue eyes who dressed in a fine black woollen suit, carried a thin wooden cane with an L-shaped gold handle at the top and wore a black bowler hat. He was like someone from a Dickensian novel. You only noticed his Lithuanian accent when he swore, which was rare. He was very smart and I had always found him to be very intense and a bit stand-offish, but Ashley was fond of him: she would hug him and sit on his knee. She even called her toy panda bear after him – Mr Bovey the Bear.

He was a bit pompous and overblown for my taste, so I could never get my head round how this very prim, proper, formal man with a bowler hat and a cane got on so well with this little girl who kept hugging him. 'Mr Bovey! Up! Up! Up!' she'd command and he'd lift her up on his knee and they'd chat away. She just loved him and he chatted away to her oblivious of everyone else.

One morning, the phone rang and Mr Bovey was on the other end. 'I have found the perfect school for Ashley, Mrs Storrie,' he said in his clipped, fast-talking tone. 'Laurel Bank all-girls school in the West End of Glasgow. I know the headmistress and can vouch for Ashley myself and be her sponsor. We will set up a meet-and-greet with the school to let you see all the facilities.'

'OK then, Mr Bovey,' I mumbled. 'You know best.' I was annoyed. I suppose what bothered me was that I never looked for a school myself. But, on the other hand, the West End was posh and not the normal drug-fucked, alcoholic, crazy, single-parent, piss-poor place. It had higher property prices and was quite middle class and what the hell did I know about private education?

'Other private schools,' he told me, 'just turn out girls who are good wives. Laurel Bank actually educates them.'

But Ashley was growing up among other types of girls. Our customers had enjoyed a whole year of late-night 'City of Culture' drinking and, by this time, we had a regular late-night crowd of five 'masseuses' – all 'working girls'. Sammy's girlfriend Sarah introduced them to us. They would arrive just as we were closing at 3.00 in the morning, the Year of Culture having increased their sex trade, and Sean would grant them a lock-in. It was strictly no customers, just 'The Girls'. Sean would put on the back kitchen grill and make them a fry-up: sausage, bacon, eggs, potato scones and black puddings. I would watch them slowly wipe off their make-up, kick off their high heels and drag long and hard on cigarettes while they figuratively and literally let their hair down, bitched, drank and laughed away the day's hard work.

Chantalle was a beauty. She stood about six feet tall, her long black hair decorated with small crystal hair clips, draped down to her bum. Her make-up bag contained all the big designer names – Dior, Chanel, Helena Rubenstein. Sometimes I used to let her make me up. I would sit there as she painted bright luminous colours on my lips, swept rainbows of exotic palettes over my eyelids, and she would finish by clipping up my hair into pony-tails or a French plait. By then, it would be 4.00 in the morning; I looked ready for a night on the town and the girls would clap as I paraded around in my new look, maybe fantasising about being on the game myself, because Sean had been my first boyfriend so I'd never had consensual sex with another man. I'd ask them: 'What's that like ... What's this like ... What's the other like?'

All of the girls had pseudonyms to hide their real names. One called herself Joy. She was tall and enviably slender. She had beautiful blonde hair cropped into a short spiky affair and a gamine face with cheek-bones which drew you straight to enormous lashes, framing almond-brown eyes and sitting on her cheeks when she looked down. I envied her feminine looks; I felt small and dumpy in comparison. Joy was also very funny: she loved to impersonate all the other girls. After a few vodkas, she would get up and 'act' like Chantalle, all prissy and stroppy at the same time.

'Darling, you do not touch my make-up! You have no idea who you are dealing with here! Dior is best! I get fucked for cash, so I only buy the best! Look at your cheap Boots lip gloss! You are so bloody common!' She had Chantalle down to a tee ... and, when Joy was well pissed, she loved to regale me with 'sex talk' from her long ten- or twelve-hour day: 'Five fucking blow jobs, three hand jobs and one tit-feel from a nervous dentist,' she would giggle.

One day, with all the other girls sitting round, I asked her: 'Huv ye ever had anyone famous in?'

'Oh, please! Please! Don't start me!' she said, waving her perfectly manicured hand as she slugged back her vodka in one big gulp. 'I mean, my dear, I have sucked off half the Rangers football team and not a few big fucking gangsters, honey!'

'Really? No fucking way!' I squealed.

'Yes I have. Yes indeed! And, get this …' She stood up and reached down to the hem of her black leather skirt, her blood-red fingernails clutching the material, and she suddenly hitched the skirt up to expose her bare thighs. There, hanging between her legs, was a penis.

'Fucking hell!' I screamed, laughing in shock. 'Fucking hell, Joy!'

I had no idea. All the other girls were looking at me and were pissing themselves laughing. They clapped and cheered as Joy strutted up and down in front of the bar with the black leather skirt pulled up to 'her' slender waist with 'her' flaccid penis slapping about from side to side against 'her' thigh. Then she started singing at the top of her voice:

I ammmm what I aaaaaahhhhhm!

Shirley Bassey never sang it that well or looked that feminine.

Sean came out of the kitchen holding two plates of – I swear to God – sausage and eggs.

'No! No!' Joy screamed as she held her penis in her fist. 'No sausage for me, Big Boy!'

Sean laughed, then turned away and served the food.

'Did you know about this?' I shouted, barely able to speak from laughing.

'Yeah,' said Sean. 'I did. He told me before.'

'He wanted to fuck me,' Joy giggled and cuddled up to Sean's back as he put plates on the table. 'But I said "You can't – I have a cock!"'

'You wish …' Sean laughed as he delicately prised Joy's hands from around his waist.

'I am joking, Janey,' Joy reassured me, 'but he did ask

me a couple of weeks ago if I was a man. I was shocked – nobody ever guesses!'

Sean just smiled, looked over at me and said, 'I knew a woman could never be that beautiful.'

All the girls started shouting obscenities at Sean and Joy started dancing, kicking her legs up, singing to Sean, 'The most beautiful girl in the world!'

'Leave me alone,' pleaded Sean. 'I was taking the piss! I was only joking! You are *all* beautiful but ...' He pointed at Joy. 'He has the biggest cock in the room!'

We all laughed and Joy was off twirling around dancing in her own wee world.

I never called her 'him' as long as I knew her.

21

Diamonds and pearls and death

That Christmas was one of the best we had had yet.

Just after midnight on Christmas Eve, Sean surprised me with a beautiful solitaire diamond ring to replace the wee engagement ring he had bought me when he was 16. I was absolutely gobsmacked, especially as he also got me a string of pearls. He thought I had asked him to buy me diamonds and pearls. In fact, I had actually asked him for *Diamonds and Pearls*, Prince's new CD.

'Where's my CD, ye fuckin' speccy idiot?' I shouted at him, then put the old and new rings together on the wedding finger of my left hand and cherished the love we had. I liked to believe it would all be fine.

The next morning, Sean and I watched Ashley open her presents. There was a doll's house, a toy fairground with tiny characters, a resplendent Playmobil caravan with tiny seats, windowboxes, flowers and a roof you could pull off and she got figurine characters from her favourite Disney movie *The Little Mermaid*. She also got loads of gifts from various family members. We relished her happiness as she sat among the heaps of toys and boxes all around her legs.

'Thank you, Mummy and Daddy,' she said as she hugged us both.

The New Year started well. Our business was doing well financially – we didn't separate the Weavers from the flats above – and on Saturdays the karaoke nights really boosted takings. I loved karaoke: I was not a good singer and got bored singing normal songs, but I sang rude alternative lyrics to songs like 'My Way', 'Harper Valley PTA' and Bobby Goldsboro's 'Honey I Miss You', and I would exchange banter with the customers. I loved the attention; they particularly liked my rendition of 'Pearl's A Minger' and my totally straight version of 'Mack The Knife'.

The First Gulf War started in February. We called Sammy and Paul down to our flat to watch the air attacks start live on TV, but it was just lots of green fuzzy pictures with white flashes; we'd been hoping for more. And Ashley got it into her head that 'The Gulf' was the Gorbals. She used to point across the Clyde to the Gorbals and ask, 'Mummy – is that where the war is?'

We also had an old face come back into the Weavers that year: Jonah McKenzie was someone I had known many years before, just briefly through my brother Mij. I liked Jonah – he was funny and very easy-going. He was the man whose left eye had been knocked out by the heavy glass ashtray in a freak accident at the Palaceum.

Jonah re-entered my life when he and his girlfriend Jackie and their baby girl Cheryl moved into a neat Barratt flat in Weavers Court across the London Road. Every other day, he would come over and sit in the Weavers bar for a chat. I knew he had been involved in heavy stuff – he had dealt hard drugs and was connected to some of the local gangsters. Whenever the phrase 'Glasgow Gang Wars' was mentioned in newspapers it seemed that his name appeared. I never asked why. I also never asked him about the strange marks on the palms of his hands; in Glasgow you just don't ask. It was only much later I heard the rumour that he had been crucified.

But I liked Jonah's choice of music, his conversation and the way he could laugh at himself.

* * *

One late night after we had shut the Weavers, we were in our flat on the first floor and heard loud police sirens through the windows and saw flashing blue lights flicker across our ceiling. I jumped to my feet and leaned on the window ledge to look down and see police, ambulancemen and medics standing around a body covered in a dark sheet, just lying there on the pavement across the road outside Jonah's door.

I grabbed my coat and shoes and ran downstairs, pulling them on as I went. The main road was still busy with big trucks pounding along the London Road, making their way south. It took a couple of minutes to dodge the traffic and make it to the pavement opposite. A uniformed policeman was by now dragging the covered body along by its ankles across the pavement and road, leaving a bloody black trail under the orange streetlights. I was horrified. Surely he didn't have to treat a dead body like that?

The policeman noticed me standing, watching. 'What the fuck do you want?' he asked.

I ignored him.

Three plain-clothes detectives were standing around, their cold breath drifting up and turning white and blue in the flashing lights of the ambulance. It all looked so surreal.

'Who is dead?' I asked, shuffling around in the cold.

'Fuck! ... Help!'

The words came from the body.

'He isnae dead!' I said out loud in total shock. I stepped into a pool of blood, bent over and ripped the cover off the body, before the police could stop me. They were just standing around like they were having a casual chit-chat about whether they wanted eggs in their bread rolls.

The body was Jonah's.

Belatedly, a policeman grabbed my arm and tried to pull me away. Curtains were twitching in the surrounding flats; lights were being switched on; windows began to creep open as the inhabitants awoke to the noise and lights at their doors.

'Who the fuck are you?' one plain-clothes officer snapped at me.

'You are hurting him, for fuck's sake!' I replied. 'Look! He's bleeding badly.' The blood was sticking to the soles of my shoes and the smell of it was everywhere. Jonah was silent again, his face ashen. I ran to his open front door. 'Take him to hospital – please!' I shouted over my shoulder. I ran up the stairway with one policeman behind me, my bloodied shoes sticking to the wooden steps as I went. I could hear Jackie's voice shouting something indistinct in the living room. I opened the door and, when I entered, there she was holding her baby girl Cheryl in one arm, trying to pull on her dressing gown with the other and arguing loudly with a policeman. Cheryl looked startled and bewildered at having been woken up.

'Janey!' Jackie screamed through tears. 'Jonah's been stabbed and these bastards are letting him bleed tae death oot there!'

I turned and ran back down the bloodstained wooden stairs, brushing past the policeman who'd been behind me, slipping on the sticky red fluid I had left behind on the way up. Policemen and medics were now bundling Jonah's body into the ambulance. They threw him roughly onto a bed in the back as if he were dead. Then medics pulled covers down to look at his arms.

'Keep oot of this, ya nosy cow,' a plain-clothes officer snapped at me. 'D'ye know who he is?'

'Aye,' I answered. 'He's a fuckin' human being, ya fuckin' bastard!'

'He's a fuckin' drug-dealing bastard that deserves to die!' the policeman shouted at me. 'He sells smack to the wee weans round here!'

'Is that right?' I screamed into his face. 'Well, he'll be no different from all the other cunts that sell drugs round here, then, except some of them get away with it more than others coz you fuckers take a cut! Whit's up? Did he no' pay ye enough, eh?'

'You watch yer step, Storrie,' he sneered at me.

'Fucking hell.' I stood my ground. 'You must be really important in the Polis round here, coz ye know people's names. You'll be the chief Masonic Master soon wi' all those brains, but ye still cannae threaten me or fucking treat people like that. I'll be a witness!'

The ambulance reversed and drove away into the London Road towards the Royal Infirmary. The officer turned his back on me and started talking to his associates. I pushed through them and ran back up to see Jackie. I had no idea what was going on. I knew Jonah had been involved in drugs, but I thought there was no way he sold it to kids round here ... We already had plenty of locals who did that. Jackie was sitting on her clean cream sofa crying; it must have been around 3.00 a.m. by now. Her eyes were puffy and baby Cheryl was crying in her arms.

'Whit the fuck happened?' I asked, sitting beside them.

'I wiz in bed,' Jackie sobbed, 'an' I heard him put the key in the lock, then I heard shouting. I tried to open the door but Jonah held it shut. He was screaming to me to keep it shut, Janey. He was being stabbed by people oot there on the other side of the door and he didnae want them to get to us. Then it went quiet an' even before I could pick up Cheryl and get ready to go oot to him, the Polis was here and an ambulance. I huv'nae even seen him: is he OK? The bastards widnae even let me oot o' here to see to him!'

Her voice was becoming hysterical. 'Is he deed? … Is he deed, Janey?' She ran around the wee flat holding her mouth. It sounds over-dramatic, but that's exactly what she did. Every time she said the word 'deed' she put her hand on her mouth as if she didn't want to hear those words coming out. She came from nice people; she was only a wee middle-class lassie who got dragged into a relationship with Jonah, so she had never faced anything like this in her life; she could only react the way she'd seen other people react – in films or on television – and throwing her hand up to her mouth when she was saying 'Is he deed? Is he deed?' was what she did without thinking. Her wooden floors were smeared with the blood that I had brought in on the soles of my shoes.

'Janey, is he deed?' she kept asking me. 'Is he deed?' She sat down and cuddled Cheryl in her arms.

'No, Jackie, he looked alive but those bastards treated him like meat. Look, I will watch Cheryl – you go and get ready to go up the infirmary…' I lifted the baby from her arms. As she stood up to get ready…

Bang! Bang! Bang! Bang! Bang! Bang!

'Police! Open up!' they shouted through the letterbox.

I went downstairs, let them in and carried Cheryl back upstairs with the detectives following.

'He is OK,' stated one detective uncaringly. 'They have taken him to the Royal Infirmary. Do you know who did this?' His attitude was that he didn't give a flying fuck.

'Why?' she snapped, as she pulled her hair into a pony-tail. 'Wiz it no' you lot?'

'No.' He spoke quietly to her. 'I think we know who this was.'

'Well, ye will need to talk to him aboot it. Leave me alone, OK?' She grabbed her bag and gave me her keys.

'Janey, can I pick the wee one up at yours later?'

'Sure,' I reassured her. 'You go. I will see you later. Just go, Jackie.'

She walked out with the detectives and shut the door of the living room behind her. I lay Cheryl down on the sofa. By this time, she was crying her head off, shocked and frightened; she didn't really know me. I walked into the kitchen, wiped the wet blood off my shoes, then mopped the wooden floors to get rid of the stains. The blood was all through the house. I grabbed the baby's nappy bag and some bottles and made my way with her down through the policemen, pools of blood and flashing police-car lights. Jonah was admitted to hospital and Jackie sat with him through the night. Next morning she arrived at my door to collect Cheryl.

'Janey, he is gonnae be OK. He had 16 stab wounds in his back and legs, but they're all just flesh wounds – nothing too bad.'

'Fucking hell!' I said. 'Sixteen stab wounds disnae sound OK, Jackie. Who did it?'

'He won't say.' She picked up the baby and thanked us both before leaving.

A few months later, Jonah was back in hospital. His other eye had been gouged out in a further attack.

After that, Ashley often used to sit up at the bar and chat to Jonah. She became very fond of him and he took time to play games with her. Ashley's favourite was for her to scour the Weavers, hold an object up to the poor blind man and he had to figure out what it was by touching it.

Ashley held up everything from a juice bottle to a domino box; I would get embarrassed and tell her to stop, but Jonah would insist.

'It's OK, Janey, this is better than the exercises the hospital give me. She's fine – leave her be,' then he would reach down, touch her head and shout out, 'Is this Ashley or a wee dog?' She would giggle and run around barking at him.

'It's a wee dog!' he would yell.

Jonah often sat with his fingers drifting over fag boxes and whisky glasses, his blind eyes working out by touch what was on the table. In time, he got used to negotiating the hazardous trip to the toilet on his own but in the early, difficult days, we would shout out the obstacles to him.

'Jukebox to your left ...'

'Customer approaching to your right ...'

'Smelly drunk man sitting at the fag machine ... Avoid him!'

'Woman with blonde hair on your left! Don't approach! We don't know her ...'

'If I touch a woman's tits,' he would shout back, 'it's coz I'm blind, OK? So don't shout at me!' He stretched out his arms at chest height and cupped his hands. Or he'd shout out to women: 'Can I feel your fanny? If I felt your face I wouldn't know it ...'

Another time, Jonah told me he wanted to go on an African safari. I laughed and replied, 'You're blind. It would be a waste of cash.' So I set a big electric fan up in the Weavers bar and turned the heaters on him and he made animal noises, and I did a commentary about wildebeest roaming the Serengeti. I had customers making strange elephant sounds and we laughed for ages.

* * *

Later that same year, Arthur Thompson Junior was shot dead in the street while on weekend leave from prison where he was serving a drug-dealing sentence and this set off a wave of bloodshed throughout Glasgow. The newspapers called it 'The Summer of Violence'. A lot of people were arrested for a lot of crimes but, inevitably, it was rarely the right people as the police were notoriously corrupt. The Storries were not involved in any of the violence and abhorred anything which would give them publicity. Old George had a man to cover all eventualities. As well as the dubious benefits of having The Gow as a family carpenter, he had a whole network of tradesmen and professionals throughout the city who would fix things for him without asking any questions.

On the day of Arthur Thompson Junior's funeral, two young men called Bobby Glover and Joe 'Bananas' Hanlon were found shot dead in a car outside the Cottage Bar in Darleith Street, next to Kenmore Street in Shettleston. The newspapers hailed it as an 'execution'. There were accusations, court cases and conspiracy theories. In the Calton, there were journalists and photographers crawling all over the Weavers and loitering outside Jonah's home. Old George came into the Weavers and asked me: 'Whit the fuck's happenin' across the road?'

'It's all to do with Thompson,' I told him, then nodded across to two men in the bar. 'They're journalists. Don't speak.'

Old George spat out, 'They're fuckin' worse than the Polis!' then, speaking louder: 'Get those cunts oot o' my pub!'

When blind Jonah and I were alone later that day, I asked him, 'Who killed them boys in Shettleston, Jonah?' as I stirred his tea and held the cup straight to his hand to let him feel the handle. He had thick, jet-black hair and wore dark glasses quite a lot, but this day he didn't wear specs; he was actually quite handsome and had an infectious smile.

'Killed who, Janey?'

'Fucking Cock Robin,' I told him. 'Glover and Bananas, ya mad fucker. Ye know who!' I sat close to his face, sticking up two fingers at his eyes. I still thought maybe he could really see and kept trying to catch him out.

'How the fuck would I know?' he replied evasively. 'I wisnae there, wiz I? Anyway, are ye gonnae open ma letters an' read them fur me?'

'Where's Jackie?' I asked, ripping open the first brown envelope.

'She fell oot with me again – haha!' he laughed. That was how he typically spoke. He acted like he thought it was all a big game – he was a man, after all, so he wasn't going to admit that anything had hurt him; he just sat there with his head cocked, looking up straight at me with his blind eyes.

'It's a Visa bill,' I told him. 'You owe a couple of hundred quid.' I read through the bill. Then I tried again: 'So who d'ye think did it?'

'Janey, when did ye become a fucking Polis wumin? Never ask anything ye don't really need to know. Never be a witness ... Did Sean never tell ye that?' He stared blindly into his tea and smiled.

'Aye,' I sighed. 'He tells me that all the time, but I just want to know stuff.' I knew Jonah would never tell me now.

'And did ye know,' he continued, 'did ye know ye talk too much? In fact, you talk more than anybody I huv ever met in ma life and I huv done time in jail and spent years with bastards who could talk for Britain in the Olympics but you beat them. Did Sean never say that tae ye? Haha! Nae wonder that man is quiet.'

'Everybody tells me I talk too much,' I agreed. 'Sean included.'

* * *

Sean and I now seemed to be back on an even keel. He had had no more outbursts for a while and it felt good to love him and not hold my breath, waiting for some unexpected explosion. I was even pleased to read newspaper stories about Prince Charles and Princess Diana's marriage being on the rocks. It reassured me to know I was not the only one who had in-laws that despised them. I could see why my in-laws disliked me. I was very confrontational. I asked too many questions. I did sometimes think I was better than them. And I did talk too much in a family that clearly hated any form of communication. But they were difficult to like. Every other week Sean's brother Dick, who had no top teeth, would come in, sit at the bar, get drunk and attempt to pick a verbal slanging match with me.

'Yer Mammy deserved to die in the Clyde,' he would mumble and spit at me.

'That's nice, Dick, thanks,' I would say. 'Yer own ma died, but at least she knew enough to call you Dick. She had the foresight my Mammy never hud when it came to men. In future, here's a tip for ye: when talking in public it helps if you actually know words and maybe get some teeth in yer heed, gumsy boy. Did yer teeth leave ye, just like yer woman, Dick?' I would sneer. He and Margaret had split up by this time.

'My da hates you, d'ye know that?' he would shout out so all the customers could hear.

'That's fine, Dick. It's no' yer dad I'm fucking. It's his

son though, in your family, that is always confusing, isn't it? I mean, you lot make the Borgias look like the Waltons!'

'Who are the Borgias?'

'A family from Shettleston,' I said, patting him on the hand.

I was a patronising bastard and I knew it, but I was fed up taking constant abuse from the Storrie family and started to just poke fun at them when I got the chance. I had been on the receiving end of this shit for years. I was sure even Princess Di took the piss out of her in-laws once in a while.

While I was doing all this banter with Dick, Sean would stand at the till and laugh along with me but, after I had had enough fun, he would frown and that was his sign as if to say *Enough now. Stop it now. Not in public.* Occasionally, he would lean over the bar and quietly say, 'Dick, leave her alone and she'll ignore you. Or you can leave. It's up to you.' When he said this, I would smile behind Sean's back and stick two fingers up at Dick. I often won the battle but never the war. I mostly had to live my life, marriage and motherhood in the full glare of the paying public in the bar – though Sean and I never argued in front of them: we always went into the back shop. But the customers always loved to pry and try to find out how things were really going. I was scared they would find out I had a secret life where I was an unhappy woman.

'Everything OK, Janey?' Big Malky would sometimes say, standing at the bar. 'Keep your chin up. Nobody ever gets anything right, remember that.'

Other customers would ask more prying questions. 'Sean is very quiet – you upset him again?'

'No, everything is fine, Sean is always quiet. And being me is fucking hard – OK, nosy arse?'

Even when we had a full-blown all-out fight, I would come out from the back shop, walk calmly through the bar, then storm upstairs, pick Ashley up, get her dressed and pack to leave. Sean would watch through the window in the Weavers' door for me passing, then he would run outside and we would have a hissed private argument while he watched over his shoulder to see if anyone needed serving. Sometimes while this was happening, customers would get out of cars and pass by us, saying 'Hello'. We would smile, say nothing to each other, then, the minute they had disappeared into the bar, go straight back into fight mode. Often Ashley would stand in the doorway holding her school bag and wait for us to finish whatever was going on. Most times, she thought it was some game her mummy and daddy played.

'Janey, please,' Sean would plead with me. 'I love you; don't leave me; don't take Ashley like this; wait until midnight, then we can talk more. Please, I hate this; I have to fucking serve and I am scared I go up tonight after closing and find you're gone again.'

I used Sean's fear as a weapon against him time and time again. Me leaving with Ashley was Sean's worst fear and it was the one hold I knew I had over him. I must have walked out of that street 40 times with Ashley in my arms, stayed over in a hotel one night and brought her back the next day. I knew this had to stop; she was going to school now and needed more stability. She needed to have her mummy and daddy together and solid.

Sean could be very charming and helpful at times and encouraged me to go out clubbing with my mates – he never had any true mates to go out with himself because he'd never made friends outside his immediate family circle. His friends were Sammy and Paul and the boys upstairs. He seldom went out. He didn't drink. He didn't smoke. And, if he went out, it was usually just for a quiet dinner somewhere. He always took me to nice restaurants. He told me, 'You should never just eat in the same places. You should always step out of your class. Always, always go to the best restaurants and enjoy good food.'

Which was weird, because he hated spending money.

* * *

To cheer me up, though, he decided to take me on a short break to Amsterdam. Ashley was sent off to stay with my Dad and stepmum and Philip Storrie and Sammy were to take over the Weavers for the weekend. The flight was great and we had spared no expense. We had an amazing big hotel suite and it was so luxurious. I was in heaven. I loved Amsterdam. The museums, canals and all the beautiful architecture just made my head swim. The hotel even had a health club! Sean loved to sit in the sauna, but I preferred to go for walks around the beautiful churches. After his sauna session we would meet for lunch and on the second day he told me how he had met some American guy in the sauna room.

'He told me he looks after a band and the group is playing here in Amsterdam. He says if we want tickets he can arrange it.'

'Did ye ask who it was?'

'No, I forgot.'

'I haven't seen any posters around Amsterdam,' I told him. 'So it cannae be anyone famous.'

'Suppose no'.' He shrugged. 'D'ye want to go to that jazz club we saw last night instead?' Sean loved jazz.

'Yep, that'll be good.'

That night, we had a great time at the jazz club. The

music was great and, even though we both rarely ever drank alcohol, we had shared a bottle of red wine and that was enough to make us pissed. We walked through Amsterdam at night so, by the time we got back to the hotel, we were exhausted. As we entered the lobby, there was a huge black man talking to the check-in staff. When he saw Sean, he came over.

'Hey, Scottish Guy! How ya doing? This your wife?' He held out his big hand; it was covered in gold rings and dominated by a huge gold Rolex watch. He kissed me politely on the cheek.

'You wanna come to the after-show party?' he asked me.

I took in his bright blue leather jacket, his huge baggy jeans and the bright red baseball cap atop his head. I thought it didn't seem likely to be my kind of party. 'No, we are really tired – but thanks though.'

'Well, Prince would love to have you there: he really digs Scottish people.'

'Prince? *Prince?*' I was gobsmacked. 'You never said it was *Prince*. Oh fuck!' I squealed at Sean. 'I *love* Prince! You know that!'

'I didn't know it was Prince,' Sean said, dragging his fingers through his hair and looking at me apologetically.

'I missed meeting Prince coz you don't ask enough questions!' I started to laugh as I realised only Sean would meet interesting people but would never think to ask them any questions. That was him all over.

'Hey!' The big black guy clapped his hands, laughing: 'The party is still on! I'll drive ya over!'

Within minutes, my biggest fantasy was coming true: I was in a big car being driven to a private party with Prince. Sean was not really into 'the purple one', but went along for the fun. There were hundreds of people outside a club shouting Prince's name and trying to get in. A path was cleared to get us through and we were whisked upstairs into a relatively small but funky room. The walls were draped in purple satin, there were big glitter balls hanging from the ceiling and the bar looked like a weird, colourful laboratory. The bar staff were throwing cocktail shakers in the air and uniformed waiters were mingling through the throng with glasses of champagne and salmon on crackers.

Sean and I sat down in a corner and I felt immediately out of my depth. These were beautiful people. I gazed at one woman, statuesque, dressed in a short red leather dress and gyrating for the on-lookers. The men all looked like extras from some 1950s Italian movie. Gorgeous young guys dressed in sharp suits chatted to equally beautiful young girls. And they all looked like they knew each other. I was a wee Glaswegian housewife in a top from Marks & Spencer's. Sean was even worse dressed, wearing a free T-shirt from Tennent's Lager with the slogan

OUR LAGER IS BETTER THAN PURPLE GROAK JUICE

in a big purple swirl all over the front. It was an advertising campaign: aliens came down and were given lager because Tennent's was better than purple Groak juice. Sean didn't seem to care; he grabbed a beer, happily smiling at me.

'Come, dance, Storrie!' He skidded onto the dance floor.

There was one thing I knew for sure: Sean could not dance, but he was drunk and up for fun. So I joined him and he actually moved quite well. I made a mental note to get him a bit drunk more often. Then, out of the side of my eye, I spotted Prince himself on the dance floor. *God*, I thought. *He really is tiny!* I am small – five feet three inches – and even I could look down on him. Yet I was so excited

I thought I was going to scream. I adored all Prince's music; I loved him like a teenager and here he was dancing right beside me. He moved even closer and pointed to Sean's T-shirt.

'Like your top!' he yelled over the music.

Sean danced, smiled, then leaned down to shout to him: 'Thanks! My wife loves your music, so why are we dancing to this crap? Can't they play your stuff?'

'This IS my new album!'

'Holy fuck, Sean!' I shouted and twirled him away from my musical idol.

Prince laughed.

Sean laughed.

I wanted to die.

The rest of the night went without incident; I was just happy to be in the same room as Prince and watch him dance. When we were about to leave, one of his big bodyguards came over and whispered something to Sean. I watched Sean shake his head and say, 'No, mate, but thanks.' We walked downstairs and felt the cold Dutch air slam into our faces as we left the club.

'What did he want, the big guy?' I asked.

'Prince was having a private drinks party back at his hotel suite; he wanted to know if I was interested. Do you think that wee weirdo fancied me?'

I spoke quickly: 'Was I invited?'

'No, just me. I said no.' Sean hugged me close. 'His music is shite anyway.'

* * *

When we got back to Glasgow, life at the Weavers went on as normal. Sammy showed me some new pictures of his kids. They really were cute children – God knows how he always got the women. He had been up in Shettleston that week, seeing them.

'I met your Uncle David Percy in the betting shop,' Sammy told me, lighting up a fag and sitting beside me. 'He wanted to know what you were doing. I told him to fuck right off. *She disnae want to speak to you, ya big bastard – an' you know why!* That's whit I said to him, Janey.'

My hands started trembling. 'Thanks, Sammy. He needs to fucking keep away from here. He never contacted me all these years until that day he thought I wiz looking fur him. He *knew* I didnae want tae look for him.'

'Janey,' Sammy told me, 'ye know when I wiz a wee boy an' my mammy an' daddy stayed wi' David Percy's dad – Granda Davy Percy? Well, one night my dad hud a fight with Granda Davy Percy coz my sister Jacqueline said he had touched her an' stuff ...' Sammy looked at me and nodded his head. 'D'ye think Granda Davy Percy wiz a perv as well?' he asked.

It seemed perfectly clear. I had seen Granda Davy Percy's penis more than I cared to remember and it had always been by ambiguous accident. I could never prove he was a child abuser, but I remembered all those uncomfortable conversations I had had with him when I was around 16. I remembered him telling me to go on the pill and have sex; I remembered the way he would sit with the zip of his trousers down when he chatted to me. The more I thought about it, the angrier I got. Sean and I had spent almost a year staying with Granda Davy Percy. I was confused. I had to talk to my sister Ann. I never actually thought about what I was doing; I just lifted the handset and dialled her number.

'Hiya! That you, Janey?' Ann answered, sounding happy.

'Aye, it's me. Listen, that bastard David Percy phoned here a couple of months ago and asked me if I was looking for him. I mean, why does he think that? I told him to fuck off. I mean, after everything he did tae us!'

Silence.

Heavy breathing.

Sobs.

'Ann ... You OK?' My heart was pounding. I realised I had just opened the floodgates. The last time we discussed this was when I was seven years old.

'Janey ... I ... can't talk.'

The phone line went dead.

I immediately called her back.

'Ann?'

'Janey? Brian here. Your sister is really upset, Janey. Please come up and see her ... Please,' my brother-in-law whispered down the line.

I told Sammy to stay behind the bar and bolted upstairs to the flat.

'What the fuck is wrong?' Sean demanded. 'Who is in the pub, Janey?'

'Sean, get the car and take me to Ann's house. Please don't ask. Just come now. Paul will watch over Ashley.'

Sean ran to get his car keys; I ran up two more flights of stairs.

I banged on Paul's door.

'Go watch Ashley till I get back! Sammy is in the bar! I won't be long!'

'Whit's wrang?' I heard him shout behind me as I ran down the stairs.

'Nothing! Tell you later! See you later!' I shouted as I almost ran into Sean who was halfway along the landing holding the car keys. As our car pulled out of the street, he turned to me and, for the first time, was able to ask, 'What has happened with your sister?'

'I spoke about Uncle David Percy to her and she flipped.'

I kept my head down.

I felt numb.

'How do you feel?' Sean asked, looking straight ahead as he drove.

My hands felt like glue sticking to each other: 'I don't know … I feel like I just … stabbed her … Maybe I should have kept my mouth shut.'

The car journey up to Ann's house seemed to take forever.

Why did I say that on the phone? I should have gone round and chatted instead of dropping that big bombshell on her down a telephone line. As the car drove on, I remembered how we sat in that toilet up in Kenmore Street.

'Oh Janey, no, no, no!' she had whispered. 'I thought if I let him touch me he widnae touch you!'

My big sister had tried to protect me and now I felt that I had hurt her by talking about it again.

I walked up to her home.

Brian was standing at the door, holding it open for me.

'She is in the living room, Janey.'

Ann was pacing up and down her living-room carpet, sobbing. When she saw me, she opened her arms and pulled me to her.

'Janey! Janey!' was all she could say as we hugged.

Ann had tried hard all her life to lock the memories away inside her head. When we were grown up, we had never spoken of the abuse, in fact we never even spoke David Percy's name. Now we held hands and sat in silence.

Ann had been through a difficult marriage and

divorce, she was happily remarried and had just given birth to the second of her two youngest daughters when I had brought all this back to hurt her. She had suffered severe depression all her adult life as a result of the abuse. She hardly ever let her kids out of her sight; she was fearful and weepy around them; her relationships had suffered; and she had never had much self-confidence. I felt horribly hurt for her.

We sat together that night and chatted and chatted about everything except the details of the abuse itself. We spoke about Mammy, we shared stories of her. She was everywhere: laughing as she dragged on a cigarette; dancing on the cold lino in the hall in her bare feet, her long toenails clicking and clattering as she skittered around; carrying all our school dinners up from the school dinner hall – she had paid for them but we all had measles that week and could not attend so she went and collected them; doling out dry mince and sloppy puddings to us on the familiar blue plastic plates from our school. Mammy was passed back and forth like a curious wee broken doll that we smiled over, told an anecdote about, then passed back to the other. Mammy was a storytellers' pass the parcel. Each tale involved peeling a layer off and looking at what was left. It was good to finally talk about her that night; Ann and I adjusted to a new truth we shared, the new version of Mammy, the honest memories of our past.

Ann and I managed to put something of our past into a perspective that we could both almost deal with. I was horrified to know how much damage our own Uncle had inflicted on her. It made me start to think about how I had dealt with my own demons. That night, I decided my Dad had to be told. I knew Ann would not be ready but, if I could tell him on both our behalves, then he might be able to get a handle on what had actually happened to his own daughters. I also felt it was time for him to take his share of the blame 'cake'. I knew he had been an alcoholic when we were abused, I knew he was unaware, but I felt he now needed to know that, while he was drinking in The Waverley, that bastard of an Uncle had been hurting us. By telling him, I would be getting some of the anger off my own chest.

As a mother I had watched Ashley grow, I had questioned every nuance of her behaviour in case she began pulling out her hair or biting her nails till they bled or getting the nickname 'Shakey Cakey' because she trembled so much – as I had. My parents had never questioned anything when I had been a child.

Sean called Dad and asked him to come over to our flat.

He arrived with my stepmum Mary.

Sean took Mary into the kitchen.

Dad came into the living room with me.

I sat at one end of the room. Dad sat at the other.

An expanse of brown carpet and a wooden table separated us. He looked at me with concern in his eyes.

'What's wrong, Janey?'

I just could not bring myself to say it. Every time I tried, my mouth felt like someone had shoved damp dough into my cheeks and it had stuck my tongue to the roof of my mouth.

'Janey, what is it?' His eyes were clouded and his brow came down. It was the look that had made my heart lurch as a child. The look that said *I don't like this*.

'Dad, when Ann and I were small, David Percy sexually abused us ...' I stammered out the whole story, I never stopped, I was scared to stop talking, I kept going on and on and on talking, I kept my eyes on the floor and started to see tiny wee white, brown and blue twists of wool in the brown carpet that I had never seen before. If you actually stared carefully at it, it wasn't actually brown at all; you could start to see how the brown broke down and the colours combined. I felt like I was getting smaller and smaller and crawling deeper into the fibre of the carpet. I did not want to look up. I did not want to see the pain that I knew would be in his eyes. I was saying things that would hurt my father for the rest of his life. I was speaking words that would change his dreams, change his past, change his feelings towards his dead wife. Me, I was doing it.

'Janey!' He was there at my knee. I realised I had clenched myself into a wee round ball as I talked. My arms had wriggled their way round my knees and they were in turn brought up to my forehead. I was a ball of pain and shame. 'I am so sorry, Janey. I am so sorry, I wish I could go back, hen, and fix it all. I am so sorry.' He hugged me and sat on the floor with me. 'I should have been there. If I had been a better father, this wouldn't have happened.' He said it. He took some blame. He told me over and over how he should have watched more, how he should have asked more, how he should have loved me more. My Dad was saving me now. He was here and he was telling me how much he wished he could have been there.

It was a huge weight off my shoulders finally telling Dad but I knew that the rest of my family would have to know as well.

Mij arrived late on a Saturday night, just as we were shutting the pub. 'Janey, whit's up?' he asked, wrapping his big grey woolly coat around his bony shoulders; he looked like my Mum now that he was thin and scraggy from heroin. I took him upstairs to the flat so we could have some privacy. The kitchen was cosy; Ashley was fast asleep in her own room; lying there she was oblivious to any pain in anyone's childhood, surrounded by teddy bears, panda bear, parental protection and love. I looked through the wee wooden window that linked the kitchen to her bedroom. Her face was cherub-like, her wee chubby hands resting under her cheek, her bed strewn with books and Whisky our new cat, fluffy and ginger, wrapped around her bare ankles which peeped out from under the blue duvet. I turned to Mij, sitting there at the wooden table beside the windows which overlooked the dark, windy London Road.

'Mij, I need to tell you this.'

His eyes were bloodshot. He looked like shit and I was about to give him ten hundred more reasons to take heroin. Again I fumbled over the words; again I fiddled with my buttons on my cardigan.

'Percy abused Ann and me when we were weans ...' I blurted it all out. Mij stood up quickly and leaned against the kitchen unit. His back was against the cupboard; he raised his eyes and held his face in his hands then slowly slid down onto the floor. He crouched against the laminate wood; his sobs were frightening.

'Ah ... am ... gonnae ... kill ... that ... big ... Orange ... bastard,' he hissed. 'I fucked up, I beat my own Mammy, I let you get abused, I am a fucking shite brother.' He sobbed and gulped into his sleeves.

'Mij, for fuck's sake, this is not about you,' I shouted. I looked quickly into Ashley's bedroom to check she was still asleep.

'I know, Janey,' Mij told me. 'But I failed everyone. I always thought he was up to something, I know I knew something but I cannae remember whit it was, I'm sorry. I love you. I'll do anything fur you. I know I wis a big bastard, I shouldnae huv hit my Mammy or you. I abused ye as well, being violent and no' helping.' He started bawling on the floor. I could see he was really hurt; he had been a big bully when I was younger; I had really wanted to hate him; but I had always felt sorry for him. Now he stood up and put his arms around me and just held me for ages. 'My two wee sisters abused by that sick fucking pervert!' Mij stared at the floor. 'I will get him fucking killed!'

'Don't talk shit,' I told him. 'If I need him dead I will knife the fucker myself; I just need you to be strong for Ann and me and no dramatics. Dad knows now and Ann is telling Vid this week, so no more secrets.' I hugged him and put on some tea for us all.

'Sean will kill him,' Mij muttered to me. 'Sean Storrie will pull that fucker's heart out.'

'No, Mij, he won't, coz Sean told me that he does not have to avenge me, coz Percy took nothing from me that belonged to Sean. He says I am a whole person who has to deal with this on my own terms.'

'Well, he *should* kill him!' Mij stood looking at me as if Sean had let us all down.

'Why, Mij? So you don't have to go back to Shettleston and defend your sister's honour? Are ye worried the Orange Walk freaks will hate ye for hitting a Protestant? I don't want anyone fighting him. I will deal with this myself, OK?'

That night, as I lay in bed and relayed the whole conversation to Sean, I started to get mad myself. Maybe I *should* kill Percy?

'Sean,' I asked, staring into the darkness, 'would you kill him if I asked you to?'

'Do you want him dead? Could you live knowing that because of you he was dead?'

I paused.

'No.'

'Good, then you are a good person. You just need to work out how you want to deal with all this and I think you are doing well. I love you and am very proud of you, Janey.' He held me tight.

It had been difficult telling my family but, when I told Sean's dad, it was very easy and Old George was very succinct in his remedy:

'Fucking bastard! He needs his balls cut off and put in his mouth. That's whit they used to dae to perverts when I was young.'

'Well, George, I really don't know whit I want done, to be honest.'

That same week, I heard Granda Davy Percy had died. I never asked how, why or when. Someone told Sean, Sean told me, and my reaction was, 'Good. That's one more pervert in the ground.' I was angry more than anything. I felt I should have confronted him while he was alive. I told my brothers and sister I would not go to his funeral. My Dad agreed with me and stayed away from his ex-father-in-law's funeral. I don't know who went or what happened. I did not ask. I had other issues to deal with. Ashley was about to start school. There was a uniform to buy, school bag to be ordered, sportswear to collect and a new part of our life was about to start.

* * *

She looked lovely in her wee green blazer and smart hat, all set to become a schoolgirl. Her very first day reminded me of the day I started school. Ashley – like I had done 25 years before – was sitting up at 7.00 a.m. waiting patiently, all dressed, so excited, so ready to burst down the stairs and start a new life outside her home.

Paul, Sammy and Sarah all got up early and came down the landing stairwell to wave her off on her big day. I was as excited as Ashley. Sean was distraught: he vomited all night and was crying as he watched her run down the stairs in her outfit.

'I just can't bear to think she will be away every single day, Janey!'

'Daddy, come on, we will be late!' Ashley shouted from the bottom of the stairs.

Sean pulled himself together for her sake and we all set off in the blue delivery van we used for the pub. Ashley sat in the back seat laughing and chattering. No nerves at all.

'Play the Hoola Girls, Daddy, please?' she pleaded, patting the wee green pinafore on her knees. Sean pressed the tape deck and Ashley sang her heart out: her head bobbed along to the music as we travelled from the decaying old tenements of the East End to the tree-lined streets of the West End.

The school looked very imposing, a big terrace of Georgian mansions leading up to Glasgow University, as if that geographical path was a predestined choice for your own wee daughter. *You start down here and you end up there.* When we arrived, all the new mums and dads were negotiating the parking, getting used to the small streets, glancing at each other nervously, watching other wee girls holding on grimly to their mums' hands, people who we would get to know so well when our daughter shared the same class. Ashley ran from our grip and dashed up the short flight of stairs. She recognised Mrs Finley, the teacher she had met at an induction day the previous month.

'Hello! I am here,' Ashley said, stretching out her tiny palm to shake hands with the tall lady.

'Hello,' replied Mrs Finley in pink, with pearls and blue skirt, kneeling down.

'I am Ashley Storrie and I don't speak slang. Nice pearls. Where is my classroom, please?' She never even looked back at us to wave goodbye. Mrs Finley smiled to us as she led Ashley inside to hang up her blazer and start her first day. Sean and I stayed standing alone in the street, watching mothers and fathers say goodbye to sad children who did not want to be left there. We stood quietly, late autumn flowers still in bloom nodding their heads all along the railings that bordered the playground. We walked down the hill together. Sunshine beamed through rust and orange trees to give the West End of Glasgow a superior glow. Big tall town houses and massive mansions lined the back streets of Byres Road. Hippy coffee shops lined the main street next to upmarket book stores and music shops that specialised in finding the one song you thought everyone had forgotten about. This was an area where couscous and mung beans were organic, coffee was served in big steaming bowls and practically no one dressed in sportswear unless they were actually running through the park or on their way to play hockey. All I could think of that day was *This is where my daughter will grow up; this is where she will meet poets and educated people and folk who don't swear loudly and come from broken homes; this is where she will mix with people who are not like me.*

Ashley loved school immediately and seemed to make friends very easily; she was a real social butterfly. Every day she jumped from bed, ran into the living room to get ready and couldn't get to school quickly enough. The teachers were very pleased with her progress and made encouraging comments on her behaviour and attitude. They organised a special Concert Day to bring all the new parents and children together. Each child would sing one verse from a song of her choice and we would all gather round and have tea in the school hall beforehand and enjoy meeting other parents.

When the big day came, Sean and I hung around at the back; he had never been very good at meeting new people and preferred me to do the talking as always. Most of the parents were slightly older but lovely people and nice to meet. The concert started, the girls sang sweetly and we clapped along, watching proudly. When it was Ashley's turn to sing, she took a deep breath, started to stamp her feet, then smiled a big smile at me and belted out: *'We don't need no education.'*

I thought my toes were going to snap inside my shoes and my womb was going to fall out with embarrassment as she sang and sang. Ashley smiled after she finished, and announced very demurely, 'That was from my favourite album Pink Floyd's *The Wall*.'

The room was deathly quiet. Ashley continued smiling at me. No one reacted. Then the headmistress broke the silence by laughing really loud and shouted from the back, 'Well done, Ashley! Anarchy at five! You will make head girl!'

She was going to be fine at this school.

22
A scary fairground ride

The Weavers was working out fine too; customers were being loyal and we tried our best to make sure they were looked after. But Sean's health suddenly took a downturn and he started to get very weak again; I was worried he would have another brain haemorrhage. He had stopped eating and was sleeping too much during the day and never enough at night. The doctor sent him for more tests but nothing was found. He was already on constant medication from the last brain problem and his mood swings were becoming more difficult to deal with. He started shouting at me again. I would run out in the middle of the night, return in the morning, get Ashley to school and then open up the Weavers and pretend nothing had happened as Sean needed to sleep the day away and would not talk about what had happened last night.

We could keep up this charade as long as Ashley was not affected. When we were alone, we veered from love to hate and anger, from affection to spitting in each other's faces only to emerge smiling from the back shop to serve a customer. It was like a scary fairground ride that neither of us was willing to get off. I had married Sean when I was only 19; I had no idea how other people lived and loved. *Did they scream and rage? Did real love have to be this intense? Was I addicted to the drama?* I didn't know but, even when it all went smoothly, I would pick at him until he exploded – I would argue with him, shout at him, remind him what a bastard he had been, how he had hit me, how he had made my life difficult, how all my dreams had had to be put aside because his dad had a pub to run – I'd pick-pick-pick until ... Here we go again! He turned back into an angry polar bear and we hopped back on the fairground ride.

I cry.

He shouts.

I run.

He searches for me in the back streets around the pub.

I return in the morning.

He shouts.

He sleeps.

I open the Weavers.

That was my marriage. I made it like this or, at the very least, I accepted it. My own family was up in arms. I seemed to have a knack for upsetting everyone. I had talked openly about the abuse. My Aunt Rita was very disturbed. I was talking about her brother. She never actually said anything to me but she did go and see my sister. Ann and Aunt Rita were very close, much closer than Ann and I were. Aunt Rita asked outright if what everyone was saying was true. It must have been hard for Ann to tell her the truth, because Aunt Rita was a very sickly woman, always in and out of hospital with breathing problems, cystic fibrosis and lung disease. Ann later told me that, when she told Aunt Rita the truth about our past, the woman was distraught. I hated hurting everyone with this scabby knowledge. It was like I held a key to everyone's misery.

* * *

My brothers Mij and Vid also had to deal with the fall-out from our revelation. Both of them lived near Uncle David Percy and both had to face him either up at our dead grandfather's house or in the local pub. It caused particular problems for Vid, who had friends in the Orange Lodge and who hung out among Rangers football fans, usually including David Percy. Vid told me he avoided and never really confronted my Uncle, which was fine by me; I realised Vid was stuck in a difficult position, caught between his friends, his Protestant culture and his sisters' honour. Ann and I both made it clear to everyone we did not want violence or to be 'avenged' in any way. I told people we would deal with it in our way which, to be honest, was actually to do nothing, not even talking to each other again about what had been done to us when we were children. I felt Ann didn't need to know the details of what I had gone through and I didn't really need to face her story in depth. We both knew he had abused us and that was all we needed to support each other. But Ann attended a psychologist and I started group therapy.

My group unfortunately met in Kenmore Street – just yards from the house where it all happened. Having to deal with the location on top of the memories themselves upset me at the time, but the women in the group were amazing and we all pulled together. I did benefit from those therapy sessions; I felt better each time I left Shettleston and returned to my world back in the Calton.

Occasionally, on my way back down Kenmore Street, I would throw a glance up at my Mammy's old window, half-believing she might still be sitting there, blowing out her spindly smoke circles and gazing out towards the big gas tanks and Barlinnie High Security Prison and all the houses of High Carntyne. I wished she were still there for me to talk to. I could ask her so much, tell her so much, and hope that, this time, she could face the truth like her two daughters were now trying to.

23

Cleaver and Polis and pills

Sean and I had booked another holiday in Florida because, now that Ashley was older, she would enjoy the trip more. Sean was much easier-going during the trip and seemed to be enjoying himself. One night, we sat on a beach, Sean, Ashley and me, all curled up in a blanket inside a big blue cabana, watching the Florida sunset and, after darkness fell, Sean let Ashley get up and paddle in the moonlight.

'Daddy, come on! It's midnight swimming time!' she squealed as she ran splashing along the shoreline.

'She might die in there!' I yelled out – I could hardly see her in the darkness – She might fall in and drown – I ran down the beach – Searching through the darkness – I couldn't see her – I could hear the ocean – Not see it – I was scared.

But she *was* there, holding Sean's hands and tip-toeing through the surf, humming and singing:

She's gone with the Hoola Hoola boys ...

I could see Sean's wide smile: he was holding her hands, singing along and making his wee girl happy just by being there.

He made things easier for me at times; when I was confused and scared he could always calm me with his reassuring words. I had always believed in my heart he never really wanted to hurt me. I knew he loved me dearly. Yet he was the one person who did hurt me most. I had never really understand why he felt so destructive at times. Somehow the love we shared either ripped us apart or pulled us together.

'Janey,' he told me in Florida, 'never accept things you can't live with. I know I fucked you about. I'll never deny that.' He held my hand. 'One day you will know where you want to be and – if it is not with me – trust me, I will make it easy for you. I won't fuck you about any more.'

When Sean said those words to me, I remembered a regular in the Weavers who loved to play word games with me. He was very educated and loved crosswords. He worked at the new computer company across the road in the Templeton Business Centre. He sported long greasy hair, big goggly spectacles and clothes that implied he liked to dress in the dark at a jumble sale. He was the archetypal nutty professor.

'Janey, what word is spelt the same, sounds the same but has two opposite meanings?'

'Don't know, you tell me,' I replied, unsmiling, looking at a row of unwashed glasses.

'Cleave,' he announced smugly. 'It means to pull apart and to stick together.'

That single word described my relationship with Sean. We were 'cleaved'.

I wanted to love him without fear and look forward to a lifetime with a man who didn't scream at me and make me climb out of windows to escape his rage. I also wanted to hate him, but I had to keep reminding myself he was Ashley's daddy and I could no longer genuinely wish him dead because she would be fatherless. I knew I could not take her away from him and I knew I could not leave without her. *What point would my life have if I left my daughter?* So the bond between Sean and me became much stronger but much more volatile. I needed our relationship to work so that Ashley's mind would not be fucked up. I almost wished her life away; I would look at her and think: *Hurry up and be 16!* The minute she was 16, I would leave Sean; I would only be 40 – not a bad age. I had it all planned.

* * *

Ashley still loved her school and so did I. There, I was just Janey Storrie – I wasn't Sean Storrie's wife and that felt nice. Ashley made friends easily, felt secure in her world and was often invited to tea at other girls' homes, some of which were huge mansions with gravel paths and enormous gardens she could play in. It did make our pokey wee flat above the Weavers feel very inadequate. Ashley never mentioned if she felt overwhelmed by the superior financial status of her new friends though she spoke with pride of her pals' big cars and swimming pools in the garden. I worried we might not be good enough for her and became stressed in case Ashley would feel 'the poor girl' of the class, exactly as I had.

Fortunately, this never seemed to happen; she loved the world of the Weavers bar with the flats above and the garden on the roof. Although she lived in our flat, she had access to most of the other flats and rooms in the building. Her playroom – specially decorated for her – was actually in the flat next door to ours – a whole room next to Old Wullie's. We never kept the doors locked during the day and she would drag her toys back and forth all over the landing stairs which were very often carpeted in dolls, toy cars and tiny pots and cups. It became so bad I had to keep making sure she cleared part of the stairs in case someone stumbled over the toys when coming up or down. If the boys who lived upstairs came across her on the landing, they would be held emotional hostage. She was the only child in the building and she knew how to manipulate that situation to her advantage.

'Steve! Play with me for a wee while, please? I will be the teacher and you can be the good child who gets to read!' Before he could react, she would put a book in his hand. 'Please! You are my best pal! Please play for just this many minutes?' Her hand would hold up five chubby fingers and she would smile her biggest smile. 'Now sit down and I will get all the teddy bears and Mr Bovey the panda bear to listen to your wee story!' She would point to the old grey stone stair, smiling and pleading with her big eyes. 'Please?' Her world was full of obliging, happy people – young men who danced to her songs, read her books and swung her up high any time she asked.

* * *

Sammy had been her favourite uncle for the longest time but, lately, he had been avoiding her – in fact, avoiding all of us. He was hardly offering to work any shifts in the pub and any time I knocked on his door to see him, he made me feel like a stranger standing there. I was concerned as Sean and I had taken out the loan for him in our name to buy his car; he was paying it back as agreed but it seemed to be the only time we ever saw him. After a few weeks of this, Sammy came to us with news that he and Sarah would be moving out and going to live up in Coatbridge, 20 miles outside Glasgow. Sarah's family lived out that way and she seemed happy with the move. But I was very suspicious. Sammy did not get on well with Sarah's family and he had never seemed keen to move away before. When I pressed him for further details he just brushed me off.

'Sammy, whit the fuck is this all aboot?' I persisted. 'You belong here with us. Who the fuck do you know in Coatbridge?' I handed him a mug of tea, watching as he scooped the fat ceramic mug between both shaking hands to steady it.

'It's aboot nothing, Janey. I just feel like a wee change, ye know?'

He moved out the following week. It was all too fast for my liking; Sarah, too, was very evasive on details of where they were going; neither would tell us the actual address. Within weeks, Sammy's payments on the loan had become sporadic. It was unlike him and alarm bells immediately rang in my head. There was only one thing that would stop Sammy keeping up with his loan repayments and that was heroin.

One night, soon afterwards, he stood in my kitchen. He had always been skinny, but now he looked like every bone in his body could rattle against the others. His hands shook; his face looked in pain; he could not make eye contact with me; he stood shivering and uncharacteristically shouting. I had never heard Sammy shout in my life.

'I have no fucking money to eat!' he shouted at me. 'I am skint! I can't afford this fucking car!'

His hand clutched a wad of 30 £10 notes. He kept moving forward with the cash, as if to give it to me, but not actually letting go of it. His thin hand would hover over my pine kitchen table but never once did his bony fingers open enough to scatter the money onto the table top. He paced up and down the kitchen, shouting, 'Janey! I cannae pay ye!'

He suddenly stuffed the money into the pocket of his blue denim jeans. I reached out and grabbed him by the shoulders. He looked straight into my face. His eyes were cloudy, not the clear bright blue they used to be. I knew then. For certain.

'You are on smack, ya cunt!' I shouted. 'Fucking hell, Sammy! You! Why?'

'No I am no' Janey!' he spat out, wildly throwing his arms up and releasing himself from my grip. 'Ah promise, Janey. Fucking hell, I'm no' a junkie!'

'Ye fucking are, Sammy!' I shouted. 'Jesus! Fuck! Why? After everything you fucking know, *you* took smack?' I sat at the table and put my head in my hands. Sammy stood there, shivering, looking down at me. 'Take it, Sammy,' I told him, exhausted. 'Keep the money, but you will huv to explain to Sean why he will need to pay £300 this month oot of his own pocket for a car you own, not fucking him.'

Sammy did not move.

He slowly pulled the 30 £10 notes out of his pocket. I watched him as he held the bundle in his grip and then put it on the table. His eyes did not leave the brown notes. He turned his back on me, then actually ran out the door. My stomach lurched like a leapfrog game had taken place inside it. *Sammy was on smack.* I felt so fucking angry. His own denials, his anger and the look on his face as he screamed at me confirmed it all.

Sean took Sammy's fall from grace very well, considering he would now have to pay a lot of money for a car he didn't own and couldn't sell – Sammy had already done that the week before without telling us.

'Well,' Sean said. 'That's my fault for giving a loan to a junkie.'

'Fucksake,' I told him. 'You slapped me for not defrosting the fridge, ya weird bastard! Sammy fucks you for a couple of grand and you just shake yer head?'

Sean looked at me through narrowed eyes, reading a newspaper. I didn't really want him to hit Sammy, of course, but I never could understand why I always got the shit and no one else did even when they clearly deserved it. I felt overwhelmed by everything and deliberately started a fight with him.

'Sammy fucks us both for cash and you accept it! Your fucking family slag me off and you accept it! If *my* family hurt *you* that would be a different story, wouldn't it, ya fucker?' I ripped the newspaper from his hands and threw it on the floor.

Sean always ignored me when I went into a rant. He just picked up the newspaper, resumed reading it and smiled quietly, saying: 'Sammy *is* your family.' This calm pedantry really annoyed me. Sammy had taken Sean's side in so many arguments and situations that I had almost forgotten he was my cousin.

'Well, he has been here so long he behaves like a fucking Storrie!' I yelled. 'And you never asked me if we could lend him the cash! You just did it! You make all the decisions! I never get any say!' I grabbed the newspaper off him again and this time I ripped it up to make sure he couldn't read it. I grabbed his hair and pulled him off the chair onto the floor. I was so angry that he was just smiling and ignoring me. I needed a reaction. My left foot came up and kicked him in the head. I heard the thud as my foot made contact with his skull, breaking his spectacles which went flying off. He lay there, motionless, for a few seconds. I watched him move to get up and kicked him in the head again. Sean lunged forward and grabbed my leg as I threw another kick. He pulled it so hard I fell backwards onto the floor. He jumped over me and pinned me down with both his hands on my wrists. I was petrified; my heart thumped so loudly I could hardly hear him speak.

'Stop this, Janey! Don't become me! Don't fucking do this.' His eyes were pleading and full of tears.

I didn't understand what was happening; I wanted him to hit me then so I could run and he would feel bad and want me back, then we could all live like this till next time. *Isn't this how it works?* I thought. He let go of my wrists and lay on top of me on the floor and wrapped his arms around me. He was crying, his tears sticking to my neck.

'Don't, Janey. I love you. If you need to hit me, then we are both fucked.'

I lay there holding him.

We eventually got up and he sat holding my hands on the sofa.

'You were never the bitter and angry one, Janey; don't hate Sammy; he fucked up. I will pay for the loan, don't be like this.' He stroked my hands on his knee.

'Sean,' I blurted through tears, 'I feel so mental. All we do is fight or shout or have sex or scream then I leave and you plead then I come home and it all goes fucking round and round in circles ...'

Sean looked into my eyes and wiped my tears with his thumbs and said: 'I thought about us going for marriage guidance, what do you think?'

'Well, if it stops you hitting me, then I would be happy about it.' I tried to sound enthusiastic. I was worried Sean would never really open up with a stranger but, if he was the one to suggest it ... So Sean called the Marriage Guidance Council place in the city and we had an appointment set for the following week.

* * *

It turned out to be at Glasgow's Catholic Cathedral, an awesome Gothic spiral affair of a building that stands right beside the River Clyde. It made me feel that I had no right being grumpy with my husband in such a place. On the other hand, I felt it was all wrong to have marriage guidance there. As all Catholic priests are single, what the hell would they know about marriage? I felt they might even say my marriage was in tatters because I was not a Catholic – that if Sean had married a lovely Catholic girl, everything would have been fine. But, despite this constant nagging in my head, we walked together into a cosy wee room with cushions and sofas all arranged at what seemed like erratic angles. I stumbled and tripped over a footstool, landing on my palms. It was not a good start.

The walls were all rainbows, doves and hearts. This immediately set off warning bells. Anywhere that displayed a rainbow and a dove shouted shitey tokenism to me. Never in my entire marriage had the thought of a fucking rainbow or a white bird salved my pain. I was totally defensive. I decided I hated the marriage guidance man sitting there and hated Sean even more for suggesting coming to see some nutty Catholic who painted doves on the wall. I had wished a brain haemorrhage on this bastard and had actually got one to strike him down.

'Hello, my name is Harry,' the marriage guidance man said, smiling, friendly, patronising, reaching out and shaking my hand. It was a very soft grip and his palm was very dry and warm.

'I know you both need to do some talking, so I will sit here until you are comfortable enough to tell me what you feel.'

He spoke like a man who normally tells people they have cancer. His voice was immediately annoying. I sat there staring at my shoes. I gripped both hands together very tightly and felt the blood pulsating through my knuckles, trying hard to get some form of circulation going back into my fingertips. Sean did not speak. The man did not speak. Eventually, I felt it was up to me to fill the dead air and give Harry the juice he needed to get this show on the road. Without even knowing it was happening, my mouth went into full throttle.

'I married him when I was really young. I tried hard to be a good wife. I don't smoke. I don't drink. I don't fuck other men. He shouts at me, he makes me feel scared, he hits me, he never praises me, I work in his pub, yes it is *his* pub, I never even got asked if that was a job I wanted, I just did what I was told, I wanted to be an actress or an artist but, no, I wasn't given a choice, he told me to work in the bar and I did, I try hard to be patient but he makes me feel like shit, I was abused as a child and he made me feel bad about it as well, even though he was kind of supportive, I felt as though my family and my past were an inconvenience to him ...'

By this time I was on a roll. I took a deep breath and launched into what I can only describe as my 'Freedom' speech:

'I hate his family, they make me feel like I am some sort of freak, he lets them put me down, I would never let my family say a bad word about him, we have a daughter and she loves him and I would never turn her against him, but he can frighten her when he gets angry, she knows when to walk out of a room and occupy herself and keep out of his way and she is only six years old, he is like a petulant child and demands attention a lot and gets grumpy if he doesn't get sex on demand, I am tired and I have to work a lot, I starve myself coz he hates fat people, I wear the clothes he likes and I fucking hate myself for being what he likes and what I hate.'

I finally shut up. I kept my head down and stared intently at my shoes. They were black, leather and low heeled because Sean liked my shoes to be flat. I decided that, first thing tomorrow, I was going to buy my first pair of stiletto-heeled shoes. Then I remembered that I could not walk in high heels. Sean was going to be angry with me for saying all that stuff; I could feel his presence beside me. He was very still and quiet.

No one spoke.

The room felt very small.

Harry looked at me and finally said quietly, 'You do talk a lot, don't you?'

'Yes, well sometimes I get a bit carried away,' I replied. I spotted a wee scuff mark on my shoes where my big toes had been pressing against the leather from the inside. Then I thought, *Cheeky bastard! How dare he judge me? I was just trying to get it all out!*

'Maybe Sean would like to say something?' the cancer announcer intoned.

Sean looked at me and silently shook his head.

'He just shook his head at me,' I told Harry. 'That means I have to tell you he is not going to speak. He even gets me to communicate with other people for him.'

I sat back smugly now. Sean just looked at me. He slowly took off his glasses and put them on his knee and rubbed his eyes with his thumbs. I thought he was going to explode.

'Maybe you should stop speaking for him.' The patronising cardigan-wearing Catholic smiled at me. 'Maybe you overwhelm Sean; don't you think that may be a possibility?'

Sean leaned forward and looked Harry straight in the eyes.

'Actually, everything she says is right. I am a bastard. I make her sad and fuck up her life and maybe the best thing is to accept I did a lot of things wrong here?'

'Well, this is a good start,' said Harry. He was happy he had two puppets to play with now. He nodded and smiled and started to write stuff down in his wee book. This really annoyed me because he had never written down anything *I* said!

Then our appointment was over.

Sean and I walked straight out into the cold dark night.

'Fucking hell,' Sean laughed as he took my hand and walked me to the car park. 'That was weird, Janey. He was nutty, eh?'

'Sean, I meant all that stuff: you are so hard to live with an' I get scared you will just lose your temper and kill me.' I kept looking down at my feet as I walked; I was scared to break the spell. Sean was being so co-operative and honest.

'Janey, I would never kill you. I don't know why you think this.' He pulled me towards him and lifted my chin up as he spoke.

'My Mammy was killed,' I said. 'Killed by a man who frightened her, so it can happen, Sean.' I felt tears choking in my throat.

'Janey, I'm not him; I can't believe you think I would really hurt you. I don't mean to scare you like that; if *you* scream at *me* I don't get scared, so just laugh at me when you feel I am scaring you: it's your fault for letting me mean that much to you and getting into your head.' He cocked his head to the side and smiled.

'*My* fucking fault? It's *my* fucking fault *you* scare me? I *let* you scare me?' I was now shouting at him in the cathedral car park. 'How the fuck did *that* happen, Sean? I let you scare me? Fuck you, ya arse! Take yer holy fucking Catholic weird therapy and your blame theory and stick it up yer retarded arse!' I stomped off into the dark. I started to run. Now I remembered why I always wore flat shoes: it was because I could run faster in them. I ran all the way down to the side of the Clyde. *MY fault? Everything MY fault?* Thoughts and anger just ran out of control inside my head. *I must be stupid and shite at everything ... I let him scare me ... I did all this.* I was out of breath and my breathing was clouding up in front of me in the cold air, as I walked fast along the grass verge that ran alongside the wall that stopped people from falling into the river. Wee drunk men sat on the ornate benches that were built for tourists back in the City of Culture year. I was muttering under my breath, swearing and grinding my teeth.

A voice shouted out: 'Men are all cunts!'

I looked round. An old drunk man wearing a black coat over at least three jackets, smiled at me and held up his can of lager. His smile was wide; he had teeth that looked like a row of condemned buildings.

I smiled back and shouted: 'Yeah, they're bastards and *fucking* cunts!'

Sean was at the end of the walkway. I ignored him, continued towards the car and took my place in the front seat. I wanted to go home. He got into the driver's seat and tried to hold my hand; I just gripped my fingers into a ball and made him hold the stump of a fist.

* * *

After this episode at the cathedral, Sean decided to consider my opinions more.

'I am sorry I never asked you if you wanted to be a

barmaid, Janey,' he said. 'No one asked me if I wanted to be a barman, you know. Anyway I think we should buy the whole business. It will be security for Ashley in the future – and for us. What do you think?'

'What do you want me to think? If you think this is the best way to spend and invest our savings then I agree.' I smiled blankly at him. I was planning to run away when Ashley was 16. I didn't really care what he did.

Sean and Old George decided to draw up a contract through which Sean and I would buy the building and flats above. We had proved we could run it successfully. We already owned our flat so we just had to buy the other eight and the pub. So, one day soon afterwards, Sean sat with Old George and the Storrie family lawyer Mr Bovey making plans and working out prices. I, of course, made tea for the men. After a long day of paper shuffling and teacups it was all settled – Sean and I would be buying the whole place. I was not told the total price nor the method of payment. I don't think any of Sean's brothers were told we were buying the building; that was the Storrie way – nobody should know anything unless they had to.

We celebrated by going to an upmarket hotel for the night. Ashley stayed with my Dad. Sean and I were booked into the same suite Michael Jackson had stayed in a year before. The bedroom was huge with a big four-poster in the middle; the bathroom housed a huge Victorian bath with claw feet which took up most of the white-tiled room. We had a great time, dinner was fantastic and we went to bed and booked breakfast in our room for the next morning. As I lay there that night and watched Sean's face, I wished I could sleep that peacefully. I still had my nightmares most nights. Dark corners in my head, evil demons chasing me, sniggering at my attempts to wake myself up to escape their pointy-nailed clutches. *Wake up, Janey! Wake up, Janey!* I would whisper like a mantra in my head as I ran naked, slipping on blood-drenched cobblestones along streets I had never seen before, unsure of who was chasing me but knowing I had to keep running. Cold winds would slap my exposed breasts as I tried to cover my lower body with my hands and blood flowed through the gaps between my fingers. I can't see where I am bleeding from, but pain sears through my head and sweat drips from my body as I fight with cotton sheets in a struggle to tell the difference between sleep and real life.

Sean lay there, his dark lashes resting on his cheeks, brown hair flopping on the white cotton pillow and his mouth reminding me of Ashley when she had her cheeky face on. I got up out of bed and walked to the bathroom, filled the huge bathtub with hot, steaming water and a luxurious bubble bath. The smell and steam relaxed me. I lay there in the depths of warmth, listening to Hall and Oates and Prince on my Sony Walkman, being careful not to get the headphones wet.

I loved it when Sean treated me like this and, lying there in that bath, I half believed he would look after me like this for ever. Maybe. If things got better I would not have to leave him when Ashley was 16. Maybe by then it would all be OK. I lay and wondered how the Weavers would look in ten years' time. *Would I still be there? Would Sean still be chasing me barefoot?*

Later that morning, just after breakfast, Sean and I sat and read the newspapers. I opened up the *Glasgow Herald* and read an article about a woman who had been sexually abused as a child; she had her face blanked out in the newspaper to protect her identity, but she told of how her family and neighbours were angry at her for speaking out. I was enraged. *Why was her face blacked out? What had she done wrong?* This kind of article annoyed me because it re-inforced all those beliefs that to be abused means you should be ashamed. I called the journalist, Maggie Barry, at the *Glasgow Evening Times* (sister paper to the *Herald*) and told her how I was angry at the whole piece, that people should not black out their face as if they had to be ashamed of their past. It was not them who should be ashamed but the abusers. She listened to me, then suggested that I help her write my story with my face exposed and tell how I felt about the issue of the 'shame' of sex abuse. I stopped for a second and thought about what I was actually doing, then agreed she could come and meet me. I was ready to talk about it openly and be damned anyone who was not ready to talk about it. Sean and Ashley were supportive. Ashley was just a child but her feelings were important as well.

Maggie Barry came to meet me and brought along as her photographer Ray Beltrami, my old mate who used to drink at the Weavers.

'Janey, Ray can sit in the kitchen and you can tell me everything,' Maggie explained.

'No way,' said Ray, clutching his camera and sitting down. 'Why did you no' tell me, Janey? I never knew all this happened to you. I want to sit here with you.'

I told Maggie everything I could – the whole story. She explained that I could not name my Uncle because he had not been charged with the offence but, if I charged him, I could mention him by name.

'But it's too late to charge him now, that's the problem,' I said.

'It's not too late. There's no limitation. If you and your sister go speak to the police then they can decide if there's enough evidence to bring charges.'

I was stunned. It had never entered my head I could still report it.

I read Maggie's article before it went to press and it was ambiguous about who the abuser was. I was worried that my lovely old Uncle John would be suspected as the culprit, because he never married and was childless. He was very ill in the Royal Infirmary at the time, so I made sure Maggie Barry added in that my abuser had children and was married. I also mentioned in the article that when I told my Uncle John about my abuse he was horrified, which would further clear his name.

On the day before the article was to be printed, I was at the *Glasgow Evening Times* building checking over my picture and discussing the piece when I suddenly felt this overwhelming need to go to the hospital and see Uncle John. I ran out of the building. The Royal Infirmary was only minutes away on foot, but I spotted an old mate of mine in his car. I ran across, opened his door and shouted above his music:

'Thomas, can you drive me up to the Royal?'

'No worries, Janey!' he shouted, then turned his Irish rebel songs down to a minimum and drove up the hill towards the hospital.

I ran through the main building and up the red staircase; I knew Uncle John's ward was on the third floor; I had a terrible feeling of impending doom; I had to get there now! I was breathless when I finally reached his bedside. The curtains were pulled right around the bed and my heart lurched.

'Don't be too long with him – he is very tired,' a nurse said, swishing the flowery curtain back to reveal an old man looking very small and childlike with a white sheet tucked under his chin. I was shocked. He looked very ill and slightly dazed. My Uncle John had been a big man with a sparkly character; he was famous for his witty asides and funny anecdotes. The man in the bed had a skinny wee body with parchment skin and scared eyes. *When did he get this ill? Did I not visit him enough?* Immediately I felt guilty and selfish.

'It's me, Uncle John – Janey,' I whispered near his face. 'I am getting the article published about Uncle David Percy tomorrow.'

'Nail him, Janey,' he said. His voice was weak. 'Don't let him get away with it and make sure the papers know how I feel about that bastard, though I might no' be here to read it, hen.'

I sat and watched him for a while. He was shivering; I leaned over and tucked the covers around him. His pale face turned to me; his big brown eyes followed me as I walked around the bed and patted the covers over his bony body. Uncle John was never one for hugs or affection, but I did love him so much. He had always been there in my life when I was a wee kid and would visit often when I had the Weavers. I reached over and held his hand. He let me do this without any fuss.

'I am scared, Janey,' was all he said.

I felt my throat choke as a lump of emotion suffocated my words: 'I love you, Uncle John.'

'That's good, hen,' he replied.

'You have to leave now,' the nurse's voice interrupted. 'He is due a test.'

'I will see you soon, eh?' I tried to smile to him.

'You keep your head up, hen, an' never let anyone get ye doon. Yer a Currie, remember?' He smiled as he let my hand go.

I looked back at him and, as I walked towards the door, he smiled and lifted his bony hand up to wave at me. That was the last time I saw him: he died later that day when my brother Vid was visiting him.

Before I even got time to deal with his death, the newspaper article was published. There, for all to see, was a big colour picture of me wearing a smile and a pink jumper declaring my abuse to the world. My immediate family already knew the whole truth; now everyone else would. I felt terrible about losing my Uncle John and Dad was in a terrible state about his death. He didn't care about the article. He had always told me:

'If ye want to dae anything, Janey, just dae it.'

I had to carry on working in the Weavers as usual. That afternoon brought in my regular old men who sat in the corner, drank their drinks and went home at teatime, just like normal. But this day was different. One old man, Jack, who normally mumbled his order and shouted at me if I played the jukebox too loud, actually leaned over the bar, took my hand and smiled at me.

'Ye were very brave to talk about your past. Lots of us just keep oor heeds doon and get on wi' life. Good on ye, hen.' His old hand trembled with emotion as he held onto mine. Jack had eyelids that were so slack you could see the red rims at the bottom of each milky eyeball; the smell of drink and piss on him had often appalled me, yet never once did I think he might have been a small boy who had been sexually abused. I always forgot men were abused as well as girls.

'Thanks, Jack.' I gripped his veined hand tight and gave him my biggest smile.

My brother Vid came to see me that same afternoon and told me that he had gone up to my dead Granda Davy Percy's flat where he suspected my Uncle had been staying. When he went into the flat, the *Glasgow Evening Times* was lying spread on the floor with the picture of me staring out. The electric fire was warm but nobody was there.

'It was like the *Marie Celeste*,' he told me.

My Uncle David Percy was nowhere to be found. Vid had checked around with my Uncle's friends and it seemed he had gone down to England to 'visit some old friends'. He had been separated from his wife by this time and had taken up with another woman, but she said she didn't know where he was either. I decided that I wanted to get him reported to the police, so I went to see my sister.

Ann was still a mess. She was trying hard to hold her life together. Her husband Brian was a rock to her. He was a great guy, hard working and lovable. He helped bring up Ann's two kids from her previous marriage and the two wee baby girls they had from their own union. I knew that dragging up all this pain about our past and her having to deal with Uncle John's death was dragging her down. She had looked after Uncle John; going over to his flat daily to cook and clean for him before he went into hospital. I knew she had been on anti-depressants for about two or three years and was getting therapy, and I was loath to add to this burden, but I wanted to report it all to the police for my own sanity and to get closure.

'Janey, whit if naeone believes us?' Ann pleaded, wringing her hands around a towel she was hanging up in her kitchen.

'Well, we can only tell the truth. I want to dae this and I need to know if you do as well. I cannae talk ye intae it, Ann. It has to be your decision.' I stood looking as her wee girl held onto her skirt. She agreed with me that we needed some closure and this was the best way to deal with it. So I called the London Road Police Office and arranged an appointment with the Female and Child Unit.

When I arrived with Sean at the square grey concrete building, I started to shake with fear. I remembered the night I had been here with Old George when Paul had been involved in the glue-sniffing trial. I did not like the police from experience and Sean disliked them by genetics.

'Janey Storrie! In here, please,' a smartly dressed, slim policewoman commanded me. When I walked into the back office with Sean, I was taken aback that it was a male detective I was sitting opposite. I had expected to be seen by a woman.

'Hello Sean,' the man said, 'I am Detective Jarvis, I know yer dad well.' He reached over and shook Sean's hand. 'And you must be Janey.' He smiled, shaking my hand almost as an afterthought. 'Tell me what's been happening, Janey – and take your time, please.' He looked down at a piece of paper and poised his pen above it to write his report.

I slowly told him about my childhood, where I was born and what happened. He interjected occasionally, asking me to confirm names of brothers and uncles and who stayed where and who was in the house and what age I was at the time. The interview seemed to take forever with his constant interruptions. My brain felt ragged with the constant need for age reference and school times and where my Dad was and where my Mammy was and why had I taken so long to report this story and did I know the legal ramifications of my statement. It went on and on. He took his time, making sure he got all the facts, and pressed me to tell in detail the actual sexual nature of the attacks. I did feel very uncomfortable although he was very reassuring throughout it all. Sean would look over from time to time and hold my hand. The office was painted that typically horrible pale Police Office green though, on one wall, cheap wood panelling seemed to have taken over. I secretly wondered if Old George had sold them that very familiar fake wood panelling.

Eventually, the detective closed the file and smiled at me: 'The bottom line is, Janey, we now send all this to the Procurator Fiscal along with your sister's statement and we wait to see what happens then. You did very well, Janey, this must be really hard for you.'

He turned to Sean and asked, 'Will this man ever get to court or will he be found dead before the trial?' He asked the question in a jokey tone of voice but one that implied that, if it was taken seriously, that was fine too.

Sean spoke very quietly but stony-faced: 'Janey and her sister need to get this out of their system and my family don't do violence.'

The detective smiled.

'Why would we want him dead?' Sean asked.

The detective nodded his head. 'OK, then, as long as we know where we all stand.'

Old George came down to the Weavers for a quick visit after having been at a car auction. He was looking smart in a new blue shirt, smiling with Sandra at his side. She was playing the attentive girlfriend, brushing imaginary dandruff off his shoulder, her blonde dry hair pulled up into a severe pony-tail, highlighting her pale pinched face. Old George asked me to make some coffee for him and stood quietly as I stirred it for him. I knew he wanted to say something by the look on his face.

'Did you make a statement at the Polis Office aboot yer uncle?' he finally asked.

'Yep,' I said and carried on stirring his coffee on the bar.

'Why did you do that?' he spat at me angrily. 'We don't go to the Polis, Janey!'

I looked him square in the face and replied: 'We? Who the fuck is We? We were not raped, George. I was. Me. Not you. Not we. Me. And I want to deal with this my way. I don't want him beaten by anyone. I don't want him killed. I want to see him in court so everyone knows what he did to me and my sister.' I did not want the men to solve this problem for me; this was something I had to do myself.

'That's all very well,' George said, 'but I am not so fucking sure I like the Storrie name in the newspapers as a victim of anything. We don't huv victims in our family.'

Sandra leaned forward and spoke in a hushed tone. 'I wiz sexually abused as a child and I don't go shouting aboot it to everyone and I'm fine.'

'Really?' I snarled at her. 'You consider yourself to be fine, do ye?' George shot me a dark, warning look which I ignored. 'Maybe the next time ye have to spend time in a mental ward ye should remind yourself ye are so fucking OK!' I told her. I knew this was cruel, as she was continually in and out of the mental health care system due to her depression, but I was not about to be placated by her advice on sexual abuse. 'George,' I told him, 'the first chance I get, I will change my name so it's not Storrie any mare. And, in case ye huvnae noticed, this is aboot me and no' aboot yer precious fucking fucked-up family!' I slammed the coffee down in front of him and walked to the other end of the bar.

I didn't care if he jumped the bar and strangled me; I was determined to keep focused on the main issue. It was enough to be up against the abuser himself without being sabotaged by people who just didn't like the police or a little spot of publicity. And Sean backed me all the way. He was happy I was doing what I wanted to do. He was so moved by the whole issue that he volunteered his services to the local Victim Support Group and was given training on his afternoons off. He enjoyed the work, threw himself into the whole scheme and was happy taking part in something he felt gave real help. Things between us were slowly getting better again. Despite our one attempt at marriage guidance, we managed to resolve issues between ourselves. I still was scared when he got angry, but not as scared. I had decided inside myself that I definitely would leave when Ashley was 16 and up till then he could do all the shouting he wanted. If he hit me, I would take him to court as well. I was not about to be bullied again.

That New Year brought the best news I had heard in a long time. The police let me know the Procurator Fiscal had decided that, on the basis of the statements my sister and I had provided, there was certainly enough evidence to have my Uncle charged. The only problem was that the police could not find him.

* * *

By now it was early January and I stared through those big windows at the front of the Weavers, looking at the beautiful mosaic on the side of the old factory opposite; the spirals and majestic turrets of that building always cheered me up. It made me wonder if I would ever get to Venice and see the real Doges' Palace, not a replica on an old carpet factory in Glasgow. The frost and snow capped all the trees that lined Glasgow Green, making the place look like a wee Christmas card. I loved that view. Ashley was out playing happily in the snow, rolling big snowballs down the wee hill opposite the Weavers. I went out to keep her company and met a young man who was walking his two wee terriers. We got chatting and I told Colin to come into the pub for a beer and to bring the dogs that Ashley seemed to have adopted within minutes of meeting them. Before long he was a regular and brought over his partner.

Colin and Andrew were a lovely gay couple who had moved into the Barratt homes across the road. Colin worked as a wigmaker and hairdresser for theatrical productions; Andrew worked in an upmarket Glasgow city-centre restaurant. They had initially been a bit worried about coming over to drink in a 'rough' East End bar – the Calton tolerated prostitutes but not so many homosexuals except Gay Gordon, who was still a Weavers regular, drinking more and more, getting more and more bitter, going downhill fast. After one visit, Colin and Andrew became regulars too. I loved Colin's wicked sense of humour: the sarcastic, scathing remarks that he whispered under his breath about locals had me pissing myself laughing.

'Oh my gawd!' he'd say, combing his cream wig. 'Why that woman thinks acrylic dresses covered in flowers is cool I will never know; she is the reason men fuck other men!'

He stood nearly six feet tall, with blond spiky hair, and was always dressed in the latest outfits to hit Glasgow's fashionable expensive designer shops. He was really very kind and he loved hanging out in the bar; his partner Andrew was very hard working but more subdued. One night, they took me out to a gay club and introduced me to all their friends. I loved the whole gay scene. The music and the guys all hanging out having a laugh and being very risqué suited me. One of their gang was Findlay, a tall, brown-haired, big smiler, who was outrageously funny and was just about to go off to work in one of Conran's new restaurants in London. He and I hit it off straight away. He spent his last six months in Glasgow hanging out in the Weavers and made good friends with Ashley. He could hardly believe she was so up to speed on the whole gay attitude even at seven.

'Do you have a boyfriend, Findlay?' she asked him within minutes of meeting him. 'Do you like Doris Day?'

I explained she had been looked after by Gay Gordon, our customer and friend. She regaled Findlay with all the gay torch songs Gordon had taught her. Findlay was fun to be around and I enjoyed going out with him and the boys. But I missed one old friend. Sammy had not come down for Christmas and this was hard for me. We had always got together at Christmas. Ashley missed him as well. His new flat was not that far away – only half an hour. He could have paid us a visit, but I supposed the cash situation made it all worse. He had given Sean a few payments for the car despite the hardship that came with it but, because he owed us so much money and was on heroin, he could not bring himself to visit us socially. Whenever I saw him, his face was severely drawn and gaunt. Whenever he made a sporadic payment, he never spoke to us. He simply walked in, held out an envelope to Sean, then left. It still hurt me. I wanted to sort out his life, maybe stop him from taking heroin. But I knew that was stupid thinking.

My brother Mij had now been HIV positive for over five years and was still on smack, though his health was on a fairly even keel. Ashley was still very fond of him. He was still childlike and funny and played card games and magic tricks and kept her imagination fired up with his crazy stories of how he had fought that big shark in Shettleston swimming pool. I let Mij know I was charging Uncle David Percy with the abuse. He was all for it and reassured me that, if I needed him to back me up, he would say anything to the police.

'Mij,' I told him, 'you didnae *know* anything. You spent the best part of the seventies believing you were Bryan Ferry and were a man who fought with a shark, so for fucksake the last thing I need is for you to lie on oath. I have Ann to tell the truth and me to tell the truth. I don't want you to add lies to this story, OK?'

'OK sis,' he said. 'But I want ye tae know I am proud of ye.' He put his thin arms around me and held me.

Sean's brothers were another matter. Young George had taken to calling me 'Oprah' in honour of the American talk-show host who often highlighted sexual abuse cases on her show. Dick went one step further and, in the middle of another one of his pointless arguments, declared, 'You wur no' a virgin when ye married Sean. Ye hud slept wi' another man; ye lost yer virginity tae yer Uncle!' Then he laughed loudly through his gums.

* * *

There was good news, too. Ashley told us that her school was holding auditions for a London production company and she wanted our permission to take part. Of course, we allowed her to go and only found out later that week that the auditions were for a Fairy Ultra soap powder ad directed by Ken Loach. As a teenager, I had loved his film *Kes:* it was one of my all-time favourite movies and, by the end of the week, we were told that Ashley got the part. I was so proud and could not wait to tell the family and all the customers. Everyone was well chuffed. Even Old George gave her a big hug at the news.

'You are gonnae be a big star, Ashley Storrie!' he said, swinging her up high as she ran into his arms.

'Grandad! I am going to be on television and then you can see me all the time!' Ashley told him, her eyes wide with excitement.

We were all really excited and Sean, Ashley and I were flown to London for four days and collected at the airport by a big fancy car. We were taken to a hotel near Hampton Court Palace and met the other cast member. This was a young Glaswegian woman who was to play Ashley's 'mum' in the advertisement. Ken Loach came to the hotel and gave Ashley an idea of what was to happen the next day on set. She was up bright and early the next morning and was introduced to all the crew and shown around the big house at East Molesey, near Hampton Court Palace, that was to become her 'home' for the shoot. Sean and I sat in a burning hot sunny garden watching the action on one of the monitors.

She spoke her script to camera: 'Mummy! Daniel dirtied my T-shirt!' and, every time she said 'Mummy' to the actress, I felt weird inside.

Ashley was told to improvise her reaction to situations that Ken set up for her. For one, she was taken up to the top of the stairs in the hallway of the house. Ken threw blackcurrant juice onto her T-shirt and said, 'What do you think has happened to you, Ashley?'

She stood, looked down at the big red stain spreading all over her white top, spread her arms out wide and shouted: 'I have been stabbed!' Sean and I burst out laughing; the crew all giggled and Ken came back into shot to explain more about what he was expecting her to say about getting her clothes dirty for the Fairy Ultra ad.

At the end of the four days' filming, just as we were leaving, Ken took Ashley aside on the pavement. He knelt down and spoke quietly to her. I could see her nodding, chatting and smiling as he talked. She hugged him quickly and ran towards us, shouting her goodbyes to him.

'What did Mr Loach say to you?' I asked as she climbed into the car that was taking us to the airport.

'He told me to be a wee girl again and that making

films is all silly nonsense.' She looked at me, smiling. 'Then I told him I was going to be a movie star when I grow up and he said I have to get an education in case it all works out differently and I said that's nice but I am going to be a movie star and he said that was good, but educated movie stars are always much better.'

I laughed as the car drove off towards Heathrow Airport, but Ken had no need to worry: we were going to make sure her education always came first. When we got home, we also had to make arrangements for her first Holy Communion. Because her school was Non-Denominational Christian and not specifically Catholic, we had to do this independently. The nearest Catholic church was Glasgow RC Cathedral down on Clydeside, where we had been for marriage guidance: it had a beautiful Gothic chapel with awesome stained glass and wonderful wooden and stone carved interiors.

Ashley had never really attended church much. Some Sundays one of the Catholic regulars from the bar would take her to Mass. I had once taken her to a chapel; she had walked all around the Stations of the Cross with the young priest then, after slowly looking at images of Christ dying all around the room, she turned to the priest and asked, 'Don't you have any pictures of him having a happy picnic with his daddy?'

* * *

One night, shortly after Ashley's Holy Communion, Sean and I had an argument. I walked out and came back an hour later then went to bed in a huff, leaving Sean in the living room and Ashley sleeping in her bedroom. About another hour later, I got up. Sean was still in the living room, just sitting staring into space.

'What's wrong with you?' I asked, then noticed what was lying on the table beside him. 'Have you taken tablets again?'

'I really do want to die, Janey,' he replied. 'I'm never going to be the right man. I'm always going to be bad. I did everything wrong. I'm a bad man. I am really bad. A bad man.'

Sammy was in the building, so I ran and got him.

'Sean's taken something,' I said.

Sammy took him to the hospital while I found someone to look after Ashley. They kept Sean in for two days. He just kept repeating he was bad and wrong and depressed and wanted to die.

24

Running out of time

I had decided to start running to keep fit. All my adult life had been spent being on one diet after another. I was never terribly overweight but I wanted to be skinny. I would get a pang of jealousy when Sean looked at the long skinny limbs of the young women who drank in the bar and I wanted to be like them. How I wished I was tall and slim; unfortunately I stayed small, dark and curvy. No matter how much weight I lost, my breasts refused to diminish in size. So I started running. I ran every night for six weeks until I was doing four miles a day. Sean encouraged me all the way. He took me out shopping to get running shoes and even backed me up when I enrolled in an expensive gym. I started to get really fit and healthy. I loved the feeling and energy that I had gained since I started my regime. It also gave me an immense confidence boost. My hair was shiny, my legs were toned and I looked better in my clothes. Life was looking up. Sean and I were getting along fine and the money was being paid to Old George for the building. I never took much notice of the fine details and left all that to Sean. He seemed to be in control again.

Then, one night, Sean and I were woken up by fire engines' sirens screaming through the streets and we saw flames across on the other side of the London Road. I jumped up, pulled on my housecoat, ran down all the stairs and fled across the busy main road. There on the pavement was blind Jonah, standing in his bare feet and underwear, looking shocked and disorientated, his right hand raised, trying to find something to hold onto to give him stability. His partner Jackie was standing beside him, shivering in a coat over her underwear, holding their wee baby Cheryl in her arms. The only neighbours who offered any help were Colin and Andrew who, just as I approached, ran down and wrapped them up in blankets from their bedroom.

'Fucksake, Jonah,' I asked. 'What happened?' I tried to lift baby Cheryl from Jackie's arms but she was scared and held onto her mother tighter.

'I think it was an electrical thing,' Jonah mumbled. 'I could smell it fucking burning, Janey. Jackie wouldn't listen to me. Aw day I huv been telling her I could smell it.'

'Yeah. He *did* say that, he *did*,' was all Jackie could say, shocked.

Sean and I led them across the busy main road to our flat. Behind us, Jonah's flat still belched smoke and flames from every window. We took them up to our flat that night. Jonah sat in my living-room chair, smoking and drinking tea until morning came, then an ambulance took him to hospital for observation. Local people claimed his house had been firebombed but I think, if it had been, the whole block would have gone up in flames.

* * *

By now, yet another Christmas was approaching and I realised another year had passed so quickly. Sean went to the hospital for one of his regular check-ups because of his diabetes insipidus. That night, he told me, 'I saw my dad today at the hospital; I saw him walk from his car at the car park.'

'What was he there fur; did ye ask him?'

'No he was a bit away and I just watched him go into the main building at the hospital. Must be his diabetes, I suppose. But I kinda wished I had caught up with him and spoke to him.'

I pulled out my running shoes and lay them on the floor for the morning.

'Well Sean, call him now; it might make ye feel better.'

He looked at me as he took off his glasses and rubbed his eyes. I had watched him do this so many times; it had become a ritual that, when he was worried or stressed, I would wait for him to pull off the spectacles and rub his eyelids with his thumb and forefinger.

'I did call him, but Sandra said he wasn't there. I asked why he was at the infirmary today and she just hung up on me.' Sean stared at the floor and added, 'He called me yesterday and told me to keep an eye on Old Wullie as he wasn't very well.'

'What's wrong with Old Wullie then?' I asked.

Sean sat staring, still fiddling with his glasses. 'He looks ill, Janey. I did call the doctor and it's his blood pressure, but he just keeps on smoking and drinking.'

'He does look more and more like *The Ribena Man*,' I agreed. 'He is almost bright purple at times: that cannae be a good thing, Sean.'

Old Wullie's room and Ashley's playroom were next door to our flat. I often heard her chatting to him as he went in and out with his big blonde Alsatian dog Sara. I shook my head remembering the state the old man got himself into recently, climbing just the one flight of stairs to his flat.

Over the following two days, Sean became more and more worried about his father. Despite calling four times a day, there was no answer or explanation from Sandra as to where Old George had gone. Sean eventually called his brother Philip to be told bluntly that their father had gone into the Royal Infirmary on the day Sean saw him – for a major heart bypass operation. The operation had gone fine but Old George had had a major stroke during recovery and was now lying very ill at the infirmary. No one outside the immediate family was to know: 'Absolutely no one,' Philip impressed on Sean. That same night, all the other Storrie sons were informed of the situation. We did not tell Ashley or any of my family. I suggested that maybe Old George's old flame Patsy Paton should be told or even some of Old George's brothers or wider family. If he was very ill then this might be their only chance to see him again alive.

'No, Janey, tell no one,' Sean shouted at me. 'OK? No one!' He went to visit his dad that night. When he came home he was very pale and drawn.

'Janey, he is incapable of communicating. He looks angry and frustrated just sitting there, but the doctors say he can make progress with the right treatment.'

I could see the fear in Sean's eyes. My heart lurched, I felt dreadful for him, for Ashley, for his six brothers and for all the other children in this big fragmented family. They were all held together by Old George. The brothers had never really got on; their father bound them all together like human duct tape. *If he goes, God knows what will happen*, I thought.

It was a nightmare trying to remain calm and focused on the bar while worrying sick about Sean's father. As it stood, we were told that only his family could visit him. I assumed that meant only his sons, not me, and was annoyed when I discovered that Sandra and other daughters-in-law had been to the hospital but I was not allowed.

I accepted that Old George had never really liked me much, but I had never heard him say many nice things about his other daughters-in-law either. When I thought about it, though, I didn't really want to visit him: the thought of seeing Old George incapacitated actually scared me. I had always known him as this big strong man who took control of any conversation and every situation. But I couldn't understand the need for secrecy. If my father had been ill in hospital, I would have had no problem telling his close circle of friends. Perhaps it was to prevent anyone knowing George and his family were terribly vulnerable. I tried to talk to Sean about it: 'What if he stays in hospital for a long time recovering from the stroke? What will you tell people to cover up his absence?'

'Shut the fuck up, Janey. He will recover. He looks better every day. He can move his fingers now,' Sean told me, pulling off his glasses and rubbing his eyes.

I had to carry on getting ready for Christmas. Ashley had written a letter to Santa asking for a train set and it was now my job to buy and assemble the thing. I decided to set it up in her playroom on Christmas Eve. That way, she could keep it on the big board it was fixed to and play with it at her leisure. Meanwhile, Old George was into his second week of intensive care and Old Wullie was getting sicker. He had never liked anyone coming into his room and I respected his privacy.

'Wullie, d'ye want me to take the dug a walk?' I would shout through his door.

'Naw, ahm fine!' he would shout back, then his whole body would break into a deep hacking cough. I would stand there and wait for the coughing to subside then shout again:

'Wullie! It's Janey! D'ye need anything?'

'Naw! I will put yer pot ootside the door later. The mince wiz shite – even the dug didnae like it!' he would growl from what used to be my living room when I first moved into the building 13 years before. I would stand out there in the hall laughing: he was a cantankerous old bastard who loved getting a dig at me.

'OK, ya ungrateful old fucker!' I'd yell. 'Let me know if ye need anything. I will be next door an' ye know the doors are always open!'

Sean was barely holding it all together; he became more distraught each time he visited his father. Old George was not progressing enough to even contemplate coming home for Christmas. The other brothers were getting increasingly annoyed at Young George and Sandra's closeness; everyone knew Sandra had been Young George's girlfriend for years before his father took over the saddle; they suspected that they might be 'seeing' each other again.

I just kept running. Each morning, I would pull on my running shoes and pound along the Glasgow Green, down towards the River Clyde. The Christmastime cold would shock my lungs as I started into the run, I would dodge the traffic and run across the Salt Market and make my way down the Clydeside walkway to run along the hard cobbles that lined the dockside all the way beside the river to the Glasgow Exhibition Centre. There I would take off my backpack and go into the Moat House Hotel and swim for an hour before I headed back towards the Weavers in my running shoes. This kept me focused and busy. I loved running and it really did help me beat the stress.

I was also trying to keep Ashley's spirits buoyed up. She was now aware something was happening in the family but I could not tell her that Grandad George was ill as she might tell someone else by accident. I told her that Grandad

George was away at his caravan at Wemyss Bay on the Firth of Clyde and would be back home after Christmas. She seemed to accept this, but became very clingy to her dad. Each night she would sit on his knee till she slept. Sean would sit there and hold her in silence. It was as if they were both comforting each other without knowing why.

When Sammy came over to see us, Sean did tell him about Old George's illness. He sat in my kitchen and hung his head in silence. Sammy had always called Old George his uncle and Old George was fond of Sammy. He looked on him as one of his family and he knew that his son Paul and Sammy were very close as they had lived and worked together for so long with Sean and me. I felt awful for Sammy and, despite the grief he was giving me, I hated knowing he was in pain.

The Weavers was fully decorated for Christmas and the old tree dressed with all the old familiar ornaments. Sean was on a huge emotional rollercoaster. He was happy with his dad's progress one day and shocked to the core the next. I was also getting more concerned about Old Wullie; he was very quiet and hadn't shown his face for a few days. I would regularly bang on his door.

'Wullie? Ye OK?'

If there was no answer, it would scare me because I knew he hadn't left the building – I would have heard the dog bark as he went downstairs.

'Wullie! Are ye OK?' I would yell again and, eventually, he would shout through.

'Ahm fine! … Noo fuck off!'

I knew he was getting worse. Then one day Ashley came in to see me: 'Mummy, Old Wullie wants you to come right now,' she told me, standing holding her tiny wee teapot. 'Is he going to die?'

'Ashley no. What makes you say that: he is just ill.'

'He shouted: *Ashley tell your mum I am gonna die!* I heard him say that, Mum.' She fiddled with her wee teapot. I could have shot Old Wullie, the insensitive old fucking drama queen. Ashley was only seven. I went onto the landing and into the flat next door, striding up the long hallway, making sure he could hear my footsteps, and then I opened his door. I stepped into his room. It smelled of stale smoke and old fish. Wullie had always shoplifted tins of salmon. The opened cans were now gathering together up at the window and he didn't own a fridge.

'Wullie, fucksake! The smell in here! Let me get a bin bag and I will clear this room a bit!' I put my hand to my mouth. He was generally clean and always kept the bathroom tidy with his razors and stuff all up high as he knew Ashley used it when she was in his flat playing.

'OK,' he mumbled. 'And then can ye take the dug oot fur me? The doctor is coming later. Sean called him fur me.' Wullie stood there, frail, in a bright blue Paisley-patterned satin housecoat. I used to joke this was his 'smoking jacket'; it looked so posh on this old purple-faced, hard-drinking Glaswegian.

'Wullie, do me a favour? Stop shouting yer gonnae die, will ye? Ashley is freaked.'

'Aye, but it made ye come here quick eh?' he said, his big purple face creasing into a smile and then he laughed and coughed while he held his chest and laughed and coughed again.

I cleaned his room and took Sara the dog for a walk with Ashley. She tried in vain to stop the gentle yet very big blonde Alsatian from dragging her along. The dog was desperate to pee and ran along the grass looking for its favourite place.

Christmas Eve eventually arrived and, after teatime, I sneaked next door and walked up Old Wullie's hallway with Ashley's train set under my arm. I spread the instructions out and set about clipping it all together. I had a big green board and miniature trees, tiny people and wee pretend brick bridges all to set the scene of a country village with train station. I was loving it. It was a great present and she was going to adore this toy.

Whisky the cat sat quietly and watched me; I stopped for a break, picked him up and looked out of the big bay windows. I could see all the way across Glasgow Green and into the Gorbals. The big flats were gone; they had been demolished with explosives the year before, but I could see the twinkling lights of the houses beyond the beautiful church spire of St Francis in Cumberland Street where the gangs used to fight. Frost was starting to sharpen up the corners of the windows, making the street lights twinkle. I looked around the room; it was covered in toys, dolls, crayons and loads of paper and children's books. Although this was Old Wullie's flat, this was Ashley's playroom. The walls were painted with bright Disney characters, some done good (mine!), some done squiggly (Ashley's), loads of coloured hand prints (Ashley's), lots of high-up hand prints with Celtic and Rangers written on them (Paul and Sammy's). This was her room to enjoy and play in as she wanted. I finished putting together the train set and tried it out. The old-fashioned steam train went off round the track and trundled towards the wee brick bridge.

All was well until Whisky leapt off the cupboard and landed hard on the board with his paw firmly trapping the train as it came through the bridge. 'It's not a mouse, it's a train!' I exclaimed, but the cat was so excited, his eyes were flashing, tail twitching and his hunting instinct took over as he tried to bite the train. He sat with his mouth open waiting for the train to come round again. It went straight in between his teeth and the cat looked at me, surprised and embarrassed. I laughed and thought of all the trouble this was going to cause Ashley when she played with her trains. Whisky was never going to stop stalking the train and, even when I held him, he struggled to get out of my arms, claws bared trying to stretch out to catch the wee moving toy. I took Whisky with me and closed the door to the playroom, then walked over to Old Wullie's door to see if he needed some tea or supper before the busy Christmas rush took over downstairs in the bar.

I banged on the door.

No answer.

I could hear Old Wullie's television blaring away in the room. I kept knocking louder.

No answer.

My heart missed a beat. I felt a strange shiver at the back of my neck. I could hear Bob Geldof's familiar Band Aid song, written for the starving in faraway Ethiopia, blaring clearly on television.

I walked back down the hall and went into our own flat. Sean was sitting at the kitchen table reading with Ashley.

'Mummy! I can read "The Night Before Christmas" all by myself! Ask Dad!' She smiled up at me.

'Go into the living room and stick on the telly, Ashley,' I said, lifting her from Sean's knee. 'A big Christmas film is about to come on. I need to speak to Daddy.'

Ashley ran off happily towards the living room.

'Sean, I think Old Wullie is dead. There's no answer at his door and I am really scared to go in there.' I reached out to pull Sean's arm and get him up off the chair. 'Please get the keys and go check, eh?'

He got up in silence and left the room. He lifted the set of master keys off the hook behind our door and walked into Old Wullie's hallway. I followed, after making sure Ashley was settled in our living room. By the time I caught up with him, Sean had Wullie's door open only a crack; he was crouched down, trying to keep the dog calm on the other side of the door; he turned to me and said, 'Janey, the door seems to be jammed and the dog won't let me in. She is growling. She likes you. Come and talk to her and see if we can get her out into the hall so I can get in there.'

I leaned down and looked through the crack in the door. The room was in semi-darkness but I could see the television was lying on its side flickering grey and silver, shimmering on the brown carpet; it was still playing the Band Aid song very loudly.

The dog's nose came poking through and sniffed at me. I instinctively put my hand to her and she licked my palm.

'Hello Sara, how's my girl, eh? There's ma good big lassie, eh? Coming oot, hen, eh?' I tried to push the door wider, but it felt as though something was jammed behind it, though not stuck fast. I could see the soles of Wullie's feet in his slippers facing me on the floor. I tried to encourage Sara to come out to me, but I watched through the crack in the door as the big dog turned away from me and lay beside the old man and whimpered.

'Come on, girl! Come on,' I shouted to her.

She looked at Wullie, then looked at me, then back to Wullie and slowly pushed her way through the slim space that the jammed door created. I left Sean behind as I ran quickly down the hall with the dog, avoiding colliding with her as we both leapt down the stairs, her long claws clicking all the way and skidding on the grey stone slabs that led to the outside door. I pushed it wide open; she ran through, jumped the wee red fence, stood there, squatted and seemed to piss for ages. The poor dog had held that urine inside her for who knows how long, because she would never do her toilet indoors, no matter what the circumstances.

I was sure Wullie was dead. I stood outside with Sara and hugged her when she had finished pishing. I didn't want to go back upstairs as I did not want to know about the death. I somehow thought if I stayed outside, I would not need to know. But I also knew I had to go up in case Ashley wandered through looking for her daddy. So I went into the Weavers bar and asked a customer to keep an eye on the dog for me. Big Sara slouched under a table in the corner, looking forlorn. I climbed back up the stairs very slowly and, as I reached the top, I heard Sean walking down Old Wullie's hallway and he met me as I reached the door.

'He is dead, Janey. He is just lying there on the floor. There is some blood where he hit his head. He must have fallen or collapsed – I don't know – but I have already called the police.' Sean pulled off his glasses and rubbed his eyes. He sat on the cold stone steps. 'Ma dad was worried about him as well, Janey. Maybe I should have kept a better eye on him … Fucking Merry Christmas, everybody!' he sighed.

I tried to reassure him but I knew he was not listening: 'There is no way you could have known he was gonna die, Sean. We did wur best.'

'I can't tell ma da,' Sean sighed. 'This will set him back. And Wullie didn't know my dad was in hospital. It's all fucking falling apart!' I could hear his voice cracking as he put his arms around himself and sat hugging his tummy.

Two policemen's radios broke the silence as they mounted the stairs.

'Sean Storrie?'

'Yes. The body's in there.' Sean stood up and led them down Old Wullie's hallway. I went back into our flat and made some tea. I arranged for the staff to stay on a bit later to give me time to get organised for the late shift. Ashley's babysitter had turned up – Clare was a daughter of my Dad's cousin and she was told what had happened. She was in control within minutes, lifting a curious Ashley up and away from the door.

'Why are there policemen in at Old Wullie's?' I could hear Ashley ask.

Clare spoke quickly. 'You are not allowed to ask that many questions on Christmas Eve – didn't ye know that, madam? So let's get the mince pies ready for Santa!'

I went down to the bar to work. I stood watching all the late-night revellers smiling and singing along to their favourite Christmas songs from the jukebox and went round to pick up the empty glasses. When I got to the wee tables round the side where the telly was housed, I stopped and almost broke down. There was Sara, still lying under a table, watching the door, waiting for Old Wullie to come through and join her; she never let him even go to the toilet on his own, she was always with him, even when he sang on the karaoke; she even stood faithfully at his side, like an uncomfortable child averting her eyes whenever Wullie belted out 'Love Is A Many Splendoured Thing'. I recalled how I used to laugh at the look on the dog's face as Wullie sang that song with his baggy pockets full of tins of salmon. I had never seen an Alsatian embarrassed before then. I walked over to her and stroked her soft blonde tufty coat. My first priority would be to get someone to look after her; Wullie was dead but Sara was alive. I made a few phone calls and that same night Sara had a new home.

Sean came down later and told me the police doctor reckoned it looked like a heart attack; there were no suspicious circumstances but they needed to talk to me to finalise statements. I sat and told them everything I could remember and they took notes.

'We will probably be in touch to let you know what is happening. We will take his body away and deal with the paperwork as soon as we can. Christmas is not a good time to die, y'know,' the big policeman told me as he tucked his notebook away. 'Though is there ever a good time to die?' he added sarcastically, then he looked sheepishly at Sean: 'Sorry, Sean, that was stupid of me. How is yer dad? Does he know about Wullie?'

Sean looked shocked then looked away; he realised the policeman knew nothing about Old George's situation and was just being polite.

'I will tell him in the morning,' Sean said flatly.

Christmas Day was hard for us all. We videotaped Ashley opening up her presents and kept smiles on our faces at all times. We took her next door to see the train set all arranged. I looked at Old Wullie's door. I knew his body had been removed but didn't want to freak Ashley out by telling her he had died in there. She still thought Old Wullie was alive.

'Mummy! Daddy! I *love* this train set! Thanks so much!' She sat mesmerised watching the old-fashioned trains glide around their miniature town. Sean managed to lift it all up and bring it next door for her to sit in our hall with, but Ashley was having trouble stopping Whisky from dragging the trains off the track: he was still convinced the small moving objects were prey and deserved to be attacked.

After lunch, Sean went to visit his dad in hospital and came back knowing he would have to tell Ashley about Old

Wullie dying – we had by now informed all the people in the building and the customers were all talking about it. Sean looked beaten. He told me he felt he had let his dad down by not looking after Wullie. He felt in his suspicious Scottish heart that deaths came in threes and that his father might be next. Old George was not getting any better and each visit only confirmed Sean's fears. The seven Storrie brothers were now all back in Glasgow except Michael, who was serving time in a German prison. I hadn't been told what the crime was but knew through overheard conversations that he would be home soon, so I presumed it could not have been that serious.

When we told Ashley about Old Wullie's death, she cried in my arms. I went through to his room with the police to check out some of his documents.

'Were you his daughter?' the policeman asked.

'No, I just lived next door and always knew him. As far as I am aware Wullie never had any family, though I might be wrong; he was very private.' On Old Wullie's wall was a big colour photo of Ashley as a baby; he had hung it up beside his calendar. He was fonder of her and Sara the dog than he was of anyone I knew. He had never had much time for me but would chat away to Ashley whenever she played in the hallway. She stayed out of her playroom all over the Christmas holidays.

'I don't like being in that flat alone,' she explained to me. 'I feel like someone doesn't like me. When Wullie was there I always knew he would look after me.'

I tried to talk her round, but she begged me to bring her toys through into our flat and even the cat could not be persuaded to go back into Old Wullie's flat. The next few days were spent organising his funeral. I could see Sean was worried that this might be a rehearsal for his own dad's death. We put an obituary in the *Glasgow Evening Times* to make sure Old Wullie's old cronies would know and former workmates from the council where he had worked as a welder/blacksmith. The funeral went well and loads of his old friends turned up to say goodbye to the old character. We invited them all back to the pub where we laid on his favourite music and lots of salmon sandwiches.

On the morning of his funeral, a letter had arrived for him from the Salvation Army. It said that they had traced and were contacting him as William Kerr – Old Wullie's real name – on behalf of a woman in Leeds. She thought she was his daughter by a relationship with a Glaswegian woman and William was invited to write back and make contact with her. They had included a copy of a very old picture the woman had of Wullie and her mother smiling together. The picture was, indeed, of Old Wullie as a young man and it broke my heart to call the woman in Leeds and explain to her that he *was* her father but he had been cremated the same day her letter arrived. After the call, I posted off Old Wullie's wallet, watch and pictures of him that we had gathered over the years. I hoped it gave her some peace. In a strange way, it made me feel good that there was a family member somewhere missing him as he had had no family at the funeral service.

Now New Year approached and Old George's health was deteriorating; Sean explained that it was OK for me to go visit him now. The other daughters-in-law had all paid visits. I was very apprehensive. I felt that, with seven sons to visit him and the emotions that they would all be feeling, the last thing they or he would want was for an outside witness to the pain. Least of all me. I was easily the least liked by his sons. I decided not to go and Sean accepted it well. But I was worried that Ashley might be horrified if she found out she could have said goodbye to her beloved grandad and I was torn between not telling her and pushing Sean into telling her about her Grandad George and maybe even taking her to see him. Sean decided she should be told he was in hospital but there was no way she was going to be taken to see him.

'Janey, he gets angry and struggles. He is in a wheelchair. He has to be hand-fed, for fucksake. Ashley would scream if she saw him like that!'

Sean patiently explained to Ashley that her grandad was very ill in hospital and needed to stay there till he got better. He told her it had to be a secret and not to let anyone know just yet. It always amazed me that, whenever Sean told Ashley something had to be a secret, she never questioned him or debated it, she accepted his word. More importantly she never ever told anyone. Not a soul.

On New Year's Eve, we all gathered at Toad Hall for the traditional Storrie 'party'. There was different music playing in each room you entered – the kitchen was blaring with local radio, the main sitting room where George always sat had Scottish Television's New Year celebrations belting from it and, in the dining room, the stereo was blasting out some strange rap music. It felt like the music was there to fill the void that George had left behind. The brothers wandered from room to room, stalking each other like cats who had forgotten or were checking out their territory, touching old ornaments that had lain on the shelves for years.

'Was this the china thing my ma had in Greenhead Street?' asked one, as he delicately inspected a fine figurine between his thick fingers.

'Naw, Da bought that at a sale, remember? You were there – it wiz the day the Pope came to Scotland. You bought a silver cake slice that day; there wiz millions of crap china stuff and nick-nacks an' you hud to stop Da from buying loads o' shite. He really liked mad ornaments, didn't he?'

Sean said, 'Stop talking like he is dead, eh?' and walked from the room.

Tension crept around the house, which still smelled of dogs' piss, and spread like a virus from brother to brother, from wife to child. Everyone was exhausted by trying to keep a smile on their face, laughing at the antics of the kids through gritted teeth. As the booze, cannabis and various other drugs seeped into their hosts, the night slowly ground to a halt. At one point, I sat on a sofa, holding Ashley's hand as the house, filled with around 20 people, slipped into total silence. A little later, the mood changed to paranoia and deep suspicion and, as always, the Storrie family broke off into splinter groups and snatched, angry conversations started to fly around. Shouts were heard from upstairs. Young George had been defending Sandra as one brother accused her of not looking after his father more; another brother had then shouted at Young George, 'You were shagging her as oor father lay dying!'

The tension got worse, Ashley started to get upset and Sean came downstairs to drive us home. He had never wanted to be there in the first place.

'Janey,' he snapped. 'Get your coat; Ashley, get your shoes; come on.'

We were ready in double-quick time. I looked into the dining room as I stood up to get my coat and saw Paul Storrie standing there looking desperately sad. His girl-friend Shona held his hand. I liked Shona; they had been together for years off and on. Shona had stood by him through the best and worst of his behaviour, and some-times I wanted to take her aside and tell her to run as fast as she could in the opposite direction. But probably, like me, she would stay and see what happened next. I walked over to Paul and put my arms around him and told him we were going and, if he wanted, he could come with us. He shook his head and kissed Ashley goodbye.

Sean and his brothers were still visiting their dad daily at the hospital. I kept my head down and carried on working hard at the bar. January was always a hard, cold month in the Calton. The view through the window again became one of freezing branches on bare trees above frost-covered grass as people wrapped against the wind scuttled past.

Patsy Paton came down from Easterhouse to see me. I was sure she knew about Old George because she was unusually quiet and sat staring at me as I polished beer glasses. Nothing got past her sharp eyes and ears. I was terrified she might quiz me, might spot any hesitation, deviation or the very least aversion of my eyes. Eventually, she ran her hand through her fine blonde hair, let out a sigh and tapped her fingers on the bar. 'So where is old George, Janey?' Her blue eyes followed me as I leant beneath the bar, pre-tending to look for something. I had to avoid eye contact with her.

'Why are you asking me? Your own sister Mary is married to one of his sons, Patsy. Ask her. Give me a fucking break, eh?' I tried to act as brusquely as I could with her. She leaned over the bar and grabbed my left wrist. She had never hurt me before in her life; she always protected me and stuck up for me when I needed her.

'Patsy, ask someone else, please,' I pleaded with her. 'In fact, just ask fucking Sandra.'

Sandra hated Patsy. They were friendly in front of Old George whenever they met, but Sandra was desperately jealous of her as Old George's ex and gave George a hard time whenever she came to visit. Patsy did not give a fuck about Sandra and would descend on Old George whenever it suited her. He was no longer her lover but they had a long history and there was a bond between them that lasted. Now Patsy sat at the bar staring at the wall behind me, her eyes filled with tears.

'I know there is something and he is fucking ill and no cunt in his family is telling anything!'

There were a few wee men sitting at the far end of the bar minding their own business. They casually looked in her direction when she said this but any female emotion was akin to the plague for these wee guys in dark old suits who sat and tapped their toes to Frank Sinatra as he sang from the jukebox.

I came out from behind the bar and faced Patsy, then wrapped both arms around her shoulders as she sat on the tall bar stool. She pushed me a little away from her then held my face between the cold palms of her hands. It was something Patsy always did when she wanted your undivided attention.

'Is he dead, Janey?'

'No, Patsy, he's no' dead. Please go ask someone else. I get the blame of everything. Go ask one of the boys, eh?'

When Sean came back that day from the hospital, it was clear Old George had taken a turn for the worse. Sean leaned against our big industrial microwave in the back shop and slid off his glasses to rub his eyes: 'He looks angry, Janey – just fucking angry ... He is not ... not really there at times and I feel ...' He broke down, tears choked his words and he slowly slid down the fake wooden panelling that covered the back kitchen area to sit crouched on the floor, his shirt and tie crumpled up around his knees as he hugged them to his chest. He looked like a wee lost boy. I tried to touch him, reach over and hold his head but he just put his hand up defensively, to fend me off.

'Go serve, Janey. I just need a minute and I can hear old Albert out there shouting for a pint of cider.'

I seemed to spend most of those days watching people cry and rushing around tending to customers. At night, I would run, even in the snow; I was getting up to six miles now and was pleased with my progress. I loved the feeling of pounding along, leaving everything behind me, my Sony Walkman thumping into my ears – no more dealing with crying people, just Steely Dan, Supertramp and Hall and Oates to soothe my soul as my bouncy trainers strode along the concrete in the cold. At home, I would hear Sean on the phone debating, arguing or calming one or another brother. It was one suspicious conversation after another.

'Dad bought land from Johnny Jones. Let's see about that.'

'We'll go and start to dig up these people who owe my dad our money.'

Each son started to make decisions about Old George's various businesses in his absence, cutting the cake before he was dead. It was causing huge rifts. They would fight about Toad Hall and the other pub Old George owned and his collection of cars and vans, the caravan at Wemyss Bay on the Firth of Clyde, the money lent out to various men for various deals … it went on and on. I kept out of it. I knew we were secure; we had paper-work to show we were buying the Weavers bar and build-ing. Sean assured me we were fine and safe and I trusted him. I had no reason not to. Despite all he had ever done to me I was sure he would always look after us financially. He was smart at this money stuff. This was the man who had budgeted £20 a week for everything when he was 17 and stuck to it. I felt safe amidst a sea of Chinese whispers that stuttered poison.

Early January saw my long-delayed visit to Old George's hospital bed. I had just been swimming and Sean took me straight up to the ward. Sandra was with us; she and Sean walked fast with the familiar comfort of people who had taken this route every day. I was constantly trying to catch up and almost walking off in wrong directions as they strode ahead, turning corners and pushing apart quiet hissing doors in the endless Royal Infirmary corridors. My heart was beating loud. I hated hospitals. I did not know what to expect. I was afraid to see him. Eventually, we reached a corridor where the nurses started smiling at Sean and Sandra. I hung behind; I saw Sean turn into an open ward and stop. I could see his back bend over and hear his voice as he spoke to his father. I stepped in and looked beyond Sean's shoulder.

Everything was white.

Old George was pale, bloated and his skin was very white – his hair was white – his gown and the surrounding bed were white – the strong, bright lights over it were white – all white – and it dazzled my eyes. Old George was sitting up in a wheelchair by his white bed, staring straight ahead. His eyes looked dead. My immediate reaction was one of complete and utter horror. Sean smiled at me, saying, 'He looks good eh?'

I turned on my heels and walked out of the ward; I had to gulp hard to stop the lump in my throat from choking me. No, he did not look good – in fact, he looked like fucking Death to me. I screamed inside my head. But I managed to pull myself together and walked back into the ward again, more for Sean's sake than mine. He and Sandra sat there smiling at the white man. Old George's fists were gripping into the arms of the wheelchair; his white face was contorted with anger and his sharp blue eyes looked like he was silently screaming behind them, screams of complete horror – ripping, deadly, venomous howls of anger leapt from his eyes as I looked at them.

He was not the kind of man who waited for a stroke to sort itself out, or who would want to spend months having physiotherapy in the hope of managing to finally feed himself. He was the kind of man who fucked younger women, ate big breakfasts, bought fancy cars and lived life his way. His eyes bore into me; I could feel the frustration well up every time he moved his eyes and they darted desperately around the shiny white room.

A male nurse was chatting over his head to Sean and Sandra explaining how well George was doing today and rubbing my father-in-law's big white right hand. I looked, half-dazzled by the bright overhead lights, at George's old white arm and could see the pale blue fading tattoos that boasted of his love for his mother. The white hairs on his arms made the letters blur. His shins were peeping out the bottom of his pyjamas and I knew that, underneath his pyjamas, his white legs were covered in mottled blue bruises from the savage beatings he got from the police in his early twenties. Sean and Sandra chatted away to Old George. I just wanted to leave. I was horrified by what I had seen – the big, powerful man I knew, sitting there glaring at a world which could not hear his silent screams. Afterwards, I was glad to get back to the bar and was desperate not to discuss Old George.

The second time Sean and Sandra took me to see him, as soon as we entered the ward, a doctor took us aside and explained that George had had a further stroke that morning and was now gravely ill; he was on a machine to help him breathe. Sean and Sandra sat staring at the floor as the doctor explained.

'You have to get the rest of the family up to the hospital soon.'

Inevitably, a day or so later, there came the decision to switch off the machine that was keeping him breathing and this had to be made by his surviving children. It was heartbreaking to see his sons all sitting in that hospital ward with his daughters-in-law. At one point, there were eleven people around his bed watching and listening to him breathe noisily without a machine. He rasped out each breath and his chest rattled. Everyone waited in case that was the last breath he took. I felt overwhelmed. This really was no place for his son's wives to be.

I finally decided to go, but first I had to say my goodbyes. I leaned over, took his white, clammy hand in mine and quietly whispered to him, 'Thanks for everything, George. Thanks for giving me Sean and thanks for loving Ashley. I will miss you.'

I quickly turned and left his bedside and walked out into the hallway of the ward. That was it for me. No more visits and no more waiting for him to die. I had a pub to run and even Old George would have agreed with me on that score. He died the next morning with his family around him. Sean was on his way to the hospital and missed being there for the actual moment of death but, within minutes of his father's death, Sean was on the phone organising the funeral – that was the best way for him to cope. Ashley became hysterical when she found out her beloved grandfather had died and she had never got to say goodbye to him. She ran out of our living room and crouched under the kitchen table and covered her head with her arms like she did with her jacket when her daddy was beating the man in the car. As a child, I did handstands; Ashley did head-hiding. 'No! Don't tell me!' she cried. 'Don't tell me! Don't tell me, Mummy!'

The funeral was set for the following week, a week in which there were so many arguments and shouting matches it made me smile, because Old George would have loved the fuss he caused.

His funeral took place on a sunny January morning and was well attended: several 'Faces' came up from London to pay their respects. They dressed the same as their Glasgow counterparts. They all had slicked-back hair or shaved heads and wore sun-glasses with the ubiquitous uniform of grey or fawn camel-hair coats or black cashmere Crombies. Onlookers and ordinary people from the pubs and clubs Old George ran swelled the crowd in the street outside the funeral parlour and streams of cars followed the funeral procession all the way to the crematorium. There were no security arrangements as there were in some equivalent London funerals. George had seven sons and they were all there. Perhaps 200 mourners lined the seats inside the full building and there were others who couldn't get in as Mr Bovey, the family lawyer, conducted the service. Old George's sons sat in the front pew, all with heads bowed to the ground, remembering their father. Outside, on the grass, big floral wreaths sat, plump and bulging with ferns and flowers, amid the January frost. Ashley wore her green school uniform and was so upset during the service that I had to leave early with her. As I stepped out of the crematorium and walked to the car, I heard some woman say: 'That's a wreath from the Kray Twins.'

25

Toad Hall, London and Ocho Rio

With the funeral out of the way, we all just carried on as best we could.

There were various Storrie family meetings to which I was not invited: always 'just the boys'. Sean usually returned from these meetings with an angry face and sometimes a black mood. It transpired that Old George had left a 'tape' to explain his will. He could read but was not good at writing, so this had been the easiest way for him to do it. The tape caused much pain and in-fighting, mainly because it was in the hands of Young George and Sandra; they kept telling the brothers that they would allow it to be heard only when it suited them, feeding on everyone's insecurity. The fact that Sandra was in on it with Young George further fuelled suspicion among the other brothers that she and he were sleeping together again. When he got drunk, Young George would yell out at anyone near him, 'I heard the tape! You are getting fuck all. Wait till you hear the tape! You'll fucking shut up then, won't he, Sandra?'

She would sit there and nod her head in agreement.

But, when the much-hyped tape was eventually aired, it just sounded like Old George making a long inventory of his possessions, his cars, his cash, his bank accounts, his property, something he referred to as 'hard-working money' and his 'various miscellaneous materials' – I wondered what those were; I thought perhaps pieces of jewellery, a watch and some of his Masonic regalia. Although a Catholic, Old George, like many of the policemen he encountered, had been a Freemason all his working life. The tape said that 'the deal still stands with Sean', meaning, of course, that Sean was still buying the pub and the Weavers building. This was no shock, as everyone knew it already. We would continue paying into the account Old George had set up for our building. We would own and run the Weavers. Philip would continue to run the Palaceum. Old George also mentioned that Sandra was 'to be looked after' although he didn't explain how and left her no money at all in his will.

The cash the seven brothers knew about was divided equally seven ways, but the tape finished abruptly. There were no goodbyes or any natural end to his conversation. Old George's voice just suddenly stopped in mid-sentence. This aroused suspicions all round. The other six brothers were convinced their father had mentioned cash he had put aside for them and they now assumed Young George and Sandra were conspiring to keep it.

* * *

In early March, Sean stood behind the bar in the Weavers as he opened an envelope. I watched him smile and then saw big fat tears drip down his face: 'Janey! We got the grant from the council to renovate the building!' He turned from the bar and walked into the back shop. 'That's good news eh?' But his tears perplexed me. Sean realised I was looking at him and explained, 'My da never got to see it. All those years he talked about what we would do when we got the grant and now he won't see it.'

Within days, architects and builders were all over the

building and plans drawn up years ago were now set in motion. We, of course, had to put up cash as well and the first sum of money we put in matched the cash that Old George gave Sean in his will. It was a huge financial investment and, at some moments, it scared me just thinking about how much we would have to pay, but the end result was that we would get a good living from the hard work we had put in – and a shiny new place to stay. Slowly and diligently, we managed to get temporary homes for the people who lived upstairs and we got the whole building empty; the pub itself was not due to be evacuated until October, in about six months' time; then it, too, was set for renovation. Sean and I started to look for somewhere for us to stay ourselves. I wanted to go up the West End nearer to Ashley's school but, then, we got a phone call from Young George.

'Sean, just come up here an' live in Toad Hall. Da would have wanted that.'

'Erm, I will ask Janey if that's what she wants, OK?' Sean replied.

It was most certainly what I did *not* want.

'It will be free,' Sean tried to persuade me. 'And George is moving out. Sandra will go to the caravan in Wemyss Bay and we will have the place to ourselves. Come on, Ashley will love living near Tollcross Park!' he pleaded with me.

I was sure this was going to be a bad move, but I eventually agreed. Ashley and Sean loved it. I spent three days hauling boxes and bags filled with all our possessions into the big house and put our ginger tom cat Whisky's box down in the back hallway; he was very excited to have such a big house to explore. He ran from room to room, his back slung low as he anticipated danger around every corner, his tail twitching, ready to pounce, possibly stimulated by the distinct aroma of dog piss. Sandra's two wee Yorkshire

Terriers had pissed or shat on every surface they could find. The carpets in the hallways still felt constantly damp with dog piss and the smell was sometimes unbearable. I scoured and scrubbed those hall carpets till the dye leaked but never got rid of the smell. Still living out in the pound at the back of the house were Old George's two dogs Brindle the black evil vicious Alsatian and Junior the blond passive happy Alsatian. Brindle had an outhouse right beside the back door. To feed him we had to shout over the half-stable door at the back, 'In dog! Get in!' and he would run in, barking, snarling and growling at us, then turn his back and gobble the food. Junior would watch the whole scene with genuine canine bemusement. With his big blond head tipped to the side, he would wait for Brindle to finish and only then would he risk eating his own food. I would let Junior come into the house and sit by the fire as I stroked him. One night, he sat by the fireside with me and leaned his big chin on Old George's armchair. His soulful brown eyes looked at Ashley and he whined sadly.

'Mummy,' she said gently, as she stroked Junior's neck. 'He is crying for Grandad George.' We both sat on the floor with him and wept. Ashley hugged the dog and wrapped her arms around his middle. 'I miss him too, Junior,' she said to his tummy.

Ashley had moved into the bedroom that used to be her daddy's when he was a teenager: she loved it there and, when she got home from school, sat at the windows that overlooked the dog pound, looking into the massive back garden and, beyond, across into Tollcross Park. Sean and I settled into Old George's bedroom, which quite freaked me at first, but I changed all the bedclothes, re-arranged the furniture, washed down the wardrobes and soon made the room ours. The wardrobes were still stuffed with Old

George's belongings and Sandra still had stuff lying around, but I made space where I could.

Living in Toad Hall was fine so long as we had no Storrie visitors. We were a family not used to people staying in the same house as us and I liked to be able to sit in my T-shirt and knickers and watch TV. But, despite all assurances that we would have the house to ourselves because Young George would be in London and Dick would be staying with his friends, we always got them or another of the six brothers coming to stay. When we came home from school with Ashley, the familiar smell of toast and hash smoke would greet us. I hated her being surrounded by cannabis and heavy cigarette smokers. No watching cartoons on TV for her, no playing downstairs, she had to go up to her own room to avoid the drugs and confrontations.

'Holy fuck!' I moaned to Sean. 'I cannae cope with this. Ashley has tae hide away and do her homework in her bedroom coz they bastards cannae stay away. Fuck it all, tell them they huv to go or I go!' I shouted loud enough for them to hear.

Later, as he passed me on the stairs, Young George smiled, blew smoke in my face and sniggered, 'If you go and take Sean with ye, I will fucking take yer pub!'

Sean heard this and ran upstairs screaming at Young George. A shouting match ensued. It sounded like blows would be struck. I was horrified. Ashley started screaming for her daddy. Young George came running downstairs and shouted at me, 'This is no' your hoose! We can stay here if we want!'

'I didnae want to come here,' I snapped back. 'Ya fucking dope heed! Naebody likes ye, ya big weird cunt! No wonder yer mammy didnae want ye and gave ye to yer granny!' Old George had told me he always felt guilty about Young George as he had been given away to his granny as a child. 'Even yer mammy hated ye!' I screamed at him. 'Fuck off!'

Young George stopped shouting and stood stock-still, stunned. There was complete silence. He looked up the stairs at Sean, who was looking down at him. He looked at me in shock, then stormed off.

After that, the fighting never stopped. Young George would let Brindle the evil Alsatian stalk the house and Ashley hid, terrified, in her room as the big dog panted at her door. Young George would spit on her and call her names.

'Mummy! Uncle George says bad things to me!' she told me one day, holding onto my hand in the kitchen. Something inside me snapped. I had had enough. It was time to make Sean choose. Them or us.

'I don't know what they're planning behind my back,' he explained to me. 'I need to be here where the threat is. I want to keep my enemies close. I've got them plotting; I've got you fucking screaming at me; I don't know what to dae.'

I thought maybe he was planning his own suicide.

* * *

The pub was still ticking over, although the whole place was now covered in scaffolding and workers wearing yellow hard hats and blue overalls were everywhere. It was strange to work there but not live above. I had got used to running upstairs if I needed to see Ashley or Sean or get something to eat and it drove me mad having to carry a change of clothes each day when I went to work. The builders' bills came in regularly and we kept up with the payments. The good news was that soon we would have a great new place to stay and lovely new pub to go with it. The bad news was that Sean was becoming overwhelmed by builders' plans, architect meetings, fights with his brothers, trying to stay calm in his dead father's house and keeping me happy. He just didn't have time to grieve properly. Something was always happening either with Young George or Sandra or some brother was moaning to him about another having more money or more property than him. I had my own way to deal with it all: I put on my shoes and ran for an hour round Tollcross Park. I was determined to get fit enough to run the annual ladies' 10,000 metres street race through the West End of Glasgow in under an hour.

When the actual day of the race came, I was so excited my legs felt like jelly and I was not sure how I would fare because I had never raced against anyone during my training. But I started well and my legs carried me all the way around posh Kelvingrove Park; I never stopped or got out of breath once; I just kept running and running. Sean, my Dad and stepmum were all waiting at the finishing line for me and I came in at just under one hour. Getting that medal round my neck felt like a huge personal achievement for me because, any time I'd won anything before, I'd never got the prize.

Immediately after the race I had a shower, then caught a train to London: my gay friend Findlay had invited me down to see the new Conran restaurant he was running near Tower Bridge. I couldn't wait to see him; it was ages since we had laughed together and spent time bitching about the world. As soon as I got off the train at Waterloo and into a cab, I relaxed. My legs still ached a bit, but the excitement of getting away for a week on my own soothed my strained muscles. When I arrived at Findlay's flat in a big Victorian house in Clapham, he came running out to meet the cab and hugged me in the dark street.

'How are your old Scottish legs then?' he laughed as he lifted up my bag and led me by the hand through his big blue door. It was a shared flat and there were four people sitting around on the floor and on the few chairs in the living room. 'Everyone! This is my mate Janey Storrie from Glasgow!' Each person looked up and said *Hi* to me.

I recognised one: 'Oh, hello, I know your face!' I blurted out.

'Oh here we go, the big superstar!' Someone laughed out loud.

Andy was an actor from Scotland now working in London. I had recognised him from the *Take The High Road* TV series back home. They were all a really nice bunch of people, mostly working in television acting, wardrobe or production. Findlay was the odd one out as he worked in catering. He took me into his own high-ceilinged room, sparsely furnished except for one wardrobe and a big double bed. I was taken slightly aback: I was expected to sleep with him! It had never entered my mind he would not have a spare room. I realised I had a lot to learn about living in London but I was determined not to let my stupid naivety get in the way of being with all these exciting people in this exciting city. I had never slept beside any man except Sean. Of course, Findlay was gay but it was still weird. I was so tired after running that day that, by the time I was in my cotton pyjamas and lying down, I was fast asleep and I awoke the next morning to find myself wrapped around Findlay's back.

'Yuk! Get your breasts off my back, Storrie!' he giggled as he turned round to hug me front-on. 'People will say I am straight and throw me out of London! Men with whom

I have not yet had sex will shun me for letting your boobs touch me!'

I loved his humour; he laughed at all my wee jokes and impersonations of people from the Weavers and loved to listen as I ranted on about Ashley and Sean. He knew me well enough to take the piss out of me, which was reassuring. I phoned home each day. Sean was coping well, the Weavers was fine and Ashley assured me she was happy enough, but I missed them so much.

* * *

One day, Findlay organised lunch for me at the restaurant he managed: Sir Terence Conran's new eatery The Chop House was housed on the South Bank of the Thames, amidst the cobblestones and fancy upmarket new flats at Shad Thames. The staff were all dressed in starched white and blacks and appeared to float around as if on wheels, delivering large white plates of delicious food. I was overwhelmed by the sophistication. Findlay's staff and friends were very cosmopolitan, very well spoken and very tastefully dressed. One woman I sat chatting with was dressed in a fashionably expensive long black linen dress, wore a silver twisted chain around her uniformly tanned throat and her long elegant fingers were adorned with platinum rings and red-painted fingernails. I sat with my hands on my lap and kept my head down, staring at the solitaire ring that Sean had bought me and at the dull clothes which made me feel old-fashioned and very unworthy. I was wearing cheap jeans and a cheap black blouse tucked in with a brown belt. I had a cheap handbag. Findlay saw me frown and slid in beside me on the leather banquette:

'You all right, sweetheart?' he asked, lifting up my chin. 'Missing family?'

'No, I am OK,' I whispered to him. 'I just feel really old-fashioned and I'm scared I will say something wrong in front of your fancy pals. Fuck, Findlay, that woman is so posh – it scares me a wee bit.'

'Posh my arse, Janey!' he giggled, twisting my curly hair and playing with it as he told me, 'She is a 35-year-old corporate wife. She looks good and fucks hard because she wants a new Aga cooker from her husband. Her handbag is worth more than my monthly wages, but she has to stay skinny and have sex with a man who is 57 years old, so she can keep her house in Chelsea ... Chin up, Storrie, at least you work for your money and love Sean!' I smiled at him. We lifted up our two expensive champagne flutes and chinked glasses. 'Cheers!' said Findlay. 'To the woman who married through choice and who is married to a man who has skin that still fits him and makes her smile.'

'He also makes me cry, Findlay,' I replied. The champagne was getting the better of me. I was feeling slightly tipsy. 'It's not all that it seems, you know.'

'Let's get out of here,' Findlay said, grabbing my arm, making his excuses to the crowd and leading me out onto the riverfront walkway. Across the water, the lights and towering office blocks of the City of London twinkled in the balmy early evening; beside us, people walked along holding hands, a lone fat man jogged and couples strolled with babies in prams. We caught a cab to Quaglino's, Conran's new upmarket restaurant in St James's. Findlay knew the front-of-house staff.

'Janey, this is Sophie, the receptionist and sexiest lesbian all the way from Soho.'

'Hello, Sophie,' I laughed, shaking the blonde girl's hand. 'I must apologise for my friend here: Findlay is the most indiscreet homosexual in London.'

'Is there any other kind of homosexual?' She winked.

I turned to follow Findlay and immediately balked inwardly. The entrance was a grand twisted staircase that took you down to the floor below. I was terrified I would stumble, fall down the entire flight of stairs and land flat on my arse at the bottom. But he took my hand, we stepped down together and took our table safely at the bottom. He flirted easily with the wine waiter and ordered a bottle of white wine.

'I don't really drink much, Findlay; don't get a whole bottle.'

'Darling, this is a really good white and, if you don't drink it, no worries – I will!' He lit a cigarette and flashed his eyes over the menu.

Over the first bottle and first course, we chatted about how Old George's death had been affecting us all back home. I went into my usual 'Ashley this' and 'Ashley that' routine.

Just as I was about to tell yet another funny story about her, Findlay interrupted me. 'Janey, for God's sake shut up about your child. How are *you*? What is happening with *you* and Sean? Who *are* you, Janey? You're not just some-one's mother, someone's wife. For fuck's sake, tell me the last time you had fun just being *Janey*?'

I stopped in my tracks. The wine had trickled into my soul and made me feel slightly floppy and warm and he had caught me off-guard.

'I don't know *who* I am, Findlay. I am just a woman who works in a pub and tries to keep talking quickly enough so nobody knows what's happening inside me when it all goes quiet.'

'Janey, you are lovely and funny and intelligent and you need to try to remember who you were before you got married. Did you always want to live in Glasgow? Who was your mum? Did she smile like you? Do you get your sense of humour from her?' Findlay probed into my head with a barrage of questions, all the while smiling as he talked.

I told him all about my life with Sean. I talked about my Uncle, my fears, dealing with the Storries, how I actually missed Old George. We talked and talked. I even learned to listen. I sat there with him and we both downed two bottles of wine and three glasses of brandy. Drunk, happy and full of good food, I let my big defensive attitude go; I admitted aloud for the first time that I was not happy with my life; I did not have to pretend; I had never told anyone this stuff before; I had always kept up the Janey Storrie mask, the attitude that nothing got me down. Old George had told me, 'Never show weakness. Then they will get you,' and I had never shown weakness; even when Sean slapped me hard on the face in the back shop, I came out smiling, telling jokes and covering my tracks. I always felt I didn't really deserve much in life and worried that sometimes people might see inside me the weak 'bad girl' – the description that my Uncle used when he raped me regularly over all those long years. Findlay held my hand and smiled.

'You don't need to let anyone rule your life.'

I was beginning to feel different about myself. I did not have to go home and accept Sean's bullying. I would stand up to him more. I thought, *I hope my head remembers all this*; I was taking mental notes, because I knew I was sure as hell likely to forget how to be brave. That night, when we went dancing, it was in a seedy, smelly, Soho gay club. I was exhausted and had never drunk that much in years – I had been, in effect, teetotal throughout my life because I saw the effect of drink on my parents. I danced twice, sat in a corner and sweated for an hour, until Findlay decided it was time to go. I had a great time.

* * *

The following week, I was back in Glasgow's East End, back in the war zone of Toad Hall. Sean updated me on the latest round of arguments. His brother Philip was making decisions about the Weavers – like what staff should be brought in and how many barrels were used – and this disturbed Sean no end. We were buying the pub and it was our money that was paying the builders. Why was his brother Philip taking such an active interest in our private investment? The six brothers had quickly spent the cash their father had left them and the minute it started to run out, they had started to ask questions about how much we had. *How much did their dad pay us over the years? Why did we have savings and they had none?* Sean and I got nervous at these probings and tried hard to just keep working and planning our future. But there was also the annoying fact that Sandra was starting to arrive at Toad Hall unannounced, declaring her stake in 'the Storrie fortune'. Young George had already warned us all to treat her with kid gloves: 'She knows too much aboot Dad.'

Sean had replied: 'Well, that's what happens when you tell women your business. I don't fuck Sandra, I've never fucked her and she knows nothing about me. If she knows too much about you, George, then take her somewhere else and treat her nice. Just keep her away from Toad Hall and away from my daughter.'

In my absence, Sandra had been upsetting Ashley by telling her that her Grandad George never really liked her and had always preferred to spend time with Sandra's kids whom he really did love. Ashley had run straight to her dad with this revelation and Sean immediately threw Sandra out of Toad Hall onto the main street. Literally. He grabbed her by the back of her neck and pulled her out of the house as she held one of her small shitty dogs in her arms. The other dog was yap-yapping behind them. Sean opened the gate, threw Sandra out, shut the gate and expected the second dog to follow through a gap, but it didn't; it was still yap-yapping around his heels; so he picked it up and threw it over the wall.

'Don't come back here!' he screamed at Sandra, as strangers at the bus stop outside enjoyed the free entertainment. 'Go to the caravan, ya mad cow! There must be men down there that haven't had sex with you yet! Don't ever speak to my daughter again!'

Sandra had called on Young George to 'sort out' Sean, but it never happened. He knew that, if Sandra had upset Ashley, there was no going back with Sean.

Ashley had started to ask questions about our future: 'Mummy, will we be getting our flats back above the pub? Will we be going back to the pub? Uncle Dick told me the Weavers wasn't Daddy's any more and Daddy will have to get a new job.' Her anxious eyes searched my face for reassurance.

'Uncle Dick was just being difficult and annoying,' I told her. 'Ignore him and, if he says that again, tell him to go buy teeth with the money his daddy left him.'

'No, Mummy, that's cruel. Uncle Dick is shy about having no top teeth.'

We could not go a single week without either Young George or Dick descending on us. I just wanted to leave Toad Hall and get a temporary flat somewhere: 'Sean, they said they would let us live here alone. I am fucking sick of it! The place is a mess, the smell of hash would knock ye oot and they keep being fucking snide to Ashley. I want to go!'

Sean rubbed his eyes as he sat in his father's kitchen. 'Well, now, you are letting them win by being upset. That is what they want, Janey. So calm down. It won't be long until we move back to living above the Weavers.'

'I fucking hate them! *You* hate them! They told Ashley we don't own the pub and we need to look for a new job! Dick told *our child* this, Sean! I want to go now!' I was not going to back off, not after my talks with Findlay.

'Look, why don't we go on a holiday?' Sean asked.

* * *

He thought a good two-week break in the Caribbean would chill me out and give him time to decide what we were all going to do. I guessed the holiday was a good idea; it would make Sean relax. Indeed, as it approached, he became more and more excited about the trip and asked me if I wanted to renew our wedding vows on the beach in Jamaica. I was thrilled and put aside all past fears. *He really must love me!* I thought. *He's been putting up with all this stress, dealing with the renovation, his father's death and still he wants us to have a beach ceremony to honour our wedding vows!* I thought I would burst with happiness. Ashley was over the moon too as, finally, she would get to be a bridesmaid. I set up cover at the Weavers, organised everything at Toad Hall, locked up all our personal paperwork, switched off our computer and locked our bedroom door. I told one of my sisters-in-law: 'Please keep it locked. It's hard to keep anything personal in this house and it already feels like I'm living in a hostel.'

The flight to the Caribbean was long and tiresome; it seemed to take forever to get from the airport into Ocho Rio by bus and, by this time, Ashley was fast asleep on my knee, all hot and sticky. But the hotel grounds were beautiful and, when we woke up the next morning to explore our surroundings, we were amazed by the beauty. It was everything the brochure had claimed: white sand that stretched for miles on our own private beach, the blue sea dotted with tiny boats and catamarans for our personal pleasure!

Ashley squealed with delight and immediately ran down into the ocean in her pyjamas: 'Mummy! The water is *warm*! Come in quick!' She dived under the first wave and stood up in her pink top and soaked cotton trousers shouting, 'It's lovely! Come in!' It was great to see her unwind and enjoy life for a wee while. She was only eight and I knew she was under strain as well. She had had to deal with missing her beloved Grandad George; she too had been uprooted from her home and had had to live with people who were always very difficult and rude to her.

Sean and I made plans with the Jamaican Wedding Supervisor for our beachfront wedding: the food was all-inclusive and a special Scottish Wedding Barbecue was arranged for the evening to celebrate our special day. I was surprised how much effort Sean was putting into it. Normally, he would balk at any display of public affection or anything that involved him talking in front of people. But he was enthusiastic, helped choose my flowers and picked one of the Jamaican bar stewards as his 'best man'; he had champagne and flowers delivered to my room, just before the ceremony.

And it was an amazing day! There was a crowd gathered round a white gazebo erected on the hot white sand and children ran around bare-footed, singing and throwing flowers onto the white sheet we were to be 'married' on. The old Jamaican minister came to greet me as I walked down the sand, dressed in a white off-the-shoulder summer top and flowing white skirt. Sean was dressed in white linen shorts and shirt and all the guests were bare-foot. Ashley wore the brightest fuchsia cotton dress with pink flowers tied in her light brown hair, smiling and giving flowers to people as she passed. The ceremony felt quietly spiritual and the minister asked us to both declare we would continue to respect and cherish each other as we grew in spirit and in age. Sean stood in front of all those strangers sitting on the sunny sand and declared his love for me as loud as he could, then he kissed me on the lips as the crowd clapped and cheered. We drank champagne, cut the two-tiered white cake and chatted on the beach with our congregation who had taken pictures for us. I thought I would burst with happiness. Sean had bought me a new wedding ring and I gave him a new watch, as he never wore rings. We sat and watched the sunset over the Caribbean and both temporarily forgot the Storrie family.

But they hadn't forgot us because, while we were away, they opened up our room and went through every single box, drawer, paper folder, handbag and – finally – our computer. When we got back to Toad Hall and walked into our bedroom, I was horrified.

'What the fuck happened?' I asked. 'They never even had the decency to tidy up after them.'

'The kids wanted in to play and we thought it would be OK,' Sean's brother Stephen tried to explain.

Our computer displayed file after file that had been opened, as the person/s doing the prying obviously had no idea how to shut them back down. The computer only held information about takings at the Weavers, the list of tenants' identities and how much was paid to us by the Government. This was not secret information and it was easy to work out if you could count your own ten fingers, but it was the fact that someone had tried to go through our files to find information that bothered us. Sean closed the computer down and sat with his head in his hands. The holiday had been great for us but now the pressure was on him even more. He had to admit his brothers were hounding him. All his working life, he had dealt exclusively with Old George; he had never had to explain himself to his siblings. Now he was being questioned on every aspect of our business, even though it did not concern them – they had not bought the Weavers, we had. For 14 years we had built up the business and worked daily in that bar, pretty much sacrificing our marriage, health, relationships, friends and everything else that goes with committing yourself to a business full-time.

And now we both felt it all slipping away from us.

26

The handstand

Living up in Toad Hall had one advantage – my sister Ann lived just round the corner. It was good to see and be near her, though we both worried about the day when Uncle David Percy would be tracked down by the police – he was still on the run. Neither of us knew what would happen when the case went to court – we just tried hard to be supportive of each other's pain. Ann was going through a terribly depressive time; her husband Brian told me she was not coping with even small domestic issues. It was hard watching her constantly fall apart then get herself together then fall apart again; she had two very small children and two teenagers to deal with. I tried hard to put on a brave face when she asked how I was coping at Toad Hall. I wanted to be strong for her; I did not want to tell her how hard the six Storrie brothers were making my life.

Eventually, with most of the flats' renovation complete we had to close the Weavers pub itself for renovation and that was a weird night. Sean arranged for all the bottled beers and various cases of spirits to be taken up to Toad Hall. Tables and chairs that might be sold or recycled to other bars owned by the Storrie family were stored in the shops we owned next door. So, that night, all our old and new customers gathered round the bar and we let them drink what was left in our draught beer stock. We even let them pull down the fittings and walls. I watched as people

I had served for 14 years ripped up tiles and dragged carpets about. Friends and customers hauled couches, toilet pans and sinks outside until 4.00 a.m. Even the bar units were ripped out.

Sean wanted to pull the place down himself; he felt it would provide closure for him. Every piece of the Weavers had been part of him since he was a wee boy and he had either renovated or designed or built each piece. Now he took it all apart, destroyed it and threw it into the rubbish skip. By midnight, the place was a cloud of dust and Sean was filthy. By early dawn, the bar was a black shell, the fake wood panelling ripped away, revealing all the scorch marks on the walls and ceilings that had survived a mysterious big fire in 1970 which had almost destroyed what was then the Nationalist Bar. By morning, the place where the bar once stood just housed a single beer tap (still connected to a barrel down in the cellar) on a scorched, bare wooden floor. Electrical wires drooped from various wall sockets where wall fittings had been ripped off and the place looked like it had been bombed. Finally, Sean left the bar – he looked deep and longing, like something had died – and locked the door behind him.

We lay in late the next day, unsure what we were supposed to do now that we did not have a job to go to. Ashley was off school for the October week holidays and we planned to go out in the car with her. At about ten that morning, Sandra called from the caravan at Wemyss Bay, near Rothesay on the Isle of Bute, and demanded that Sean pay her phone bills and give her money. Young George was in London and she needed money right now! Sean told her, 'Fuck off!' and promptly made sure the phone was disconnected at the caravan.

Later that week, she retaliated by calling the house from a phone box and shouting down the line, 'You will be sorry, ya fucking bastard!' Sean hung up on her.

On the Thursday of that week, Dick came over to stay (again). I tucked Ashley into bed and gave her Whisky the cat. 'Goodnight, chicken,' I whispered as I kissed her head.

'Goodnight, Mummy. Kiss the cat, please.'

I did kiss the cat, his soft furry head feeling warm on my lips.

I was woken early the next morning by noises. It sounded like Brindle the evil dark lord of dogs had finally caught some poor bastard in his jaws around the backyard. His deep growling barks were interrupted by human screams of agony. I jumped out of bed and crept through to Ashley's room which overlooked the back yard. Whisky the cat was already at the window, bemused, watching the dogs. It was only 6.00 a.m. *Who the fuck would be daft enough to go into that yard at this time of day and face that nasty psychotic dog?*

I could hardly make the figure out in the early morning light but it looked like a man dressed in black. As I saw him, he leapt back up onto the wall and disappeared over it with Brindle snapping at his heels. The dog looked up to me in the window and began barking his head off, slavering and snapping madly; even amiable Junior was going mad barking and he normally just stared at Brindle when he went off on a barking rant. I ran to get Sean and, as I reached the bedroom, heard a hammering on the downstairs door. The bell was being pushed constantly, as the hammering continued. It sounded like someone was trying to kick the door down.

'Sean, get up! The dogs are going mad! Who the fuck is kicking the door?'

Sean sat up, his hair sticking on end, reached for his glasses and spoke very quietly. 'Police,' he said simply.

I jumped into our bed, naked, trying to figure out what was happening, as Sean walked calmly downstairs to open the front door. Within seconds, two police officers were in my bedroom, dressed in black with stab vests and armed with sub-machine guns. They never spoke, just stood there. All I could think was *Oh my God! They will be in Ashley's room and she will wake up to see them!*

'Please, let me go in and get my daughter – don't you wake her.' I tried to wrap the sheet around me.

'Get out of the bed!' a police officer spat.

'Let me get on my housecoat.' I tried to reach down to the ottoman that sat at the foot of my bed. He pulled me roughly from the bed, naked, and made me stand there. I was horrified but more worried that Ashley would be awoken by this vision of men with guns. 'Please let me go get my daughter next door, please.' I grabbed my housecoat and wrapped it around myself.

'Which room is it?'

I pointed through the wall. He nodded and let me pass him.

I could hear Sean downstairs explaining who was in the house and where they were. 'Let me go wake up my daughter and give her through to my wife,' I heard him say as I passed Whisky the cat sitting, still bemused, at Ashley's doorway. Ashley was on her side tucked up in her favourite sleeping bag. She had always refused to sleep in any bedclothes that belonged to her dead grandad's house and insisted on being wrapped up in her sleeper on top of the big double bed. She looked so happy and cherub-like lying there. Whisky suddenly leapt up on the bed and curled defensively beside her head, hiding her face from my view.

'Ashley,' I said gently, 'get up, baby, come on.'

Her eyes snapped open. 'Is it school time?'

'No, but the police are here and they want everyone in the living room,' I answered.

'Are they here for my grandad?'

'No, remember Grandad is in heaven?' I smiled as I tried to lift her gently out of the sleeping bag.

'Then why are they here, Mummy?'

'Ashley, just get up, please, and don't ask anything.' I spoke quickly as I realised there was now a police officer standing behind me at the door.

'No speaking!' he barked.

Ashley dipped her body to the side to see where the voice was coming from, looked at the police officer standing there and then her big brown eyes opened like saucers and she looked straight at me: 'Are they going to take my daddy away?' She suddenly leapt off the bed and ran for the door. The policeman stopped her as I tried to catch her from behind.

'Let me go! I will speak if I want! This is my grandad's house! You can't make me stay here! I want my daddy! Daddy! Daddy, where are you?' She struggled from his grip and ran downstairs with me still trying to catch her; she met her father halfway down the stairs.

'It's OK, Ashley. They are just here to look for stuff; no one is going anywhere. Let's get breakfast, eh?' and, with that, he picked her up. She wrapped her legs and arms tightly round him and stayed there until he made her sit at the kitchen table. The police brought Dick down and sat us all together in the kitchen, including Ashley. There were three policemen standing over us. The men with sub-machine guns had melted away somewhere.

'We have information that there are weapons and

explosives hidden here in the house and in the surrounding grounds.'

I looked at Sean with enquiring eyes that begged him to reassure me with a smile that there was nothing to find. Sean looked at me, then looked straight down at his feet, a sure sign he could not assure me of anything. *Fucking hell!* I thought. *There are guns in this fucking house? Where?* I had let Ashley play everywhere out in the yard and all around these grounds. *There are explosives?*

The plain-clothes officer continued. 'Also there is an accusation of abduction and rape against you, Sean Storrie, from a Mrs Sandra Storrie. We will be taking that enquiry further as soon as we search the place.'

I looked at Ashley, took her out of the kitchen and was allowed to take her into the living room to watch television.

'Don't speak to your daughter,' a policeman told me. 'If you want, you can get someone to come and take her away from the house.'

I ran upstairs with Ashley and a policewoman and packed for her to go. I took out her panda bear and told her to 'speak' to it.

'What are you saying to her?' the policewoman demanded.

'I just told her to speak to Mr Bovey if she was worried about anything.'

'Who's Mr Bovey?'

'He's her panda bear.'

Ashley looked at me, smiled, then grabbed the bear, hugged him tight and waited for me to call Sean's Aunt Betty to come collect her. As she kissed her dad to leave, she held up her panda bear and said: 'Say hello to Mr Bovey, Daddy ...' Sean looked at me and laughed as we waved goodbye to her. The real Mr Bovey would be called as soon as she got to Aunt Betty's house; the panda had Mr Bovey's Edinburgh telephone number on its collar.

The police took apart every box we had painstakingly packed when we moved from the Weavers. I saw, lying all over the floor, my pictures, wedding dress, Ashley's Communion frock and loads of personal mementoes that we had carefully kept. They overturned Old George's big work desk and pulled all the paperwork out of it. They demanded that we lock up the dogs and even Whisky got into trouble for hissing at a female officer who hated cats. My nerves jangled as they pulled out each drawer, each cupboard, and pulled up yet another mattress as they searched for the 'weapons and explosives'.

'Look, we know what this is all about,' said Sean, standing with his arms folded, casually chatting as if he were behind the bar at the Weavers. 'Sandra was my father's girlfriend and she never got any money after he died and she is set on revenge. I never raped her.'

'Well, we will see about all this later, Mr Storrie,' the unsmiling officer replied.

The officers took us upstairs to search our bedroom and, from the back of the television mounted on top of the wardrobe, one officer pulled a large padded envelope. It was placed on the bed in front of us. *Mrs Storrie* was typed on the front. The policeman pulled on rubber gloves, peeled the top open and felt inside. I watched his face for any clues as to what he was touching. I looked at Sean for any sign that he recognised this package, but he just shrugged at me. The policeman delicately pulled the item out of the bag and I giggled. It was a huge black ribbed vibrator and it was followed by tubes of lubricator. I threw both hands to my face in embarrassment and shouted: 'That is fucking *not* mine! I would own up to the fucking weapons or explosives you seem tae think we huv – even the rape – but I do not own a black vibrator. That is Sandra's! Remember she calls herself Mrs Storrie.'

The policeman made a really cheap side glance at me and just threw it back in the bag.

'Fuck off looking at me like that!' I told him indignantly. 'They are not mine – I mean it.'

'Everyone down here now!' someone shouted from downstairs.

We were led down and out into the backyard; the dogs had been locked up. A plain-clothes officer was crawling under a washing machine that sat in the garage space behind a big yellow truck. I shivered in the autumn chill. I realised I had not eaten any breakfast; nerves had made me keep going but now I felt cold and faint. The shock was beginning to scratch at me, like cold claws creeping upward at the back of my legs. The policeman pulled at a black plastic rubbish sack that was half exposed with the other half dug into the soft earth directly beneath the washing machine. As he pulled, two other policemen eased it out carefully. I looked at Sean. He immediately stared at Dick, who took one long drag on his cigarette and flicked it high into the yard; then ran both his hands through his hair and kept his arms up high around his head. Their body language screamed *Guilty! We have guns here!* I felt my legs buckle slightly as the bag was ripped open and three big, old-style World War II rifles spilled out onto the moist grass. The policemen kept pulling at the black bag and what seemed like hundreds of bullets came out, spattering and spilling all over the earth like steel confetti.

Holy fuck! was all I could think. *I am going down. I am going to prison and some other bastard brother called Storrie will raise my child.* My heart thudded hard inside my chest. I glared at Sean. Words I could not say in front of the coppers sat like venom inside my eyes. I wanted to leap across the guns and grab the useless bastard by the neck. I felt like picking up a gun and shooting the fucker. *Him and his fucking brother so aptly named 'Dick'.* Now I was dragged into their shitty mess. *That cow Sandra knew what she was doing.* I glanced to the back of the yard where two policemen were holding a piece of paper, turning it round and round as if trying to make sense of it, while other police officers looked smug. I ran over to look at the paper the men held. As I got close, they tried to hide it, but I recognised the handwriting.

'A fucking map! She drew you a fucking map! Did she draw you a picture of my husband raping her?' I was so angry I actually gave the policemen a fright with my sudden turn of mood. They jumped back from me, looking startled by my screams.

'Calm down, Mrs Storrie,' a big, black-haired police officer said as he gently took my arm. 'Let's get into the house. We have to formally charge you all with possession of the weapons.' He looked genuinely sorry for me. I had seen no compassion from anyone else that day, but he stroked my hand: 'Look, we know this has fuck all to do with you; this is just procedure. The sooner we get it all done, the better.'

The day dragged on as the officers kept interrogating us. My stomach dipped and churned as if it was on a roller-coaster. *I knew we should never have come to this poxy bad luck house!* I worried about Ashley. *Was she scared? Was she crying? Did she call Mr Bovey?* The timing of this raid could not have been better for Sandra. Young George and Stephen were in London, Philip was in Spain on holiday, Paul was in Thailand and Michael was probably in jail again. We were left on our own to deal with this fucking mess. Before long, they found 11 handguns, 14 long sawn-off shotguns, an automatic rifle, black balaclavas, handcuffs and hundreds of bullets and shotgun cartridges. By then, it was late into the afternoon and, after they had discovered nothing new for four hours, they decided they had thoroughly searched the place, covering all points on the Sandra Treasure Map. The police called for a van and started to carry all the stuff into it. Neighbours were hanging out of their windows watching – at least seven tall tenements looked into George's front garden – they must have had a great view of the whole scene. We were cuffed and put into the back of a police van; I was so shocked I just sat with my head down. Sean looked over at me, cocked his head to the side and smiled.

'It will be OK, Janey.'

'Fuck you, ya cunt!' I spat at him. 'I hope you die! My daughter will never forget this and here I am going to the jail coz yer useless fucking father cannae hide a fucking gun!'

The policeman sitting beside me sniggered. 'Aye,' he said. 'And he *is* getting charged with rape as well.'

'Fuck ye!' I screamed. 'Rape? Sandra was never raped! Don't ye know it is physically impossible to rape her? She shags anyone who asks! Maybe *you* fucked her yerself! She is a fucking, lying whore!'

Dick looked over and said, 'Don't get upset, Janey. Sean didnae know aboot the guns.'

'Fuck ye as well!' I shouted.

As soon as we got into the Police Office we were led to the bar – the counter – to be formally charged. Sean asked if he could share a cell with me. 'No!' the policeman behind the counter told him. 'It's no' the fucking Hilton, ya stupid bastard!'

After the charging procedure I was taken alone into a small white cell about 20 feet square with a bench running alongside one end and a small window that looked into a central observation office. It was the first time I had been on my own since this shit day started. My head was racing. *Wait a minute! They never found the explosives!* I started to go over the backyard in my head, trying to imagine where the explosives could be hidden. I didn't even know what explosives looked like! It was at this point I realised that the 'various miscellaneous materials' Old George had referred to in his taped will were these guns and explosives. My head ran round in circles. Stress was getting to me and I felt sick. I decided to do the breathing technique that helped me when I was running. I sat on the floor and took long deep breaths. I could feel my pulse slowing down. I could feel my heartbeat becoming more regular. This felt better. I did not want to hyperventilate in a fucking police cell. I stood up and looked at the bench. I went and stood at the furthest wall, ran forward and slammed both my palms down on the bench then threw my body up into a handstand. I could see everything upside-down. The blood rushed to my head, my breasts hurt a bit. It had been a long time since I had done a handstand. At that exact moment, a detective opened the door. I stayed upside-down.

'What the fuck are ye doing?' he asked. 'Are ye a junkie?'

I threw myself off the wall, off the bench and did a perfect landing on both feet with my hands raised in triumph in the air, like some Olympic champion. 'How many junkies de you know who can do that, ye fuckwit?' I laughed.

He lifted his hand up to slap me in the face.

'You fucking hit me, ya cunt, an' I will report ye!' I

shouted as loud as I could. His hand stopped in mid-air, as a female detective came to the door. He dropped his hand.

'He tried to slap me there,' I pleaded to her. 'That cannae be right.'

'Yes and we care deeply,' she sneered. 'A woman who has been charged with possession of guns.'

I knew this was not going to be a good day. I was taken to another room to be interviewed. I was worried that they would beat me up badly. I sat at a table as two detectives came in. One was the officer from the back garden who had calmed me down. I smiled at him as he sat beside me.

'Janey, we have to tape everything for the record – OK?'

'OK,' I replied.

The other dark-haired man leaned over the table and stared as he smiled. I felt slightly uncomfortable now; he was staring right at me.

'Just confirm your name and details then, please,' he said quietly.

I gave my name and address.

'How long you been married, Janey?'

'Fourteen years now.'

'Why were there guns at the house?'

'I don't know. I huv never seen them before, honest.'

I sat with my hands on my lap and started to pick at my nails. This dark-haired man was making me feel very uncomfortable. He would stare and smile and reach over and touch me gently on the hand and then stare at me blankly, without emotion, as I answered.

'Who owns the house?' he asked.

'Well, I don't know, to be honest,' I replied. I knew that whoever owned the house owned the guns. That was Scottish law, for sure, so I had to get my head around this.

'You live in a house and you don't know who owns it? Who pays the bills for gas and electricity?'

'I don't know. I am a woman. If bills are being paid, I don't question it.'

'Liar!' he suddenly shouted, leaping across the table at me. The edge of his hand hit me full force on the side of my head. I had no time to duck. My ears rang with pain.

'Fuck you, ya big arse!' I screamed back at him. 'D'ye like hitting women? Eh? Do ye hit yer wife?' I rubbed my ear and looked at the tape machine hoping it had caught all that noise on it. But the spools on the tape recorder were not moving at all. My heart started to thump wildly and I tried hard to breathe slowly; I knew now that they were going to beat me up badly. The other detective sat impassively and stared as I cried, holding my ear.

'Janey,' the dark-haired man spoke. 'Just tell us everything and you can go home, eh?'

'I don't fucking know anything and that belt to my head has just given me real mental problems. Now I am in shock, so I cannae speak.' I didn't care if they kicked me to death now, the pair of bastards. *I am not being scared by anyone any more*, I thought to myself. They got me up from the table and led me to the other side of the room, where all the guns and stuff they had recovered from Toad Hall was lying on the floor. I noticed for the first time that two of the handguns were very old and ornate; they had pearl inlaid handles and fancy-looking metalwork on them.

'When did you last see that gun?' one of them asked as he saw my interest in the weapon.

'In a fucking Dick Turpin film. You *are* joking, eh? Can that actually fire bullets? It looks like something Rabbie Burns carried when he was a customs official. Fuck, it must be ancient.'

'Look, you,' the dark-haired detective said, grabbing me roughly by the arm and spinning me round to look at him. 'I am fed up with your fucking behaviour. Do you know your husband at all?'

'Aye, I know him,' I snapped back. 'I have known him since he was 16. I know he never raped Sandra. I know this because he helped me cope with a rape I had suffered. I know he would not touch that mad cow and I know anything you say will probably be shite to get at me because I married a Storrie!'

'Your lovely wonderful husband – that quiet man, as you think he is – has been fucking other women. Did ye know that, eh? We huv been watching him for a while. What do you think of that, eh?' He smirked at me.

'I could not give a fuck if he was shagging your wife!' I shouted into his face. 'I huv other issues to worry aboot here – like all these guns and stuff! My man fucking other women is the last thing I care aboot! I am worried aboot the fact he let me and my daughter live in a hoose wi' guns in it, mate!'

The detective grabbed me and threw me roughly back into my seat. 'You think you are a fucking smart one, eh?' Then he stormed out of the room. I was led back into the small cell and left alone with my thoughts. I wondered how long it would be before Mr Bovey got here. I had not been offered the phone call I was legally obliged to be offered. I started to bang on my cell door and scream, 'I'm entitled to a phone call! I've seen it in the movies! I saw it on *The Sweeney*!'

The door opened and – as if by magic – Mr Bovey was standing there in front of me. He waved away the desk sergeant and came into my cell. I rushed to him and hugged him, I was so happy to see the wee Lithuanian man dressed, as usual, in stiff pinstripes and starched collar, holding a cane and bowler hat.

'Mr Bovey, how is Ashley? Did you see her?'

'Yes, I chatted to Miss Storrie on the phone,' he answered in his clipped, fast-talking tone. 'She did call me, you know. She is fine and staying with Aunty Betty. She is clearly worried. You know nothing of these weapons and I will try to get you released. There is no reason to keep you here other than spite. Forensics are looking at the weapons to see when they were last fired and they have ascertained that Sean did not rape Sandra, although he did have to go through the forensics for that just half an hour ago, poor boy.'

'Poor boy, my arse, Mr Bovey! I hate him for putting me in this position. He must have known the stuff was there and yet he let Ashley and me live there. That is fucking unforgivable.'

'Janey, he was brought up living like that, so it was not unusual for him or dangerous. Don't give him a hard time; he is a good boy and a decent father.' He stared at me with his hard, glassy blue eyes. 'Look, the main thing is, let me sort this out. You stay tight and don't talk about anything.' He straightened his shirt and jacket as he stood up.

'They slapped me, ye know.'

'Bastadds!' he said, his Lithuanian accent coming out as he swore. 'I will arrange for food to be brought in.' With that, he left, his cane tapping on the floor as he went.

I sat and waited for what seemed like hours.

Eventually, a policeman came in and told me I was to be taken to an overnight cell.

Overnight? Why? Had Mr Bovey not sorted it out?

I felt my heart sink as I was taken to a wide, square room with a metal toilet and flat bed with one stinking cover. I felt exhausted and scared. There was an eyehole on the door and I needed to go to the toilet but was scared in case someone started watching me. I worried how Ashley was coping without us. She would be very worried if we had had to leave her overnight with someone. She would know that meant real trouble. I did not want her going to school tomorrow and having to explain that her parents were in prison for hiding guns in their house. I lay on the hard bed and refused to pull the skanky cover over me at any time. It got very cold and I lay there thinking about how the hell I had ended up in London Road Police Office.

* * *

Eventually, morning came and a large policeman escorted me out to a big grey bus parked at the back of the Police Office. I sat quietly all the way to the Sheriff's Court in Glasgow city centre. I was led into the court cells beneath the main building. This was one more step nearer prison and I was scared as shit. They took me into a cell which looked exactly like the sheriff's jail in a cowboy movie: three brick walls with bars floor-to-ceiling at the front. Four other women were already sitting on the benches inside, watching me as I came in. I kept my head high and tried to look confident.

'Storrie, here's tobacco and matches,' the warder said, holding out a plastic pouch with a pack of matches.

'I don't smo-' I could feel someone's fingernails suddenly dig hard into my back. 'OK, I smoke – give them to me.' I held out my hand to take the pouch.

The warder left.

'Fuck off. I got the fags,' I said, turning to face my nail queen. 'Here, take them.'

The young girl's hard eyes creased into a smile, blue

eye shadow smeared high up to her eyebrows. Her dyed blonde hair was pulled up into a big high pony-tail that stretched her skin tight, as if she had had a facelift. She snapped the pouch quickly into the tight elastic waistband of her black velvet leggings.

'Whit huv ye done?' she asked. 'Why ye here?'

'Nothing,' I told her coldly. 'Fuck off. Ye got yer fags, ye don't need to know my life story, do ye?' I sat confused in the corner and looked around at the other girls in there with me. One looked about 30 years old, clearly an addict. Her eyes were red-rimmed, with black circles scooped out beneath, her pupils dilated, her body shaking as she sat alone in the corner.

'You OK?' I asked gently and sat beside her.

'Am I fuck? I need ma medication an' the cunts won't give me it,' she mumbled. As she drew her legs up to her chin, a strong, suffocating stench of urine and sperm came belting off her and hit me straight in the face. I turned away to hold my breath and try to stem a retch that threatened to overwhelm me. *I need to get out of here*, was all I could think. The other women sat swapping backgrounds and sneered at me as I made small talk with the smelly addict.

'Janey Storrie!' a policeman holding a clipboard shouted in my general direction.

'Yes!' I stood up quickly, my heart thumping loud. Was this me finally going upstairs to court to plead not guilty? Or was I going straight to prison on remand?

'Possession of 11 handguns, 14 shotguns, one automatic rifle, 376 rounds of ammunition and an electric stun gun ... Is that you?' he asked. As he spoke, his fat chin wobbled. 'Is that you, eh?'

'Aye, that's me – Janey Storrie,' I answered.

I looked around. All the women just gawped at me.

'Fucksake!' one of them said. 'An' she sat there like Mrs Posh Arse!'

'You're free to go,' the policeman said as he pulled out a big bunch of keys and started to unlock the door. My heart jumped into my mouth. I felt vomit and bile rise up my throat as I stood there and almost leapt to the door.

'How the fuck is she free to go?' the red-eyed addict complained. 'I only hud three jellies and some coke! I didnae huv any fucking guns an' I'm still stuck in here. That's shite!'

I ran to Mr Bovey, who stood at the end of the big oak 'bar' under the court. The place was a whirl of activity: policemen and policewomen and detectives and white-wigged, black-cloaked court officials all dashing around. I was so glad to be leaving, I held onto Mr Bovey's arm tight, terrified I might be taken back again.

'All of you are free,' he told me. 'They dare not prosecute.'

Sean came walking towards me, wrapped his arms around me and kissed my hair. He smelled of damp greasy pies and tobacco smoke.

'We can go home,' he whispered. 'I am so sorry, Janey.'

We were driven back to Toad Hall in a taxi. Ashley was waiting there with Patsy Paton and Young George.

'Mummy, are you OK ... Daddy!' She ran to him and kissed him as he knelt down to let her hug him.

I tried to answer all the questions that tumbled out of her wee mouth, but it was too much for me. 'Baby, I need to have a bath. As soon as I get out, I will tell you everything ... And you're OK, eh?' I hugged her tight as I spoke. 'Tell me you're OK? Did Whisky the cat miss me?'

She smiled, nodded and ran into the kitchen to join her father. I went upstairs, ran a hot bath, poured luxurious and expensive perfumed bath gel under the gushing taps, stripped quickly, slipped under the warm, clean water and let the smell of the bathsalts drift up into my nose. I had dreamed of this all night in the cell and now I could get clean.

'Janey, you in there?' Sean called through the door.

'Aye, I'm in the bath.'

'Let me in.'

I sighed and slowly dripped my way on tiptoes to the door, foam slipping down my legs. Whisky the cat slipped in first. Sean pulled off his shirt and threw his clothes onto the heap of mine on the floor.

'Fuck, I feel so dirty!' he told me.

The bath was big enough for us both. Without saying anything, I lay in it, feeling the warm plastic against my back, Sean lying with his back against my chest. My legs went around his sides and I hugged him beneath the hot foamy water. I really wanted to fight with him. I wanted the answer to so many questions. But, right now, I also needed to feel him close. Whisky leapt up on the side of the marble bath surround, tucked his paws under his chin and sat staring at us through slitty eyes, as if asking *So what happens next?*

Much later, Sean, Patsy Paton and I sat in the living room, trying to make sense of the whole situation. One thing was clear. Young George could no longer stick up for Sandra. It was one thing being a mad woman within the Storrie family, but it was something else entirely grassing us to the police.

* * *

A few days later, a wee, almost toothless, one-eyed man called Erchie, who wore old-fashioned trousers with braces

407

over a stripy collarless shirt, arrived at Toad Hall and wandered about the back garden. He pointed up to the roof of the big, silver-skinned trailer by the wall and hobbled into the car pit. Sean and Erchie clambered and scurried under and over cars, all around the backyard. I stood as they walked back and stopped again by the trailer. The three of us stepped inside and the two of them tentatively rubbed their hands over the walls. A panel was pulled back and there, underneath, I saw slabs of a dark, plasticine-like material, perhaps one inch thick. I went to press my finger into it.

'Fucking don't do that, Janey!' Erchie's husky voice whistled through his gappy teeth as he grabbed my hand. He put his old, wrinkled face up so close to the plasticine I thought he was going to lick it, but he merely smelled the material.

'Whit is it?' I repeated.

'Explosive putty, hen. Don't touch it. I'll need to freeze ma hands to get it aw off.' Old Erchie held up both his gnarled, veiny hands and looked at them, then walked out of the trailer and headed for the back kitchen. I stood and stared at the dark stuff inside the wall, the same wall I had bounced a ball off, the same wall I had done handstands against with Ashley.

'I huv played in here with your daughter and you said nothing!' I snapped at Sean. 'Honest to fucking God, I huv no idea who you are any more. Why did ye let me stay here when all this stuff wiz here? Do ye really no' care at all? An' whit the fuck did yer da need all this stuff fur, anyway?'

Erchie came back with his hands stretched in front of him. He was carrying frozen plastic ice chillers that we kept in the freezer for picnics and cool boxes: 'This will keep ma hands cold till I pick it aw off,' he said, more to himself than to us. 'Noo, stand back an' I'll get tae work. Don't let the sunlight get on it. We don't want it too hot.' The old man started to ease the stuff off, but it was taking too long and the sun started shining through the top skylight of the trailer to point sharply into the trailer and its open wall. I worried what effect the heat of the sun might have. 'Get yer hands cold and help me,' Erchie hissed as he picked away at the stuff. 'Just dae it aw very slowly, hen. Just imagine,' he winked at me, 'that yer dealing wi' a wee baby.'

That panicked me. I was not good with 'wee babies' but I held my hands in the freezer of our fridge till they hurt and helped slowly pick off the hard, greasy putty. It kept breaking off in my hand, smelled of petrol and occasionally started to sweat as I manipulated the chunks until they broke off. It was like handling dangerous, hard fudge. Erchie supervised Sean and me and occasionally held frozen plastic ice chillers against the explosives until he was sure it was safe to carry on. It took us about an hour or more to clear the wall of the dark putty and Erchie wrapped it all up in a sheet and put it into a brown canvas duffel bag, then simply walked out the front gate of Toad Hall holding it in his hands.

That, and the explosives we removed from under the wallpaper of an upstairs room.

'Where will he put it all?' I asked Sean.

He looked at me and just shrugged his shoulders: 'I don't fucking care as long as it's out of here.'

* * *

After that, life went on as before at Toad Hall. The police incident was never discussed again; Sean became distant and agitated every time I tried to talk about what had happened. There was no point complaining about the house being full of his brothers; it was now accepted that we all had to live together; I hated every minute. Almost even worse was that I was not used to Sean being around so much with nothing to do. With the Weavers closed for refurbishment, he and I were in each other's face all the time, so we argued, shouted and threatened each other with divorce. We tried to keep cool in front of Ashley but even that deteriorated and soon we openly threw things at each other. Once, I stood in the kitchen, looking at the filthy mess left by some Storrie brother who had attempted a fry-up. Pans were all over the units and greasy cutlery lay in the sink.

'Fucksake, can your poxy family no' wash their own plates?' I snapped at Sean as soon as he came in.

'Fuck up, ya moany cow!' he shot back at me with a dark look. Before, I would have been scared but now I was ready to use any excuse to fight him.

'Fuck you, ya useless bastard!' I shouted as I threw a greasy frying pan straight at his head. He ducked and it clattered off the wall, sending the clock crashing down to the floor. Ashley came running in from the hallway and screamed, 'Stop fighting, Daddy, please! You are all *horrible* in here! Mummy, stop shouting! Everybody shouts in this house. Stop it!' She stood there looking at us, her face still angry but now looking tired and worn out. I had never seen that look on her face before. She was only eight. I walked over and tried to put my arms around her. She started to push me away and began crying. 'I *hate* it here. I want to go *home*!' She looked up at me, pushed my arms away and walked out of the room.

Sean and I called a truce. We agreed I would stop whingeing and he would get on the case of the builders and confirm a date when we could move back into our flat above the Weavers. If our flat was not ready by January – in five weeks' time – we would move to a rented flat until we got a date to go home. It was settled. He promised and we tried to focus on getting the pub and the flats organised for redecoration.

* * *

At Toad Hall, the brothers still came and went as they wanted.

They ate our food from the fridge. I ignored it.

They used my clean towels and left the bathroom in a state. I ignored it.

They kicked Whisky the cat and spat at Ashley on the stairs. I ignored it.

In particular, I tried hard to avoid rising to Young George's baiting. I knew he was spoiling for a fight. I tried my best to avoid him. *It will not be long before we get out of here*, I kept telling myself. I retreated into our bedroom. We had a television in there. I moved Whisky the cat's box in beside us. I kept Ashley occupied near me when she was at home from school. I only ventured downstairs to get food and hot drinks. We ate on the bed. Ashley did her homework on the bed. The cat slept on the bed. We all cuddled up together on the bed. Downstairs stank of tobacco, cannabis and alcohol and there was no way I was going down to clean up after them. By now, I didn't even know how many people actually lived in the house. Sean and I left early in the morning to take Ashley to school and stayed out all day. We would go down to the Weavers building to check the progress of the refurbishment, chat to the workers, and liaise with the architect on the plans. We would only go back to Toad Hall when we had to.

The week before Christmas, we planned to leave the

house and stay at the Hilton for Christmas Eve and Christmas Day. We knew there was no way we could make Ashley happy stuck in that bedroom in that house over the holidays. We never bothered to discuss it with the brothers: even Paul Storrie was becoming distant now. One day, he watched Young George spray bleach over my coat as it hung on the stair post.

'Stop it George, ya bastard!' I screamed as I tried to rush through into the kitchen to wash it. 'You are fucking evil! That's my good heavy winter coat!'

Paul just stood sniggering as I pushed past him.

'Whit ye laughing at, Paul?'

He smiled and looked at Young George. There was a new coldness in his eyes. I had never known Paul like this. Before, he would have shouted at Young George and defended me; now it seemed I had six enemies to look out for.

As Christmas approached, Ashley became more and more excited and, just before we dropped the cat off at my sister's house (I no longer left it unattended at Toad Hall), Dick Storrie barged into our bedroom and said to me, 'Yer old pal Jonah is dead.'

He smiled and walked back out of the room thinking he had shocked me, but I already knew; I had been there when Jonah died. He was in hospital and I had gone up with a card Ashley had made. Jonah always had such a great sense of humour and we had many laughs, but he must have been so sad inside.

I did not attend the funeral. I wanted to step back from it all. I knew that people at the funeral would talk about the guns incident. I did not want to be paraded as a gangster's moll for ever. That would all be put behind me.

We packed up on Christmas Eve and left without

explaining to anyone in the house where we were going. I just smiled at Young George as I went past him and slammed the door, hurried down the three wee stairs that led to the gate and got into the car. We had booked a beautiful room with a balcony up on the penthouse floor of the Glasgow Hilton, facing west. It was lovely, but it was not home. I wanted to be back in our flat above the Weavers. I wanted my familiar things around me. But I knew I would never be safe again. Old George had been acutely intelligent in his own way and had built up a big business, but these six sons were different. I knew that, back at Toad Hall or in a local pub, a bunch of uneducated thugs who could not even count the number of fingers on their hands was debating our future and now they thought they were businessmen. I was worried to the core of my soul, but I smiled over Christmas dinner. Sean tried hard to placate me. We waited until Ashley was asleep and then chatted into the night.

'Janey, I know ye are worried, but I promise ye … They will no' take the pub; they cannae. I huv all the paperwork and stuff. Anyhow, none of them know how to run it.' He held me close, then got to his feet: 'Come onto the balcony. Look, it's Christmas Day.' He pointed to the cold blue sky outside. We stepped out onto the balcony, into the cold Scottish night. Glasgow was a glittering landscape of frost and sharp electric lights, twinkling in the dark. The view was breathtaking, I could see all the way down the River Clyde and, in the far west, I could see the spires of Glasgow University on the skyline. I could not see the East End at all. Something somehow made me glad that I couldn't see 'my' part of the city; I did not want to see it tonight; I wanted to see the nice side of Glasgow.

'Merry Christmas, Janey.' Sean smiled and kissed me.

'I am going to give myself a New Year present,' I told him quietly.

'What's that?'

'I don't want to be Janey Storrie any more, because your family let me down. I don't want to be Janey Currie, because my family let me down. I'm going to use my middle name and legally become Janey Godley. The only family who haven't let me doon are the Godleys because I don't know them. Happy Christmas.'

27

Welcome to the Hotel California

Ashley loved staying at the Hilton, enjoyed her Christmas dinner, loved the tree in her room, the presents placed underneath it, revelled in all the attention from the staff. She ran around showing them all her Christmas gifts and then got dressed for her Nana and Grandad Currie coming to visit. Dad was looking better, but I knew he was very worried about us. Newspaper reports of the gun incident had omitted our names and they also changed my age by ten years which made identifying us even more difficult, but some of Dad's relatives had heard gossip and told him. He kept asking me to go live with him and Mary. I refused because I needed to keep focused on getting back into our flat above the Weavers. I was determined not to let the Storrie brothers get me down; I had been through bigger fights than this in my life. I knew Sean was going over every possibility in his head about what his brothers could do to us, but whenever we talked about it he refused to believe his family could or would take his pub and flats from him.

'Janey, how can they? Why would they? I think you are worrying too much over fuck all.' I could see in fact that he was trying to convince himself as much as me.

After Christmas at the Hilton, we picked up the cat on the way home, then drove back to Toad Hall, went through the big oak door and straight upstairs. Ashley was happy to be back and couldn't wait to unpack and show Whisky all the toys she had got. As I unpacked our cases, Sean was called downstairs. There was definitely something going on as, when we arrived, all six brothers had been in the main sitting room. After Sean went down to join them, I heard shouting and mumbled, angry voices.

'Mummy, why are they all here? Why are they talking to Daddy?' Ashley whispered. Ashley always whispered when the brothers were at home. She became subdued and never left my side.

'Never mind them, babes, Daddy will sort it out.' I smiled at her.

Toad Hall smelled of dope, burnt sausages and a hint of dog piss; there had been clothes strewn all over the banisters when we came up to our room. I sighed at the thought of clearing up after them all yet again. I opened our bedroom door and heard Sean laughing on the stairs as he leapt up them two at a time. But, when he stepped into the room, his face was ashen.

'What's going on?' I snapped at him. 'Are they leaving?'

'They want to keep the Weavers,' Sean blurted out. 'They won't let us buy it or give us back oor money and they want us to stay and work for them. They have all fucking decided to go against my da's wishes.'

Neither of us spoke. Ashley looked at us. I could feel Sean's anger and a terrible disappointment hang in the silent air. Everything we had worked for was screwed. He sat on the bed and lifted Ashley and Whisky onto his knee. I was totally shocked, wanting to blast out at least 73 arguments against their decision, but held back as I knew he had already done this. He was faced by all six of his brothers turning on him.

'Did Uncle Paul agree with them?' Ashley asked. She loved Paul.

'He never spoke, Ashley, he sat there like a sheep.'

I felt so sorry for Sean in that moment. He had lost his dad. Now he had lost his business, his home and the life he had struggled to keep for 14 years – all of it had just fallen away from him. Now he knew inside that he had truly lost any family he ever had.

'Janey, I can't do it, I can't work for them. Neither can you.' He looked at Ashley and said, 'Do you want to leave, baby? Mummy and I will move and get a new home?'

'Can we take the cat?' Ashley asked.

Sean nodded.

My brain raced. *What would we do without the pub?* My home was above that pub, my money, my plans, our plans ... Sean just stared blankly into my face. I knew he wanted to just leave. Go. We both stood up, started laughing and grabbed black bin liners. We began to stuff into them Ashley's clothes, underwear, toys. You name it, we stuffed it in. I felt like a wee child again. It was truly terrifying what we were about to do, but the relief was amazing. We no longer had a home, we had nowhere to go and the New Year was just days away, but we really didn't care. Ashley was trying to quickly pack all her school books and stuff into a big green holdall.

Young George came upstairs and stood in the doorway watching us frantically pack.

'Where are you going? Is that my black bag, ya bastard?'

Sean stopped stuffing teddy bears into a bag, dug into his pocket and pulled out two pound coins.

'That should pay for the bag. We're leaving.'

Young George stood there, trying to think of something

to say, but failed. Then he ran downstairs to deliver the latest bulletin to the family gathering. It was late afternoon, the winter sun streamed through the big bay windows, Ashley kissed her grandaddy's picture goodbye, picked up Whisky the cat and made her way down the stairway with us, past her uncles gathered at the doorway. She kept her head up, saying nothing until she reached her beloved Uncle Paul.

'You're a sheep, Uncle Paul,' she said to him, while trying to control the big ginger cat squirming in her arms.

Paul had the grace to look at his feet.

Sean and I struggled out with the bags.

'Where are you goanna live?' Stephen spoke up. 'What the fuck do you think you're doing? You need to stay to run the pub.'

At that moment, I realised they had just thrust this situation on Sean without actually thinking it through. None of them knew the alarm code, the suppliers, the stock, the banking details, the staff's names ... and now they would have to pay the remaining 150 grand to the builder from their own pockets. They must have thought we would stay on at any cost. Our money was in that building; our home was there; our life was there; why would we refuse their offer? They never expected us to say *No*. My heart was thudding in my chest. This was it. We would never get our money back. Our flat. Nothing.

I turned as we were about to close the door and said, 'You must have had Plan B, surely? You really thought we were to work for the rest of our lives in that pub for you lot? You can just get fucked!'

'You're just a fucking barmaid!' Young George shouted. 'Just remember that. You're Janey Currie! You're just a fucking barmaid!'

'Not any more, George,' I replied as I slammed the door.

We were free. Sean did not even look back. As we drove all the way out of the East End of Glasgow into the West End, he pressed the tape player and little Ashley sang along with her favourite Eagles track, 'Hotel California'.

That night we moved into our new, rented accommodation, gathered our thoughts and spent our first night in a strange house in the West End, both quietly trying to answer all Ashley's questions but too scared to tell her we just didn't know what was going to happen next.

Epilogue

One afternoon five years later, when Ashley was 13, I found an old cassette tape in a box we were going through. The two of us sat in our flat and I spoke to her about how my Mammy had died because she was too stupid to get away from a violent man. I put the worn black cassette into my new silver Sony tape deck and pressed play. Ashley heard the woman who was her grandmother laugh throatily and giggle at me giving her a lecture. In the background, Kate Bush was singing 'The Man With The Child In His Eyes'.

'Och, Janey,' my Mammy told me. 'He's no' that bad. Peter isnae that bad. C'mon, I mean he's had his problems, we've had wur fights, but I'm as bad as him.'

'You're going to end up fucking deed!' I shouted back at her. 'You're going to end up fucking deed lying in your fucking coffin, because you're going to let him fucking kill ye!'

'Don't swear,' she told me. 'Don't get upset.'

'You're going to end up fucking deed, Mammy …'

'No I won't. Peter's no' a bad man.'

'Ann and I are going to have tae explain to your grandweans that you are deed an' the reason they never got tae see you was because you let a man kill you. That's what I'm going to have tae say in years to come – *I'm sorry you never saw my Mammy, but she let a man kill her!*'

Mammy burst out laughing: 'I cannae imagine you being a mother! … You don't seem like the mothering type tae me … I don't think ye'll be a mother. You're good wi' weans but I cannae imagine it but, don't you worry, I'll be there the day you have a wean.'

'She sounds like you, Mum,' Ashley told me. 'And you sound really cheeky to your mummy. I think you tried your best.'

I cried that day. Three generations of women held together by grief and magnetic technology.

That night, I had my dreams. I hate running that much in my sleep. I hate it when I wake myself up screaming. I can hear myself scream in the morning and it scares me. I wake up shouting and screaming. When I am awake, I am in control but, asleep, the fear takes over. I am small again and try to hide under the stairs. The big man hunts for me. He slams doors open. He rants and stomps throughout my house. I sit in a wet nightdress, trying to make my legs small and folding my body into a wee corner. I keep my eyes shut as I hear his footsteps getting closer. He is calling out my name.

'Janey! … Janey! …'

My fingernails dig into the palms of my hands. I hear the blood rushing through my ears. I feel my heart pounding with fear. I feel a draught as he opens the cupboard door. The man with a demon's face is slicing into my flesh with an open razor. I see the blood and feel the pain. My big sister Ann pinches me on the knee.

'Janey turn the right way up, eh?'

'Not yet.'

Janey Godley is a 45-year-old stand-up comedienne, actress and playwright. She has taken her comedy shows *Good Godley!* and *Janey Godley Is Innocent* from the Edinburgh Fringe to London's West End. She appeared in her own one-woman play *Smack – The Point of Yes* to critical acclaim in the West End, and has performed her shows to long-term prisoners in Scottish gaols. She writes an award-winning online blog, has written for a number of print publications and is a regular contributor to BBC Radio 4's *Loose Ends*. *Handstands in the Dark* is her first book.

Read more about Janey on her website:
www.janeygodley.co.uk

Acknowledgements

I am eternally lucky to have a father who has never stopped believing in me. I have to thank my family for giving me the space and grace to write about their very personal lives.

This book would not have been possible without constant encouragement from the following people: My two best friends Monica Brown and Findlay McLeod – their love and listening skills will stay with me always; Mike Loder (top New Zealand comic), who insisted that I write the stories of my life and kept my spirits buoyed in the hard times; John Fleming, who saw me perform comedy, thought I would make a writer, then introduced me to Ebury and constantly encouraged me to write this book – he made me explore the language and enjoy the process.

I would like to thank Jake Lingwood, Deputy Publisher, Emma Harrow in Publicity and all the good people at Ebury for their constant hard work and support. I would also like to mention Campbell Deane in Glasgow for being an exceptional lawyer.

I have many wee children in my life who constantly make me smile and remind me of happier times: Shaun Smith, Abigail McPherson, Katelin, Connar and Corinne Mills, and Gabrielle Spooner.

In the process of writing this book, I had many sleepless nights. One man chased away the nightmares: Thank you to my husband.